Disease & HISTORY

SECOND EDITION

Disease & HISTORY

SECOND EDITION

Frederick F. Cartwright & Michael Biddiss

SUTTON PUBLISHING

First published in 1972 by Rupert Hart-Davis, London, and by Thomas Y. Crowell
Company, New York.

This revised edition first published in the United Kingdom in 2000 by
Sutton Publishing Limited · Phoenix Mill
Thrupp · Stroud · Gloucestershire · GL5 2BU

British Library Cataloguing in Publication Data
A catalogue record for this book is available from the British Library.

ISBN 0-7509-2315-6

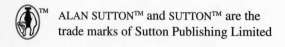 ALAN SUTTON™ and SUTTON™ are the
trade marks of Sutton Publishing Limited

Typeset in 10/13 pt New Baskerville.
Typesetting and origination by
Sutton Publishing Limited.
Printed in Great Britain by
Biddles, Guildford, Surrey.

Contents

Preface

The present volume is an enlarged and fully revised version of a work which, since its initial appearance in 1972, has enjoyed a number of reprintings as well as translations into French and Japanese. Like the original, this new edition is the product of continuing debate and collaboration between a doctor and a historian, each concerned to provide the general reader with an accessible account of some of the principal ways in which disease has made its often dramatic mark upon the past. During the process of revision we have taken the opportunity of giving fuller coverage to a number of topics, and most especially to the impact of smallpox, influenza, and tuberculosis. The concluding section on matters of contemporary concern has been entirely rewritten, particularly so as to bring into our analysis some current ecological issues as well as the recent and continuing global tragedy of HIV/AIDS. In preparing the new edition, we have benefited greatly from the advice and help of Jane Crompton, Sarah Cook, Elizabeth Berry and Andrew Lownie. Above all, we wish to thank those members of our own family whose support and encouragement have done so much to assist the completion of our reworking of *Disease and History*.

FFC/MB

List of Illustrations

Disease and History

Historians and doctors have much in common. Both acknowledge that the proper study of mankind is Man. Both are particularly interested in the influences which condition human existence. The object of this book is to study the area in which historian and doctor inevitably meet, that of the impact of disease upon history. In medical diagnosis a single cause for disease will often be found. In historical investigation the causes are likely to be complex. Nothing could be more ridiculous than to contend that disease is always the primary cause of a great historical change but, particularly at a time when the sociological aspects of history are being increasingly emphasized, it is worth examining those episodes in which the influence of disease may have been of real importance, especially when that importance has been neglected or misconstrued by more conventional historians.

Our aim in studying some of the many maladies which have afflicted the world will be to illustrate their effect not only upon historically important individuals but also upon peoples. Thus the study is relevant to History, whether conceived as a saga of great figures or as the story of social conditions and general human development. The ills that have plagued civilized man are as much a part of civilization as are their prevention and cure. If disease itself is historically important, then the conquest of disease is no less so. And, as we shall see, this conquest, though as yet only partial, has itself raised problems that are no less daunting for being different and are equally relevant to our subject.

Man is a gregarious animal and the picture of primitive man isolated in his cave is misleading. The family unit developed into the tribe living a communal life. These small communities, a few of which still exist in remote jungle areas today, dwelt in man-made clearings with little or no contact between individual settlements, for the tangled, trackless forest prevented easy communication. Each community was self-supporting, dependent upon naturally occurring food sources. In Central Africa, for instance, bananas and manioc formed the staple diet, varied by small quantities of palm oil and only rarely by flesh, either human or animal. The few enemies of these tribal communities were snakes, carnivorous beasts and pygmy humans who shot at them with strophanthin-poisoned arrows. Puerperal fever in childbirth, a high infant mortality and endemic disease, such as sleeping sickness and yaws, prevented rapid increase in population. Life span was short, partly because no reliable cure for any illness existed, partly because a high carbohydrate diet led to early obesity with fatty infiltration of the vital organs. So tribal growth remained almost static, increasing in a healthy season when live births outnumbered deaths, decreasing when infant mortality was high. Such is the natural process of slow increase in a primitive community which is adequately fed and protected from major disaster but cannot cope with the hazards of childbirth and sickness.

Disaster in the form of famine, war or epidemic disease could strike only from outside. A plague of insects might descend upon the crops and cause famine. Arab slavers, pushing down from the north and east of Africa, might chance upon one of these villages, engage the inhabitants in battle and carry off the survivors into captivity. In later years the white man would come, bringing with him new diseases harmless enough to himself, but lethal to a community lacking any inbred or acquired resistance.

Thousands of years ago the peoples of Egypt, Mesopotamia, India and China began to emerge from these self-contained communities and the chances of major disaster multiplied. A greater degree of civilization brought benefits, a higher standard of living and a fuller, more intellectual life, but it also brought hazards. As more people pushed out from their centres into less civilized areas, the chance of contact with unknown diseases increased. Tracks became roads and made for easier, faster travel. New diseases could be carried along such roads, striking down unaccustomed populations in mass pandemics before resistance to the invading organism could develop. Cities were built and, as city-dwellers necessarily rely upon an extraneous food supply, famine became inevitable if that supply failed, for there were no natural resources to take its place. Hunger, the desire for more and better living space, or the simple lust of a chieftain for power, would then set one tribe to fight against another. So man's three great enemies, Pestilence, Famine and War – the three Horsemen of the Apocalypse who bring in their train Death upon his Pale Horse – developed on an ever-increasing scale.

Pestilence, famine and war interact and produce a sequence. War drives the farmer from his fields and destroys his crops; destruction of the crop spells famine; the starved and weakened people fall easy victims to the onslaught of pestilence. All three are diseases. Pestilence is a disorder of the human. Famine results from disorders of plants and cattle, whether caused by inclement weather or more directly by insect or bacterial invasion. War, albeit arguably, is a mass psychotic disorder, a departure from accepted behaviour. In the next chapters, although the diseases of famine and war must necessarily have their place, our primary concern will be with those physical ills that have directly affected the human race.

CHAPTER ONE

Disease in the Ancient World

Disease associated with civilization is older than written history, for civilization of a kind existed before the earliest records were kept. There is evidence of disease and its sometimes important consequences at a comparatively early stage of recorded human development. The earliest known textbook of medicine, the Chinese *Great Herbal of the Emperor Shen Lung*, dates from about 3000 BC and there is a Babylonian physician's seal of approximately the same date in the Wellcome Historical Museum. Epidemic fevers are mentioned in the Ebers papyrus, found in a tomb at Thebes by Professor Georg Ebers in 1862. The papyrus has been dated to 1500 BC but much of it was probably copied from an older text. In Exodus there is an account of the plague which smote Egypt about 1500 BC, killing all the firstborn in the land from the firstborn of Pharaoh on his throne to the firstborn of the captive in his dungeon and all firstborn of cattle. This is one example of the effect of disease upon history, for the last terrible visitation upon the Egyptians persuaded Pharaoh to allow his Israelite slaves to depart. After forty years of wanderings and tribulations in the wilderness they at last reached their promised land.

The war–pestilence sequence is well described in Samuel I. We are told that about 1140 BC the Israelites went out against the Philistines in battle and were defeated. The Israelites brought out their sacred Ark of the Covenant and re-engaged the Philistines, but again suffered defeat. The Philistines captured the Ark and bore it off to Ashdod, where plague at once broke out. The Ark was then removed – by public request – to Gath and then to Ekron, both places being immediately smitten by plague. After seven months of suffering, the Philistines decided that the only hope was to return the Ark to Israel. It was delivered to the field of Joshua the Bethshemite, the return being greeted with sacrifices. But the inquisitive Bethshemites looked into the Ark and were punished by a great pestilence. It seems that the disease then spread throughout Israel, bringing death to about fifty thousand people.

The plague of Athens in 430 BC provides a striking example of the effect of disease upon history. At the beginning of the fifth century the Athenian

Empire was at the height of its power. This tiny Greek nation had defeated mighty Darius the Persian in the land battles of Marathon and Plataea and in the great naval engagement of Salamis. The enlightened reign of Pericles opened in 462 BC. Under him the temples of Athens and Eleusis, destroyed by the Persians, were restored through the genius of the architect Ictinus and the artist Pheidias. But this golden age of Greece was all too brief. In 431 BC the Peloponnesian War broke out, an internecine struggle between the two main Hellenic powers of Athens and Sparta. Sparta was a military nation with a good army but no fleet, Athens a maritime power with a strong navy and a weak army. Since her land defences were almost impregnable and ample supplies could be imported by sea, Athens could neither be brought to battle by land nor starved into submission. Fighting a defensive battle by land and an offensive war at sea, she should have been able to defeat Sparta without great difficulty. During the first year of the war the outcome seemed inevitable, for Athens was successful both on land and sea, but her defensive policy on land necessarily led to the Athenians being crowded and besieged within their city walls.

Disaster struck in 430 BC. The pestilence is supposed to have started in Ethiopia, whence it travelled to Egypt and was carried across the Mediterranean by ship to Piraeus and Athens. It raged for only a short time but caused an enormous mortality. Perhaps at least a third and possibly two-thirds of the population died. More disastrous still was the breakdown of morale, a not surprising phenomenon which we shall meet again in times of pandemic sickness. Thucydides, who left an account of this horrible time, wrote of the Athenians: '. . . fear of gods or law of men there was none to restrain them. As for the first, they judged it to be just the same whether they worshipped them or not, as they saw all alike perishing. As for the latter, no one expected to live to be brought to trial for his offences.' Thucydides added that even the most staid and respectable citizens devoted themselves to nothing but gluttony, drunkenness and licentiousness.

When it seemed that the plague had subsided, Pericles sent a powerful fleet to capture the Spartan-held stronghold of Potidaea. But hardly had the navy set sail – or, to be accurate, rowed away – when plague broke out in the ships with such violence that the fleet was forced to return to Athens. A similar disaster occurred when Pericles himself led his fleet to Epidauros for 'the pestilence not only carried off his own men but all that had intercourse with them'. Pericles may have caught the infection at this time, for he is supposed to have died of plague in 429 BC.

The nature of the visitation is unknown. No account of it occurs in the writings attributed to the master physician Hippocrates. Thucydides described a very rapid onset, raging fever, extreme thirst, tongue and throat 'bloody', the skin of the body red and livid, finally breaking out into pustules and ulcers. The disease attacked all classes, rich and poor. Physicians were helpless and themselves succumbed in large numbers. The majority opinion holds that this was a highly malignant form of scarlet fever, probably the first appearance of the infection in the Mediterranean basin and therefore especially lethal. Other possibilities that have been cited include typhus, smallpox and measles, or even a disease long since disappeared, but whatever its nature the infection must have come from another centre of population which had developed its own disease pattern or pool. The pestilence would then have taken an explosive character because the Mediterranean peoples had had no chance of developing any immunity. The survivors would gradually develop increasing resistance as epidemics of the infection recurred and so the disease became less fatal.

The plague of Athens undoubtedly contributed to the downfall of the Athenian empire. By killing so many, by demoralizing the capital and, above all, by destroying the fighting power of the navy, the plague prevented Athens striking a decisive blow at Sparta. The war dragged on for twenty-seven years and ended with the defeat of Athens in 404 BC. She was deprived of her navy and her foreign possessions and her landward defences were razed to the ground. Fortunately for posterity, the city and its culture were left intact.

One of the most stupendous events in history, in both the extent and longevity of its effects, is the downfall of the Roman Empire. The causes of this fall have been argued by historians for many years past. Here we shall examine only such causes and effects as are connected with disease and its prevention.

Public health and sanitation were more advanced in the year AD 300 than they were to be again until the middle of the nineteenth century. Rome's great drainage system, the Cloaca Maxima, was started in the sixth century BC and assumed the function of a modern sewer, the plan being repeated in many parts of the empire. The ruins of Pompeii and Herculaneum, destroyed by an eruption of Vesuvius in AD 79, have revealed an elaborate system of waterworks connected with flushing closets. Under the rule of the Emperor Vespasian, about AD 70, a building fitted with marble urinals was erected in Rome, a small charge being made for admission. In contrast, London had to wait until the Great Exhibition of 1851 before any public lavatories were provided. In 1851 'public waiting rooms', for ladies in Bedford Street, for gentleman in Fleet Street, were set up by way of experiment, the charge being 2*d* for 'lavatory privileges' and 4*d* for a hot towel. The cost of construction came to £680 and, despite their distance from the Exhibition in Hyde Park, admission fees raised £2,470 in five months.

Cleanliness depends upon an adequate water supply. The first aqueduct brought pure water into Rome as early as 312 BC. At the beginning of the Christian era there were six, but a hundred years later ten aqueducts supplied 250 million gallons of water daily. The public baths required half this enormous supply but there remained 50 gallons a head for the two million inhabitants, about the same amount as is used by a citizen of London or New York today. In 1954 four of these aqueducts had been renovated and sufficed for the needs of modern Rome. The baths of Caracalla, dating from about AD 200 could accommodate 1,600 bathers at a time. Those of Diocletian built eighty years later had no fewer than 3,000 rooms. The bath, much like a modern sauna, accompanied Roman civilization wherever it penetrated and some places became famed for the curative powers of their warm or mineral-impregnated waters. A few, such as Bath in England and Wiesbaden in Germany, retain a modest reputation as medicinal spas today.

The huge city-state of Rome had grown haphazardly, a town of crooked, narrow streets and squalid houses. Almost two-thirds of this was destroyed in AD 64 by the great fire in the reign of Nero. More fortunate than London after the fire of 1666, Rome was rebuilt to a master plan, a city of straight, broad streets and wide squares. Cleaning of the public roads was supervised by the *aediles*, a body of officials who also controlled food supply, introducing regulations to ensure the freshness and good quality of perishable foodstuffs. Among other public health measures was the prohibition of burials within the city walls, causing the much more hygienic method of cremation to become common. Cremation was not entirely replaced by burial until general acceptance of Christianity implanted belief in physical resurrection.

In its cleanliness, sanitation and water supply, Rome was much more akin to twentieth-century London and New York than to medieval Paris or eighteenth-century Vienna. The Romans were the first urban-dwelling people on the grand scale. They must have quickly recognized, probably as a result of painful experience, that a large body of people cannot live closely together without a pure water supply, clean streets and efficient sewers. A seventeenth-century Londoner existed in conditions that would hardly have been tolerated by a first-century Roman. But they met on one common ground, for neither knew the cause of disease. If the seemingly clean water that flowed along the Roman aqueduct happened to come from a contaminated source, then the Roman was as much at risk as the Londoner who drew his supply directly from the muddy Thames. This lack of essential knowledge rendered the magnificent health measures of Imperial Rome entirely useless during the long years of her plague-ridden decadence.

Imagine Rome as a bloated spider sitting in the centre of its web. That web, at the height of Roman expansion, stretched from the Sahara in the south to the borders of Scotland in the north, from the Caspian Sea and the Persian Gulf in the east to the western shores of Spain and Portugal. To north and west lay the oceans, to south and east wide unknown continents in which dwelt less civilized peoples: Africans, Arabs and the savage tribes of Asia. Beyond, in the dim shadows, lay the ancient civilizations of India and China. The long land frontiers were manned by garrisons at strategic points. From these frontier garrisons stretched back the filaments of the spider's web, the sea routes from Africa and Egypt, the straight, legionary-made roads, all of which led to Rome.

Herein lay the makings of disaster. A wide hinterland hiding unknown secrets, among them the micro-organisms of unaccustomed disease, troops who attacked into that hinterland and were attacked by the inhabitants, easy transit by ship or along the roads specially built for swift travel, a densely packed population living a highly civilized life, but lacking the most rudimentary means of combating infection. Given the conjunction of circumstances such as this, it is little wonder that the story of the last centuries of Roman power is a long tale of pestilence.

In the first century BC an unusually severe type of malaria seems to have infected the marshy districts round Rome and produced a great epidemic about AD 79, shortly after the eruption of Vesuvius. The infection seems to have been confined to Italy, raging destructively in the cities and causing so many deaths in the Campagna, the market garden of Rome, that the whole area went out of cultivation and remained a notoriously malarial district until the end of the nineteenth century.

It was primarily due to malaria, though there were other reasons as well, that the live-birth rate of the Italo-Romans fell steeply at a time when the birth rate throughout the conquered regions was rising. Further, the chronic ill-health and weakness caused by untreated malaria decreased life expectancy and enervated the nation. By the fourth century AD the mighty fighting power of the legions was no longer Italian, not just men but officers too being drawn from Germanic tribes. Possibly malaria, rather than the alleged decadent luxury imported from the East, accounts for the slackness of spirit which characterized the latter years of Rome.

Malaria may have originated in Africa but another danger came from the remote East. Towards the end of the first century AD a warlike and merciless race emerged from the region of Mongolia, riding over the steppes into south-east Europe. Their exodus was probably dictated by disease or famine or a combination of both in the lands north of China. These mounted invaders were the Huns who, by pressing on the Germanic tribes of Alans, Ostrogoths and Visigoths inhabiting the central Euro-Asian land mass, instigated a relentless westward movement which in the end submerged Rome and broke the empire into a rabble of warring states. The Huns brought with them new infections which produced a series of epidemics known to historians as 'plagues'. An interesting point is that the Huns very probably encountered a European disease unknown to them. During the years AD 451–4, under Attila, they reached as far west as Gaul and northern Italy but were turned back before invading Rome itself, apparently by epidemic sickness rather than by defensive warfare.

The Plague of Antoninus, sometimes known as the Plague of the physician Galen, started in AD 164 among troops of the co-Emperor Lucius Verus stationed on the eastern border of the empire. The sickness was confined to the east for two years, causing havoc among an army under the command of Avidius Claudius sent to repress a revolt in Syria. The infection accompanied the legions homeward, spreading throughout the countryside and reaching Rome in AD 166. It rapidly extended to all parts of the known world, causing so many deaths that cartloads of corpses were removed from Rome and other cities.

This visitation is notable because it caused the first crack in the Roman defence lines. Until AD 161 the empire continually expanded and maintained its frontiers. In that year a Germanic horde forced the north-east barrier of Italy. Fear and disorganization prevented retaliation for eight years. In 169 the full weight of Roman arms was thrown against the invaders. They were driven back but it seems that sickness carried by the legions played its part, for many Germans were found lying dead on the battlefield without any sign of wounding. The pestilence raged until 180, one of the last victims being the noblest of Roman Emperors, Marcus Aurelius. He died on the seventh day of his illness, having refused to see his son in case he should also fall a victim. After a short respite, the pestilence again returned in 189. This second epidemic was less widespread but severely affected the city of Rome, causing more than two thousand deaths a day at its height.

The name of the physician Galen is attached to the plague of 164–89 not only because he fled from it but because he left a description. Initial symptoms were high fever, inflammation of the mouth and throat, parching thirst and diarrhoea. Galen described a skin eruption appearing about the ninth day, sometimes dry and sometimes pustular. He implies that many patients died before the eruption appeared. There is here some resemblance to the Athenian plague, but the undoubted Eastern origin and the mention of pustules have led many historians to assert that this is the first record of a smallpox epidemic.

One theory holds that the westward movement of the Huns started because of a virulent smallpox epidemic in Mongolia, which they transmitted to Germanic tribes who in turn infected the Romans. Against this theory must be set the fact that the later history of the Roman outbreak in no way resembles the later history of European smallpox in the sixteenth to nineteenth centuries. But, as we shall see in some of the following chapters, the first appearance of a disease often takes a form and course quite different from that of the established disease.

After AD 189 there is no mention of a serious 'plague' until the year 250. Then appeared the great Plague of Cyprian which indisputably changed the course of history in western Europe. The nature of the infection is, however, unknown. Cyprian, the Christian bishop of Carthage, described the symptoms as violent diarrhoea and vomiting, an ulcerated sore throat, burning fever, and putrefaction or gangrene of the hands and feet. Another account tells of a very rapid spread of disease all over the body and of unassuagable thirst. In neither account is there any mention of a rash or skin eruption, unless the phrase 'rapid spread all over the frame' implies a visible manifestation. Like the Athenian plague, the place of origin is said to have been Ethiopia, from where it passed to Egypt and the Roman colonies in North Africa, which was the granary of Rome. In this respect the Plague of Cyprian resembles the Plague of Orosius in AD 125, an example of the famine–pestilence sequence, preceded by an invasion of locusts which destroyed the north African cornfields. The mention of gangrenous hands and feet by Cyprian tempts one to think of ergotism as the cause. Epidemic ergotism, caused by eating bread made from rye infected by the *Claviceps* fungus, has certainly occurred quite frequently but there is little evidence that rye, a crop of the north rather than of the south, was a staple bread corn of Rome. The very wide spread and longevity of the Plague of Cyprian are also arguments against the theory. It is safer to leave the nature of the disease in doubt.

The Plague of Cyprian resembled the 'Spanish flu' of 1918–19 in producing a pandemic; that is to say it affected all regions of the world then known to the West. It advanced with great speed, not only by human-to-human contact but by means of clothing or any article used by the sick. The first devastating appearance was followed by a remission which ended with a renewed epidemic of equal virulence. There was a seasonal incidence, outbreaks starting in the autumn, lasting through winter and spring, and fading out with the coming of hot weather in summer: a cycle suggestive of typhus fever. Mortality is said to have been higher than in any previously recorded pestilence, the deaths of infected persons outnumbering those who survived an attack. The acute phase of the Plague of Cyprian lasted for sixteen years, during which time a general panic developed. Thousands fled the countryside to overcrowd the towns and so cause fresh outbreaks, and wide areas of farmland reverted to waste; some thought the human race could not possibly survive. Despite warfare in Mesopotamia, on the eastern frontier and in Gaul, the Roman Empire managed to surmount the catastrophe, but by AD 275 the legions had fallen back from Transylvania and the Black Forest to the Danube and the Rhine, and the situation appeared so dangerous that the Emperor Aurelian decided to fortify the city of Rome itself.

It is likely that after the acute phase the infection persisted as a slightly less virulent illness. Throughout the next three centuries, while Rome slowly collapsed under pressure from Goth and Vandal, there were recurrent outbreaks of a similar pestilence. Gradually the evidence becomes more blurred, degenerating into a story of generalized war, famine and sickness, as the darkness descended over Rome and her mighty empire disintegrated. The Germanic peoples crowded into Italy and Gaul, crossing the Pyrenees into Spain, even into North Africa where an epidemic so weakened the Vandals themselves in 480 that they were

12

unable to resist a later invasion by Moors. There are rumours of a great mortality in Rome in 467 and around Vienna in 455.

Of special interest, because it may have affected the history of the Anglo-Saxons, is a visitation in Britain, apparently part of a general pandemic, in the year 444. According to Bede, mortality was so great in Britain that barely enough healthy men survived to bury the dead, while the pestilence depleted the forces of the Romano-British chieftain Vortigern to such an extent that he was unable to cope with the incursions by the savage Picts and Scots. Legend relates that, after consulting his chieftains, Vortigern decided to seek help from the Saxons who arrived in 449 as mercenaries under their leaders Hengist and Horsa. It may truly have been epidemic sickness which so weakened the British that Saxon infiltration was successful.

Meanwhile a new Roman Empire had arisen in the East. Asia Minor had been annexed by Rome in the first century BC. In AD 330 Constantine the Great founded his eastern capital at Byzantium (Constantinople, now Istanbul). The combined Eastern and Western Empires lasted about a hundred and fifty years. Then the Western Empire of Rome disintegrated but the Eastern Empire of Byzantium survived until its overthrow in 1204 by the Latin forces of the Fourth Crusade. During the sixth century Justinian, perhaps the greatest of the Byzantine rulers, had almost succeeded in translating into reality the aspiration to resurrect Rome and to reunite the two halves of the old empire. He launched an attack to the west in AD 532. He recaptured Carthage and much of the north coast of Africa, retook Sicily and crossed to the mainland of Italy. Naples fell to his general Belisarius while undefended Rome and most of central and southern Italy were captured by the imperial armies. In 540 it seemed that Germanic resistance had been broken. Justinian, having also reconquered part of Spain, formed a bold plan to carry his conquests into Gaul and even into Britain.

His victories brought no lasting gain. The Moors drove the Byzantines from most of the newly won African sea-board and in 541 a brilliant young Goth leader, Totila, recaptured the greater part of Italy. Totila was willing to make terms with Justinian but the emperor had determined upon total reconquest. There followed eleven years of bitter warfare in which Rome underwent siege five times. During one of these sieges the Goths cut the aqueducts in an attempt to force surrender. Medieval squalor and uncleanliness partly derive from this action because Rome, with her magnificent buildings and historical prestige, never wholly lost her influence upon European lifestyle. If Rome had still possessed a functioning and plentiful supply of clean water, other European cities might have followed her example.

The reign of Justinian should have been a time of imperial splendour. He girdled his domains with a defensive chain of castles and forts, and erected many magnificent buildings, including the cathedral of St Sophia. His code of laws, embodying those of ancient Rome, formed the basis of European justice for centuries to come. He recruited well-trained armies commanded by successful generals such as Belisarius and Narses. Yet during his long reign the Huns very nearly succeeded in taking his capital, the Slavs captured Adrianople and the Persians sacked Antioch. His government, which had begun in a blaze of glory, steadily declined. When Justinian died in 565 at the age of eighty-three, he left his empire considerably poorer and weaker than when he had mounted the throne in 527. For in 540, the year of his greatest success, an enemy more terrible than Goth or Vandal was about to strike.

The Plague of Justinian is one of the most lethal that has ever ravaged the world. We know something of it from the account written by Procopius, the secretary or archivist of Justinian's reign. The first known cases were reported in 540 at Pelusium in Lower Egypt from where the infection spread throughout Egypt and also into Palestine, which seems to have been the focus of diffusion to the rest of the known world. Constantinople was first infected in the spring of 542. The mortality was not at first great but rapidly increased as the summer advanced until some ten thousand people died each day. Graves could not be dug quickly enough, so roofs were taken off the towers of forts, the towers filled with bodies and the roofs replaced. Ships were also loaded with the dead, rowed out to sea and abandoned.

This is the first time that we can correctly use the term 'plague', for the sickness was undoubtedly bubonic plague. Victims were seized with sudden high fever. On the first or second day the typical buboes – swollen glands – appeared in the groin or armpit. Many patients quickly became deeply comatose, others developed a violent delirium in which they saw phantoms and heard voices prophesying death. Sometimes the buboes broke down into gangrenous sores and the sufferer died in terrible pain. Death usually occurred on the fifth day of illness or even more quickly but was sometimes delayed for a week or two. Physicians could not prognosticate which cases would be light and which fatal. They were quite useless for there was no known remedy, and by the end of the epidemic some 40 per cent of the population of Constantinople was dead. Procopius makes two interesting points. First, the plague always started on the coast, and spread inland. Second, contrary to expectation, doctors or attendants who nursed the sick and laid out the dead seemed not to fall victim any more frequently than others.

The plague returned again and again, lasting until about the year 590. It spared no town or village, ravaging the most remote settlements. If a region congratulated itself on having escaped, the plague would surely appear in due time. As in the Plague of Cyprian, there was a seasonal rise and fall in intensity, but whereas the first reached its height in winter, that of Justinian caused the greatest number of deaths in the late summer months. Many cities and villages were wiped out or abandoned, land went out of cultivation and panic threw the whole empire into confusion. Gibbon states that entire countries never regained their previous density of population. Procopius makes the observation, found in many plague chronicles, that the depravity and licentiousness during and after a visitation suggested that only the most wicked survived.

The extent to which epidemic disease contributed to the downfall of Rome and to the wreck of Justinian's ambitions must remain an open question. Incurable infectious illness is no respecter of persons but impartially attacks the highly civilized and the less civilized. The city-dweller is at greater risk than the countryman and, in a mortal epidemic, a closely knit organization will disintegrate more quickly than a looser association. Of supreme importance is the fact that failure of morale is more likely to occur among those who have lived softly than among people who have known hardship all their lives. Thus, although pestilence must have seriously affected the fighting spirit of savage tribes, its impact upon Roman and Byzantine life was very much greater. When we consider the frightful sequence of pestilences that smote the empire during the time of its decadence we need hardly search for a more potent cause of disaster.

Besides undermining the Roman state, the pestilences of the first three centuries AD produced two far-reaching and long-lasting effects which are less widely recognized. First, Christianity would hardly have succeeded in establishing itself as a world force, and would certainly not have taken the form that it has, if the Roman Empire had not been ravaged by incurable disease during the years which followed the life of Christ. Second, the thousand-year history of medicine from the fourth to the fourteenth century would have been very different had medicine not fallen under the domination of the Christian Church. To understand what happened we must go back to the beginnings of European civilization, when priest and doctor were one and the same.

In the early days of Greek legend the god Apollo killed a venomous snake, a symbol of disease. By this act Apollo became regarded as the god of health but he was also the bringer of pestilence which he visited on mortals by his arrows. He must therefore be not only worshipped but placated. Apollo passed the secrets of his healing power to the centaur Chiron who in turn instructed Asklepios or Aesculapius. The latter, possibly confused with a human healer living about 1250 BC, was honoured as a god and was worshipped in temples scattered throughout Hellas.

The cult of Aesculapius grew and developed into the ritual of incubation or temple-sleep. The patient made a sacrifice to the healing god and purified himself by bathing (lustration). Then he lay down to sleep in a long open corridor where Aesculapius himself might appear in a dream and advise him, or the god's sacred serpents might effect a cure by licking his sores. In later years the magical temple-sleep was reinforced by physical therapy consisting of exercise, diet, massage and bathing. Many patients stayed for weeks or months in the temple, which developed into something closely akin to the nineteenth-century 'hydropathic'. Treatment was no doubt equally successful in both.

The Greeks initiated the 'scientific approach'. Pythagoras (c. 530 BC) is the father of mathematics but he also founded a system of medicine. His pupils enunciated the doctrine of the four elements – earth, air, fire and water – and produced theories of respiration, sight, hearing and brain function. Their teaching was elaborated in a collection of writings attributed to the physicians of Cos, or 'Coan school' of which Hippocrates (c. 460–377 BC), often regarded as the Father of Medicine, is by legend the founder. This 'Hippocratic Corpus' developed the theory of humours from the theory of elements and tended to deny that disease was a punishment sent by the gods.

By the mid-fourth century BC Greek medicine had ceased to be mere magic and had acquired a rational basis, but how far this 'scientific approach' affected actual practice must remain problematical. The Coans cannot have been only theorists for they described recognizable diseases and the results of logical treatment. But the cult of Aesculapius certainly survived the age of Hippocrates and it is noticeable that the great physician was reputed to be a direct descendant of Aesculapius. The so-called 'Coan school' was more probably an association of physicians than a teaching unit and it is unlikely that their theories spread widely or exerted much immediate influence.

That last point is of importance in the story of Roman medicine. According to Pliny the Elder, Romans got on very well without doctors for six hundred years. There was medicine of a kind. The head of a household treated his family with folk remedies and sacrifices to the appropriate god. Both Apollo and Aesculapius had their votaries, for Rome borrowed from all countries, but citizens recognized a number of native demigods, many of whom were associated with sickness or bodily functions. So many were there that it has been said the Romans possessed an appropriate god for every part of the body and for every kind of illness, and that each god must be placated by his or her particular and exact ritual. This made the doctor's problem rather more simple than it is today. If cure did not occur, the wrong god had been invoked or the incorrect rite performed.

Practice of medicine was beneath the dignity of Roman citizens. Their early physicians were slaves of Greek extraction. About 220 BC the first of these, Archagathus, appeared in Rome. He was followed by many others who seem to have been more interested in money than in their patients' welfare. Julius Caesar granted these slave-physicians their freedom. Their standing improved under Augustus but, so far as is known, medical practice always lay in the hands of foreigners. When the great epidemics struck Rome, the citizens could call only upon their ancient gods or Greek physicians. Neither was outstandingly successful, so it is not surprising that the Romans sought help elsewhere.

Because of her contacts with foreign nations and because the empire embraced so many peoples, Rome sheltered and tolerated a great variety of religions. Not only did she have her own domestic gods but she honoured others from Greece and the East. For instance, Mithra, the most popular deity among the legionaries, originated in India or Persia. Among the conquered peoples whose religion exerted influence were the Jews. Small Jewish communities settled throughout the length of the Mediterranean sea-board and the number greatly increased after the Dispersion following the war of AD 66.

These Jewish communities were renowned for their moral code, their upright dealing, their charity and their care of the sick and poor. Many Gentiles found themselves attracted to their way of living but disliked certain practices such as circumcision and the refusal to eat meat that had been offered in sacrifice. The more liberal Jewish communities accepted Gentiles without insisting that they follow these customs. They were allowed to attach themselves to the synagogue and form an outer circle known as 'God-fearers'. The earliest Christian missionaries, among them the apostle Paul, found their first converts among the 'God-fearers' and it was in these para-Jewish congregations that the Christians of the Roman Empire first established themselves. This is why, when the emperors insisted on their own unique divinity, the monotheistic Jew and Christian were regarded as one and the same for purposes of persecution.

During much of the first century AD the apostles, the immediate followers of Christ, were still living and his story was passed by word of mouth. Eventually the basic pattern of Christian doctrine began to be summarized in creeds and the text of the New Testament. The gospels contain accounts of a number of 'miracles'. Twenty of these miracles are described by St Luke. Analysis reveals that only three are not of a medical nature. In four cases unclean spirits are cast out, in two the dead are restored to life and in eleven sickness or disability is cured. In addition, Luke positively states: 'He called the twelve together and gave them power and authority over all devils, and to cure diseases.' This authority was later extended to the seventy disciples. Thus Christ's miraculous and divine healing power was transferred to his followers.

As we have seen, the second century AD was a time of epidemic sickness. To the terror-stricken victims Christianity offered new hope, not found in any other creed. There was the promise of physical resurrection after death, coupled with the surety of everlasting bliss for the sinner who truly repented. Perhaps above all, the miracles of Christ and the miraculous power entrusted to his followers were an earnest of divine intervention that might cure sickness and even defeat death itself. Thus the growth of the Christian Church was stimulated by its specific medical mission in a series of pestilences. By the middle years of the third century the small scattered Christian communities had coalesced into an established Church and this process had been greatly accelerated by the Plague of Cyprian and by Cyprian's teaching. Conversions were more numerous at all times of famine, earthquake or pestilence. At the height of the Plague of Cyprian he and his fellow priests in North Africa baptized as many as two or three hundred persons a day.

So was formed the cult of Christ the Healer. The late third-century persecutions of Diocletian failed to stamp out Christianity and it received imperial sanction from Constantine the Great in 313. At the end of the fourth century Christianity was adopted as the official religion of the empire after enactment of laws against paganism by Theodosius. Practice of medicine passed into the hands of the Church, with priest and doctor again becoming one under the Byzantine emperors. The Christian followed the Jew in care of the sick. Sick-nursing formed one of the seven duties of the Christian and, as communities dedicated to the purpose appeared, the infirmary formed an essential part of their life. Early churches and early hospitals were designed on the same plan: a central altar with two or four long naves or wards leading from it with a number of small side-wards or chapels, each under the patronage of a saint. Treatment in these hospitals was undertaken by priests, assisted by lay brothers and sisters, all of whom combated disease almost wholly by appeal to supernatural agency.

The approach of the Byzantine and medieval 'doctor' was essentially the same as that of the modern Christian Scientist. Disease was a punishment incurred by sin, a lapse from the purity of Christian life. The cure, if God decided to effect a cure, could only be by miraculous intervention. But cure did not necessarily come from God alone. Just as the pagan gods of early Rome had intervened to cure disease, so the demigods or saints of the Christian Church could be invoked to perform the miracle. In fact many of the Roman gods and the early Christian saints were one and the same, a few with almost unchanged names. Thus Febris, the Roman goddess of fever, became the Christian St Febronia. Others enshrined the Christian concept of death, resurrection and a second death. Notable in this particular context are the two 'medical' saints Cosmas and Damian. They should be regarded as the patrons of transplant surgery, for they succeeded in grafting a new leg to replace an injured one. Accused of sorcery, they were stoned to death but miraculously restored to life, only to suffer a second death by decapitation.

The legend of St Sebastian is of special interest, although his story is now regarded as mythical. He is supposed to have commanded a company of the Emperor Diocletian's Praetorian Guard but secretly became a Christian. He converted others, including two noble youths, Marcus and Marcellinus. The two youngsters were accused and confessed under torture. They were condemned to death and their parents implored them to recant but Sebastian dissuaded them. Impressed by such steadfastness, their guards and their judges were all converted to

Christianity and all suffered death in the year 288. Diocletian himself urged Sebastian to recant, but he refused and was condemned to be shot to death with arrows. Left for dead, he was found by Irene, the mother of the boys, who nursed him back to health. Despite being begged to leave Rome, Sebastian stationed himself at the city gate and pleaded with Diocletian for the lives of his fellow Christians. Diocletian ordered him to be taken to the circus and there flogged to death. His body was flung into the Cloaca Maxima but it was found and buried in the catacombs. The church of St Sebastiano marks the site.

The cult of St Sebastian as the patron of epidemic sickness started about the year 680. The earliest representations depict him as an elderly bearded man, fully clothed, turning aside an arrow with a fold of his cloak. Later pictures show him as a youth of great physical beauty, naked except for a loincloth. Often an arrow pierces his groin, suggesting an allusion to bubonic plague. The inference is that Sebastian has become identified with the beauteous Apollo. There is also the symbolism of the arrow. The arrows of Apollo conveyed disease and Sebastian survived them. Thus, as one who had miraculously turned aside the arrows of disease, St Sebastian was empowered to protect and restore others who had been so attacked.

His legend is indicative of the ways in which Christian treatment of disease borrowed from Graeco-Roman practice. The sacrificial offering to the god became the votive offering to the saint. The temple-sleep or incubation remained unchanged but the devotee looked for the appearance of healing saints in his dreams. Ritual purification formed an essential part of Christian treatment but in time became degraded from beneficial cleansing of the body into a ceremonial sprinkling with 'holy water', a custom still observed in Roman Catholic and Orthodox churches. A less obvious transformation is the ancient practice of binding and loosing. This was originally associated with the goddess Carna who became patroness of childbirth. In Roman times binding and loosing consisted of massage or manual hypnosis. The Christian priests accepted this ritual but altered it into the laying on of hands, still practised by those who call themselves 'spiritual healers'.

So the cult of Christ the Healer became essential to both the work and the faith of the early Church. Surely it is no blasphemy to honour Jesus Christ as one of the greatest and most successful founders of a new system of medicine. His followers were psychiatrists and faith healers rather than physicians. For a thousand years they depended primarily upon supernatural intervention and only secondarily upon mundane treatment. Most of that treatment itself was frank magic: swallowing of written prayers or fragments of saintly bone, penitence, fasting and votive offerings. But there existed a solid foundation of psychological medicine and there was also a rational basis of medical theory, of anatomy and of herbal treatment.

If Christ was the founder of the Christian school of medicine, Galen was its acknowledged authority and unchallenged teacher. This is strange, for Galen was not a Christian although he seems to have defended Christianity and preferred monotheism to the Roman welter of demigods. Born in AD 129 at Pergamos in Asia Minor, Galen was appointed surgeon to the gladiators of that town and later moved to Rome. Here he practised and taught medicine, conducted scientific experiments and wrote a massive number of 'books'. He is reported to have fled the city during the plague which bears his name, but was recalled by Marcus Aurelius to Rome where he died in 216. A forceful, dogmatic teacher, he achieved a great and lasting reputation, not least as the means by which Hippocratic medical thinking was transmitted to future generations. He made many advances in anatomy and physiology but he fouled earlier and simpler methods of herbal treatment with a huge collection of noisome and useless remedies. Hence came the vile mixtures, often containing as many as fifty ingredients, by which medieval practitioners are rather unjustly remembered.

For nearly 1,200 years, and throughout the whole of the medieval period, the lamp of Greek medicine flickered on in scattered monasteries and in those small islands of culture that successfully withstood the general decline which followed the end of Imperial Rome. On the other side of the Mediterranean, in Alexandria, the school of the so-called Arabian physicians, many of them Jews and Christians, added something to the art of medicine. They, too, had learned from the followers of Christ, for their knowledge derived from the congregation of Nestorius, Christian Patriarch of Jerusalem, who had been banished for heresy in 431. The Arabs revered Galen but, more liberal than the Christians, they questioned, tested and recast his theories. In the end the two schools merged into one, but this was not to happen fully until a change in habits of thought ushered in the Renaissance at the beginning of the fifteenth century. By that time Church domination of medicine had become oppressive and the influence of Galen had waxed so great that to question his authority was no less than heresy.

CHAPTER TWO

The Black Death

The most destructive pandemic in the history of Europe occurred in the years 1348–61. This was a visitation of bubonic plague which much later became generally known as the Black Death. We shall continue to apply this familiar label to the fourteenth-century outbreak, while reserving the word 'plague' to cover later epidemics such as that which afflicted London in 1665.

The word 'bubonic' refers to the characteristic bubo or enlarged lymphatic gland. Bubonic plague is primarily a disease of rodents and is passed from rat to rat by the fleas which commonly infest them. The flea bites an infected rat and ingurgitates plague bacilli with the blood. These bacilli can remain in the flea's intestinal canal for as long as three weeks and are regurgitated when the flea bites another rat or a human. In true bubonic plague the human will become infected only if fleas migrate from rodents to humans or from an already infected human to another. Bubonic plague is not carried by human breath or direct contact.

The common source of infection is the black rat (*Rattus rattus*), sometimes known as the Old English Rat. This animal is companionable with man. It is rather a handsome beast with silky black fur and, unlike the brown rat, tends to live in houses or ships rather than in farmyards or sewers. This companionship with man assists migration of fleas from rats to humans and so permits spread of bubonic plague. The disease, whether of rat or man, carries a very high mortality among those infected, a figure of 90 per cent having been recorded in some epidemics and 60 per cent being regarded as 'normal'. The causative bacterium, *Pasteurella pestis*, now known as *Yersinia*, rapidly multiplies in the bloodstream, causing a high temperature and death from septicaemia (blood poisoning). But only relatively few human cases will occur in epidemics of true bubonic plague because transmission requires heavy infestation with fleas.

So far the story suggests a very dangerous illness, not common, occurring in isolated cases or small sporadic epidemics. But in certain circumstances, the nature of which is unknown, the infection will assume a pneumonic form which does not require the bite of a flea to infect the human but can be transmitted directly from one person to another by breath or by contact. Both forms existed together in the great pandemics, but it is the pneumonic type which produces a very rapid and wide spread, a higher incidence of cases and, since the pneumonia is usually fatal, a larger mortality.

Bubonic plague was rarely, if ever, absent from Europe during the period 1348–1666, but even over a longer time span only four world-wide pandemics are known. These are the Plague of Justinian, AD 540–90, which may possibly have extended as far as England; the Black Death of 1346–61, reaching England in 1348; 'the Great Plague' of the 1660s; and a pandemic starting in Asia in 1855 which caused high mortalities in Canton, Hong Kong and Russia, reaching England in 1900 where a few deaths occurred in Glasgow, Cardiff and Liverpool. During this last pandemic Ogata Masanori noted such a huge mortality of rats that he gave bubonic plague the name of 'rat-pest'. The pneumonic type developed in China and probably Russia, but the rat–flea–man form dominated in Europe.

In the Plague of Justinian and the Great Plague the pandemic started as a rat–flea–man infection. The spread was inland from the coast and those who attended the sick were at little greater risk than those who did not. In Constantinople the number of cases was small at the beginning but very rapidly rose until the number of deaths was too great for proper burial. A similar pattern is seen in the 1665 Plague of London. Samuel Pepys noted two or three houses in Drury Lane marked with a red cross on 7 June. From the end of the first week in June until 1 July the deaths from plague recorded in the Bills of Mortality are 100, 300, 450. Thereafter the rise became increasingly steep, reaching 2,000 in the last week of July, 6,500 at the end of August, and over 7,000 at its peak, the third week in September. The estimated population of London in 1665 was 460,000 and plague was rarely entirely absent from the city. A rise in the death rate from 200 to 300 a week can be attributed to an increase in the number of infected rats but a mortality of thousands indicates a direct human-to-human infection. Thus at some point in the Plague of Justinian and the Plague of London the type of illness must have changed from true bubonic plague to pneumonic. The same must be true of the Black Death.

The Black Death almost certainly started in Mongolia. An infected Tartar horde carried it to the Crimean isthmus, where the Tartars

besieged a small company of Italian merchants in the trading post of
Caffa, now known as Theodosia. According to one account, plague broke
out in Caffa itself, no doubt carried by rats, in the winter of 1346–7. A
second story relates that it was deliberately introduced by the Tartars
throwing infected corpses over the walls. Both sides suffered so many
deaths that the Tartars raised the siege. The horde dispersed, carrying
plague to the lands around the Caspian Sea from where it spread north
to Russia and east to India and China, which was first infected in 1352.
The surviving Italian merchants escaped by ship to Genoa. The
chronicler Gabriel de Mussis declared that no case of plague occurred on
the voyage but that it broke out in a deadly form a day or two after the
ship docked. His statement suggests a rat–flea–man infection.

From the European focus in Genoa, plague travelled in a great west
and north half-circle through Italy, France, Germany and Scandinavia,
reaching Moscow in 1352. The devastation was terrible. Historians have
reckoned that some twenty-four million people died: about a quarter of
the European and West Asian population. It should be mentioned here
that the havoc wrought in the Scandinavian countries may ultimately
have had a greater effect on world history than almost any other event.
Ships carried the infection to the Greenland settlements originally
founded by Eric the Red in AD 936. These colonies were so weakened by
the plague and by failure of supplies from enfeebled Norway that they
were wiped out by Inuit attacks. The last Viking settlers disappeared in
the late fourteenth century and Greenland became unknown country
until it was rediscovered by John Davis in 1585. It is thought that the
Viking settlements maintained sporadic contact with 'Vinland', part of
the coast of Canada or Newfoundland, so the Black Death may have
entirely altered the history of North America.

The Black Death arrived in England about 24 June 1348, probably
carried by a ship from Gascony which docked at the small port of
Melcombe, now part of Weymouth in Dorset. Infection seems to have
remained local and in the bubonic form until early August. From
Melcombe the plague travelled by land and sea, coastal vessels bringing
infection to ports on the south-west coast and along the Bristol Channel.
It moved overland through Dorset and Somerset with increasing speed,
reaching the great port of Bristol, either by sea or by land, on 15 August.
The citizens of Gloucester, learning of Bristol's plight, tried to prevent
infection by cutting off all communication, but their efforts were in vain.
From Gloucester the plague passed to Oxford and on to London,

reaching the city about 1 November. Westward spread through the sparsely inhabited counties of Devon and Cornwall was slower, for the plague did not reach Bodmin in central Cornwall before Christmas. By then the whole diocese of Bath and Wells, covering the counties of Dorset and Somerset, had been infected, for on 4 January 1349 the Bishop wrote of a great mortality and of many parishes left without a priest to administer the sacraments.

There now came a short respite during the winter months when rats, fleas and fourteenth-century humans all tended to be less active. Oxford, infected before November 1348, did not experience its highest mortality until May 1349. London suffered only a few deaths during the winter but the number increased rapidly in March, rose to a peak in April and May, then gradually declined. From London the main route led through the highly populated eastern counties, Norwich being infected in March and York towards the end of May 1349. By now the whole of the south, east and midlands of England had been attacked and the rate of spread slowed in the more thinly populated north and extreme west. Ireland received infection by sea in 1349 but Wales and Scotland were not attacked until 1350. Scotland might possibly have escaped altogether, had the Scots not decided to take advantage of England's difficulties by invading in the autumn of 1349 when mortality was at its greatest in the northern counties. Plague broke out in the Scottish army encamped near Selkirk and was dispersed over the country as the soldiers returned to their homes.

No one knows how many died in the terrible year of 1348–49. There were no Bills of Mortality as in the Plague of 1665, no Domesday Book, no census. No one in the fourteenth century was able to estimate large numbers, to strike a gross figure from investigation of a random sample. The situation is further complicated by the fact that the Black Death did not occur as a single visitation. There were recurrent epidemics on four or five occasions before the end of the fourteenth century. The worst of these, in 1361, infected England, France and Poland, among other countries. The name *Pestis puerorum*, given to this outbreak, may provide a first clue, for it suggests the presence of an abnormally high percentage of children in 1361, as would be the case if all age groups had suffered an unusually high mortality thirteen years before.

Another clue is provided by the Poll Tax levied across England in 1377. The evidence surrounding this suggests a population in the range of 2.5 to 3 million. Since the best estimates of the population in 1347 range from 4.5 to 6 million, the number seems to have dropped by 2 million or more in thirty years. The population had risen steadily between the Norman Conquest and 1300. There was also a fairly continuous increase from the end of the fourteenth century until a figure of 3 million or so for England and Wales was again reached in the middle of the sixteenth century. In both cases the rise can only have occurred because the live-birth rate outstripped the death rate. Ordinary disease, including outbreaks of epidemic illness, caused deaths throughout the whole period from 1066 to 1550 and, as the normal process of death continued, so did the normal process of birth. Thus a shrinkage of at least 2 million during roughly thirty years between the Black Death and the Poll Tax can only have been due to an abnormally large mortality. Since a great diminution of fecund adults would prevent a rising birth rate, it is safe to assume that maximum mortality occurred at the beginning of the period.

It is necessary to emphasize these rather dull facts because of a recent tendency to dismiss the Black Death as 'just another epidemic', causing at most the death of one in ten of the population. Far more probable is a mortality that exceeded one-third of the English people. This in itself is certainly high enough to dictate a social change, but it is the particular pattern of mortality as well as the total number of deaths that caused the major social upheaval of the late fourteenth century. Statistical evidence is scanty but a few monasteries recorded figures. Christchurch, Canterbury, experienced only four deaths out of eighty inmates, almost certainly from causes other than plague. The great Abbey of Crowland is another which seems to have entirely escaped, although its estates suffered badly. At the other end of the scale are Luffield Priory which lost all its monks and novices, St Mary Magdalen at Sandon where all perished, and a nunnery at Wolthorpe with only one surviving sister. Between the two extremes are eleven houses, the largest group in the series, which lost over 75 per cent, nine with mortalities of between 50 and 75 per cent and only three which record a death toll from plague of less than 50 per cent. Although this evidence is slight, it is a fair assumption that there was some resemblance between the varying mortalities of monasteries and those of town and village communities.

This pattern accords with the known behaviour of the pneumonic form of plague. There was considerable variation in the incidence of infection, and so of mortality, throughout England and Europe. The crowded walled towns would obviously have been at high risk. Density of population and ease of communication determined both incidence and rate of spread. In the thickly populated eastern counties of England, where villages lay close together and roads had been maintained for wagon traffic, the death toll must have been large. Inland waterways and coastal shipping would both have favoured rapid dissemination. In the more thinly populated north and west of Britain, and to a lesser extent in some southern counties, there must have been wide areas which escaped entirely, simply because of bad communications. But in 1348 the riches and the greater part of the English people were concentrated in the eastern and midland counties. A high mortality here would have exerted so profound an effect that the relative freedom from disease of large tracts, partly composed of forest and waste, can be almost discounted.

We must bear in mind this variation in the pattern of death when we consider the effect of the appalling mortality on English history. The impact upon England was greater than it was upon any other European country. The reason is that the English social system was already showing signs of strain and the Black Death greatly accelerated collapse. In Europe the system was more rigidly enforced and survived for many years. At the beginning of the fourteenth century England was still governed by the feudal system, of which it has been said that everything ultimately belonged to someone else. The great lord held his lands from the king, the knight held his manor from the lord, the village landowner from the knight, and the peasant or villein from the village landowner. Rental was paid by service. Thus the baron owed so many knights to the crown, the knight so many men-at-arms to his lord, while the peasant was forced to work so many days on his lord's land before he might cultivate his own. This, of course, is an over-simplification, for the system was far more complex and less complete in practice. One complication was the existence of money. So long as money was in very short supply and confined to the ruling class, the basic principle could be fairly widely applied. But, when coin entered into more general circulation, there developed a tendency to commute service for cash. The lord stayed at home instead of leading his knights, the knight found it more profitable to leave his farmers to till his land and pay a small force of professional soldiers, even the peasant sometimes managed to commute his service for a money rental or to demand a wage for additional labour. A growing population brought into being a quite large class of landless workers and these had to be paid in coin for their work.

Thus an increasing flow of money weakened feudalism. The thirteenth century saw a great agricultural boom and this led to an excess of crops above the level necessary for national subsistence. The upper classes and especially the Church, now the largest landowner in the country, devoted themselves with energy and intelligence to the business of farming. Trade and industry had both developed since the days of Norman invasion, but agriculture remained the predominant and most gainful occupation in England.

By the end of the thirteenth century more land in England had been brought under the plough than ever before and possibly than ever since. England had become a grain-exporting country, sending a steady supply of bread-corn – wheat from the south, barley and oats from the north – to the Continent in the small ships of her merchant fleet. This corn had to be collected in centres, the market towns and manorial barns, before being carried by wagon to the ports. The heavy wagons demanded well-maintained roads, and it is for this reason that the road system of England, largely Roman in origin, was in better condition in 1300 than at any time until almost the end of the eighteenth century. The agricultural boom allowed a good standard of living and this, in turn, affected the live-birth rate and expectation of life. Population, which had fallen since the end of Roman occupation, steadily increased from the Norman Conquest until the last years of the thirteenth century.

Corn exports allowed not only luxury imports but an increase in coin. Because of a flourishing agriculture and a wider distribution of money, there was considerable buying and selling of land by free peasants and exchange or leasing by the unfree as early as the thirteenth century. But the fact that a peasant possessed money did not necessarily mean that he could become a free man. His chances of freedom depended upon local conditions. Generally speaking, it was easier in the north, which was more remote from the Continental market and where there was less arable land requiring a large labour force.

Already by the late thirteenth century the basically simple structure of the feudal state had been complicated by a number of variants. The greatest weakness and the greatest danger to stability lay in the anomaly that the poorer peasants of the less highly cultivated areas had the better chance of freedom, while the relatively wealthy peasants of the predominantly arable counties found their bondage increased. A further danger lay in the very fact of prosperity. A glut of labour and a shortage of arable land developed in the cultivated area around increasingly highly populated settlements with the result that arable gradually extended on to marginal ground unsuitable for corn. Then, about the year 1290 something happened, though opinion is divided as to what that something was. Perhaps a long period of continental weather, hot summers and cold winters, gave place to a wetter and less extreme Atlantic system. Perhaps continual arable farming on marginal land, without adequate manuring or proper rotation, so exhausted the soil as to make corn-growing uneconomic. Sheep, which assumed the first place in agricultural economy during the fifteenth and sixteenth centuries, had already become a quite important branch at the end of the thirteenth, at a time when shortage of manpower had not yet dictated a type of farming requiring only a small labour force. Whatever the underlying reason may be, recession had begun in the early years of the fourteenth century, followed by a fall in the standard of living and of population growth.

Failure of a harvest resulted in widespread starvation. Only the able-bodied could hope to live through a long period of extreme scarcity until the new harvest brought fresh supplies. The very young and the elderly died of frank malnutrition or of intercurrent disease against which their enfeebled bodies could offer little resistance. The ills of damp and cold, particularly lung infections, must have carried off many older people and young children at these times, symptomatic of a general diminution of resistance which rendered the whole community more liable to attack by infectious disease. There is only one record, in 1257–9, of major famine sickness (possibly typhus fever) during the agricultural prosperity of the thirteenth century, but there seems to have been a series of poor harvests from about 1295 onwards culminating in the great famine of 1315–16.

A change to dairy farming and meat production was impossible because of the difficulty of keeping beasts through the winter. The standard of living of the peasantry therefore generally declined with a resultant fall in the live-birth rate. The peasant's economic position was further weakened by the war against the Scots in 1296 and by the Hundred Years War against the French, which began in 1337. The continental campaigns of Edward III, especially, could not be sustained by feudal levy and demanded paid or 'indentured' troops whose cost ultimately fell upon the man who tilled the soil.

Thus in the year 1347 the outwardly stable structure of the feudal system had developed a number of cracks, the economy of the realm was shaky and the subsistence of the peasantry lay at the mercy of the harvest. A network of fairly good roads linked inland communities to the Channel and North Sea ports. A stream of fighting men passed backwards and forwards across a short sea route to the battlefields of France. Given the sequence of a bad harvest, a famine-stricken people and a pestilence on the European continent, spread of disease throughout England was inevitable.

Men generally look back on world-shaking events and remember that they were preceded by signs and wonders in the heavens. There are reports of earthquakes, volcanic eruptions and even tidal waves in the years immediately preceding the Black Death but these, if they occurred, are coincidental. The one recorded antecedent that did affect the course of the pestilence is a quite appalling weather pattern which seems to have been general throughout Europe during the years 1346–8. The series of three abnormally wet and cold summers culminating in that of 1348, when it is related that rain fell unceasingly from midsummer until Christmas, imply a period of prolonged dearth with consequent malnutrition, illness and a reduced resistance to infectious disease.

So there can be little wonder that the immediate effect of the Black Death in England was a general paralysis. Trade largely ceased and the war with France was halted by a truce on 2 May 1349 which lasted until September 1355. In 1350 the death of so many able-bodied men put the realm in danger, and coastal towns were required to supply men-at-arms, ships and sailors from their already depleted resources. The cornfields had been sown or were being sown while the plague gathered momentum and a much smaller labour force reaped the harvest in 1349. Those who survived encountered unwonted prosperity: there was more money per head, more livestock, more grain. Prices fell steeply because it was a buyer's market. A good horse which had been worth forty shillings now fetched only sixteen, a fat ox could be bought for four shillings, a cow for one shilling, a sheep for fourpence. Wheat, which had been as cheap as sixteen pence a quarter in some of the boom years and as dear as twenty-six shillings in the famine of 1315–16, now sold at a shilling a quarter.

The urgent need to reap the harvest in the autumn of 1349 induced landowners to offer high wages. In the eastern, midland, and southern counties reapers and mowers are said to have received at least double their accustomed wage. The diet of the surviving labourers became unusually good as a result of all this plenty. These are the days of which William Langland wrote that Hunger was no longer Master, when beggars refused bread made from beans and demanded milk loaves or fine white wheaten bread and the best brown ale. Day labourers, who had once been content to eat stale vegetables and a hunk of cold bacon washed down with small beer, now turned up their noses at anything except fresh meat and fried or baked fish, served hot lest they catch a chill on their stomachs.

Initially the landlord suffered. He depended on agricultural products for his income and prices had fallen steeply. He used more imported and manufactured goods than the peasant and now had to pay more for them. But the labourers' time of gross plenty did not last, for only a limited number of cattle could be tended and only a limited acreage be cultivated by the reduced labour force. The continuing rise in population had outstripped the land available for cultivation in the years before 1348. The Black Death reversed the situation. Whereas there had been a glut of labour and a shortage of land in 1347, there was a shortage of labour and a glut of land in 1350.

Had the plague inflicted a uniform pattern of death throughout the country, the difficulty would have resolved itself within a short time. A smaller population would have tilled and fed off a smaller area. But the death pattern was not uniform and this is the reason for the trouble that followed. In 1350 a labour glut and a land shortage still existed on those manors which had escaped the Black Death and, only a few miles away, there would be unploughed acres and insufficient workers on badly affected estates. We know what happened in a group of three Norfolk manors belonging to Crowland Abbey. Eighty-eight peasant holdings were vacant in the autumn of 1349. So numerous were the Abbey estates that it proved possible to fill seventy-nine of these almost immediately by transferring landless peasants from manors that had not been affected. But these moves exhausted the available labour force and the remaining nine holdings continued vacant and unworked until 1352. Even then the Abbey had to increase the size of holdings on several estates so as to find tenants for the empty farms.

It is for reasons such as this that the English peasant became mobile for the first time in his history. In the autumn of 1349 the need to get in the harvest dictated the purposeful mobilization of the available labour force. This movement was at first local but became more extended as redundant labourers on unaffected manors found that they could receive wages and land on badly affected estates. The majority of landlords found it more convenient to hire labour by offering an attractive wage and the labourer soon found that he could ask a higher payment. Thus rumours of higher wages tempted peasants to travel further afield and seek new masters. The masters, though more than willing to enforce feudal tenure, found themselves so short of labour that they were obliged to hire the vagabonds without questioning their origin.

The central government took swift action. The 1349 Ordinance and the Statute of Labourers in 1351 aimed at preventing all kinds of worker from transferring their services from one employer to another, the primary target of course being the peasant. But the Statute also sought to peg prices at the 1347 level and here the law affected employer equally with employed. The Statute not only forbade the worker to ask higher wages but the employer to offer them. It is unlikely that these laws would have solved the problem in the long term but they did succeed in restoring some measure of stability by preventing wages and prices getting entirely out of control. They bore heavily upon the smaller employers of labour. The masters were not always great landlords. Many villeins had become substantial small farmers cultivating forty or fifty acres. They were not free men, in that they held their land by service to their lords or had commuted that service for a payment in cash or kind, but they were masters in that they employed hired labour, drawn from the landless or almost landless class of 'cottars and bordars' which had greatly increased in numbers during the thirteenth century.

The laws made necessary by this changed situation gave rise to hardship and a great deal of resentment, but the national economy started to recover, and it even became possible in 1355 to resume the war with France. Wages and prices never fell to the 1347 level but at least they ceased to rise. The labour shortage continued because, since all age groups had been affected in 1348–50, the normal death rate exceeded the number of children reaching working age. Population rose slowly as the number of live births outstripped the number of deaths. A statesman able to survey the national scene in 1360 might have thought the worst to be over.

There are no records of serious epidemics between 1350 and 1361. That of 1361 received the name *Pestis puerorum* because the death rate among children was especially high, suggesting that an attack of plague conferred some resistance but maternal or inherited resistance was lacking. Another theory proposes that the disease was not bubonic plague but the first visitation of some illness of childhood such as diphtheria or meningitis. Whatever the truth, a great number of children in the under-thirteen age group died. Since a boy of fourteen was regarded as of working age, the supply of labourers again fell in the next years. The landlord now found himself faced with a virtually insoluble dilemma.

Many of his service tenants had died and their holdings were back on his hands. If he wished to farm the land himself, he needed labourers. If he did not farm it, the only profitable alternative was to let the land at a rent. The only person willing to rent the land was the surviving villein, whose duty it had been to cultivate the landlord's fields. The landowning government attempted to solve the dilemma by enforcing feudal service without mercy. Not only did commutation by payment cease entirely but service was demanded from those who had already commuted.

Obviously this attempted solution created increasing hardship as the available labour declined and, equally obviously, it evoked intense hostility among that section of the labouring community which had already tasted comparative freedom. Hostility increased through twenty troubled years and crystallized in the Peasants' Revolt of 1381. Precipitated by the unpopular Poll Tax of 1380 (the third in four years), this was predominantly an agricultural rising, having as its chief objective commutation of all servile dues for 'a fair rent' of fourpence an acre. The revolt failed in its immediate purpose and was followed by harsh repression but, in the end, the landlord at last understood that his only feasible course was to make the best possible bargain with his villeins. He retained ownership of the land but ceased to farm it through his bailiff or reeve. The reeve, who had overseen the labourers on his lord's fields, became the estate steward who received the rents from his lord's tenants. The service-labourer or villein developed into the tenant-farmer.

Thus the Black Death struck such a blow to the already weakened feudal system of tenure that it lost much of its meaning within two generations and had entirely disappeared within a hundred and fifty years. But the tenant-farmer himself needed hired labour and he recruited this from the less able villein and from the landless class of cottar and bordar. The new pattern had become evident by the early years of the fifteenth century and was complete in the sixteenth. England had become a country of tenant-farmers, their fields worked by a landless agricultural proletariat. In the majority of European countries the feudal system of landlord and peasant lingered on for four or five centuries. In England the peasant ceased to exist. Farmer and landworker took his place.

The old aristocratic landlord knew of only one source of wealth – land. Finding himself impoverished, he could visualize only one remedy: to obtain more land. The new tenant-farmer lived closer to the soil and understood that an excessive acreage can only be economically farmed by methods requiring a small labour force. Thus he quickly decreased his arable and increased his pasture. Even in the strong corn-growing lands of East Anglia sheep became the farm staple, while in the north and west sheep virtually ousted all other crops. Tudor prosperity depended upon wool. So rapid was the change that shortage of labour again turned to glut in the fifteenth century and by the time of Henry VIII the complaint was heard that the sheep were eating up the men. We catch a glimpse of the starving, out-of-work ploughman and labourer in the often-misquoted nursery rhyme:

> Baa, baa, black sheep, have you any wool?
> Yes sir, no sir, three bags full.
> Two for my master and one for his dame
> But none for the little boy who cries down the lane.

So, within little over a century, the villein-farmer developed into the wool baron. He was helped by the ever-increasing strain imposed upon the landed class by nearly a hundred and fifty years of almost continuous warfare. The climax came with the dynastic struggle of 1455–85 known as the Wars of the Roses. The feudal aristocracy turned the war into a great land-grabbing operation and, in doing so, committed mass suicide. The tenant-farmer took advantage of the anarchy by buying up the estate of his ruined lord, emerging as the landowner. The large majority of older English 'county families' arose during this time and by this means, their origins lying in a Saxon and villein ancestry rather than Norman blood. These 'new men' rose to power under the Tudors. Unlike the Norman barons, they came of the same stock as their inferiors. Though sometimes harsh and arrogant and often bitterly resented, they never developed into a closed, aloof caste as did so much of the continental aristocracy. The strength of the English social structure lies in the fact that continuing shifts have prevented a rigid differentiation between classes.

Looking beyond the shores of England, we find widespread social changes although of shorter duration. The Black Death must have seemed to the ordinary man to be of supernatural origin, a punishment inflicted by a higher power upon unknown sinners for unknown crimes. Culprits were sought: nobles, cripples and Jews in turn came under suspicion. The Jews in particular were suspected of purposely spreading plague by contaminating wells or 'anointing' houses and persons with an imagined poison. Their persecution started at Chillon on Lake Geneva in

1348 and spread rapidly to Basel, Freiburg and Strassburg. At Freiburg all known Jews were herded into a large wooden building and burned to death. At Strassburg over two thousand are said to have been hanged on a scaffold set up in the Jewish burial ground. So bitter did the persecution become that the liberal Pope Clement VI issued two Bulls declaring Jews to be innocent. Numbers fled from western Europe into east Germany and Poland. Here they were tolerated and founded communities which rapidly grew in numbers, a fact which partly accounts for the very large Jewish population in west Russia, eastern Germany, Poland and north-east Austria in the nineteenth and early-twentieth centuries. Thus the Black Death intensified the medieval Christian tradition of the scapegoat-Jew and, by causing the migration of so large a number to the east and north of Europe, is linked to the pogroms of imperial Russia and the gas-chambers of Auschwitz.

The attempt to find culprits was accompanied by a general relaxation of moral values and a cynical, unhappy pursuit of pleasure, a natural reaction which was also observed in the 1920s after the horrors of the First World War. There also developed a masochistic urge to accept the divine punishment and to divert it from others. The most dramatic expression of this urge was the mania for organized mass flagellation. The flagellants were not a product of the Black Death alone, for they achieved some notoriety in Italy and Germany during a severe famine-pestilence of 1258–9. In 1348 the movement spread all over Europe and enlisted tens of thousands. The flagellants organized themselves in companies each under a master, wore a special uniform, lived under discipline, and conducted their public and private flagellation according to a set ritual. To our modern way of thinking, the flagellants are likely to be sexual deviants, but the reason for their strange behaviour is perfectly logical. The Black Death was a divine chastisement so the flagellant attempted to divert it by chastising himself. Thus it was the rumour rather than the appearance of plague which induced the exhibition. The flagellant tried to forestall punishment of his fellows by inflicting punishment on his own body.

The movement was at first welcomed by the Church as a mass penance. Pope Clement himself ordered public flagellation at Avignon in an attempt to stay the plague. But the flagellants rapidly got out of control and assumed the character of a revolutionary movement directed against Jews, the richer classes and the Church itself. In October 1349 the Pope issued a Bull condemning them. Many were beheaded, hanged or burned, and all further processions were forbidden. A curious quirk of clerical psychology condemned a number of flagellants to be flogged by priests before the high altar of St Peter's in Rome.

The Christian Church had risen to be a dominant power partly as a result of the earlier pestilences. It would be strange if so great a catastrophe as the Black Death did not exert some influence upon the authority of a religion which had now been established for over a thousand years. Its remarkable grasp upon Europe enabled Christianity to weather the storm but the authority of the Church did not survive the Black Death unscathed.

Up to a point, the Church's influence had been for the public good. It preserved a limited peace in times of strife, tried to impose a code of decent human behaviour and acted as schoolmaster. The Church harnessed and nourished intellect, provided and tutored administrators, lawyers and physicians, encouraged and preserved literature, architecture and art. But, although creative work might be encouraged, creative thought was more often sternly repressed. The doctrine of persecution formed an integral part of medieval Christianity and those whose written or spoken thoughts did not follow the rigid line permitted by the Church stood in danger of persecution as heretics.

In material matters the Church suffered badly from the Black Death. A great loss of manpower and consequent impoverishment through inability to cultivate its widespread estates rendered it a less dominant power in 1350 than it had been in 1346. But greater harm resulted from the Church's helplessness in this time of disaster, from the large loss of priests and monks, and from its failure to control their successors. Parish priests, the best-loved and most useful of church workers, died by the hundred and according to William Langland their benefices were all too often hurriedly filled by 'numbers of youths that had only devoted themselves for clerks by being shaven'. If Langland is to be believed, the friars, who had previously been renowned for holiness and charity, gave themselves up to 'gayness and gluttony' while country parsons and parish priests spent their time in London, touting for high places instead of ministering to their parishioners. Langland specifically states in both instances that these abuses had multiplied 'sithen the pestilence time'.

Further, the very fact that the Church possessed the seeming advantage of being international or supra-national imposed a threat to her power. In some countries, Germany and England for example, People and Church had been falling out of sympathy for many years. The national branches of the Church cried out for reform, but had no power to reform themselves because they lacked autonomy. In fact they were outlying parts of a foreign organization of immense power and prestige.

For all these reasons, open opposition to the Church developed in the years following the Black Death. Popular reaction can be measured by contrasting the murders of two Archbishops of Canterbury. In 1170 Thomas à Becket was done to death as the result of some hasty words spoken by King Henry II. Although Becket's policy was not generally approved, public horror at this sacrilege forced the king to submit himself to humiliating penance. In 1381 a band of rebels seized the mild Simon Sudbury and struck off his head on Tower Hill in London amid the ferocious applause of a large crowd. 'The relation of Church and people had undergone a profound change since the ancestors of these same men had knelt beside their ploughs to pray for the Holy Martyr, Thomas à Becket,' wrote G.M. Trevelyan.

The change was more profound than is suggested by the murder of Sudbury, Langland's disapproval or the deviant behaviour of flagellants. John Wyclif (*c.* 1330–84) was a notable theologian and Master of Balliol College, Oxford. He questioned Holy Church's hitherto unchallenged power, which he considered to be derived from the Caesars rather than from a divine source. As well as demanding a vernacular Order of Service and translating part of the Bible into English, he attacked the worship of images and relics, the sale of pardons and masses for the dead. Wyclif gained an immense following who became known as Lollards. They were drawn not only from the common people but also from the nobility, friars and some of the lesser clergy who had reason to dislike wealthy monks and bishops.

Wyclif was before his time. As the Church re-established its shaken authority, the Lollards were subjected to persecution and driven underground, to reappear in the reigns of Henry VII and VIII. Persecuted again, they re-emerged to combine with the Protestants of Martin Luther. Luther owed something to the teaching of the earlier reformer John Huss of Bohemia, who acknowledged himself a pupil of Wyclif. Thus it is not too much to claim that the Protestant Reformation, the sailing of the Brownist Pilgrim Fathers in the *Mayflower* from Plymouth on 6 September 1620 and the foundation of Pennsylvania by the Quaker William Penn in 1681, can all be linked with the deviation from established religion that followed the disaster of the Black Death.

One might think that so great a pestilence, in which physicians and priests alike proved useless, must have profoundly affected the development of the theocratic medical art. This is not so. The only medical advance attributable to the Black Death is in the field of public health. In 1374 the Venetian Republic appointed three officials with the duty of inspecting and excluding all infected vessels from the ports. In 1377 Ragusa detained travellers from infected places for thirty days (*trentini giorni*). When this proved ineffective the period of detention was lengthened to forty days (*quaranti giorni*) from which comes our word 'quarantine'.

The Black Death also added another saint to the calendar. St Roch is the special patron of bubonic plague. A native of Montpellier, he nursed the sick during the Black Death in north Italy and himself fell a victim. Left to die, Roch was succoured by a dog and recovered. In Lombardy he became suspected of being a foreign spy and was thrown into prison where he died. Here again is the sequence of mortal hurt, miraculous recovery, and ultimate death.

We should honour the Church for her unremitting care of the sick, but acknowledge that her influence upon medical and scientific advance was almost wholly negative. In Europe the thousand-year repression of creative thought between the fall of Rome and the Renaissance provides a miserable picture of sterile plagiarism. Great schools of medicine were founded – Salerno and Bologna in Italy, Paris and Montpellier in France – but the teaching in those schools was an uncritical reiteration of ancient theories, and research took the form of disputations upon the exact meaning of a text. The huge medical literature of this long period contains many original observations but hardly any original thought. It is little better than a series of compilations, the substance derived from Latin texts of first-century authors and their Islamic commentators. There are, of course, occasional flashes of the divine fire, for no weight of repression will ever stifle originality entirely. Thus Mundinus of Bologna defied the ban on human dissection and did something to restore the science of anatomy to the standard reached by Greek scholars about 300 BC. Another flame in the darkness is Roger Bacon of Oxford and Paris (*c.* 1214–94), a philosopher rather than a physician and certainly an original thinker, but his originality earned him imprisonment for the last thirteen years of his life.

The habit of thought engendered by theocratic intolerance stifled medical advance until the end of the fifteenth century. Galen remained the unquestioned authority. This dominance of one man would have been bad enough in itself, but the texts of Galen had been so debased as to be almost worthless. The true teachings of Galen were not restored until too late when, at the end of the fifteenth century, a new way of thinking opened up wide vistas of learning and beauty. The wonderful phenomenon of the Renaissance was not merely a revival of classical culture but a change in the whole outlook of thinking people, who demanded escape from the tyranny of dogmatism, from the limitations of thought imposed by the Church. Although the ghost of Galen was not finally laid until William Harvey disproved his doctrine of the ebb-and-flow movement of blood in the seventeenth century, it was the Renaissance that finally broke the Church's stranglehold on medicine.

Bubonic plague remained one of the more lethal European diseases for three centuries after the Black Death. It disappeared from the greater part of Europe during the early years of the eighteenth century, but remained endemic on the southern and eastern shores of the Mediterranean, in Asia, in Africa and in South America where epidemics have reached the proportion of national pandemics at times. Prevention and treatment of bubonic plague are now reasonably successful. The causative organism was discovered almost simultaneously in 1884 by a Japanese worker, Sharamiro Kitasato, and a Swiss, Alexander Yersin. The latter's name is now attached to the bacillus. Prevention was found to be possible by inoculation with a killed vaccine prepared from the organism or by injection of a live but avirulent preparation of *Yersinia*. Antibiotic drugs, streptomycin or tetracyclin, have proved successful in the developed illness. Rats and fleas can be dealt with by pesticides. But plague, especially in the pneumonic form, is still so dangerous that sick attendants must wear masks, protective gowns and gloves, just as they did or were advised to do in the Black Death or the Great Plague of 1665.

None of this explains why plague quite suddenly disappeared from Europe towards the end of the seventeenth century. There are a number of suggestions, of which the 'rat theory' is the most widely held. This supposes that the companionable black rat of houses and ships was killed out by the more ferocious brown or Norwegian rat, said to have first appeared in Europe in the 1720s, which inhabits sewers and is more commonly infested with a different flea that rarely transfers to humans. The theory is attractive but not really tenable. First, the theory that the brown rat killed out the black is a mere assumption. The two species do not appear to compete for living space or food. In the many places where they live in proximity, each stays within its own environment and keeps

39

out of the way of the other. They may even live side by side in apparent amity when the quarters are sufficiently spacious to provide each with its preferred conditions. Secondly, the black rat, if it ever disappeared which is non-proven, has returned. Since 1910 it has steadily increased in Europe. This fact has been made plain by F.E. Loosjes who commented, 'If epidemics of plague have really vanished with the black rat, it is imperative that careful study be made of the present increase in the species and if possible an end made to it.'

There is a type of animal plague known as 'campestral' or 'sylvatic' which affects wild rodents such as rats, rabbits, hares and squirrels. Rodent–flea–rodent transmission could carry infection to the urban or companionable species, black rats, hamsters and guinea pigs. There is a possibility that this is the type of plague which was once human and which transferred to the rodent. Our forefathers were quite as observant as we are, and they appear not to have noticed any unusual mortality of rats, which has been a marked feature of later outbreaks in India, China and Mongolia. Perhaps the epidemiology is correct but operated in reverse. The great plagues may have originated in the human but been transmitted by fleas to the rat.

Whatever the answer may be, and the above is supposition only, the three-hundred-year reign of plague in Europe ended by some natural process and not by any active measures on the part of men. There was no medical or scientific discovery, no advance in social hygiene, no improved standard of life, that can possibly account for its disappearance. Plague ended – or went into hiding. For we must always remember that three plague-free centuries separate us from 1665, and eight plague-free centuries separated the Plague of Justinian from the Black Death.

And if any who read these words believe that accounts of the Black Death are exaggerated and do not accord with modern medical knowledge, let them consider the evidence of Petrarch. The great poet was in a position to know, for he lived through the Black Death in Italy. Laura, his mysterious platonic love, died of plague at Avignon on 6 April 1348. He wrote of the empty houses, abandoned towns, squalid countryside, fields covered with the dead, a vast and dreadful silence over the whole world. He told of historians who remained silent when asked to describe similar disasters, of physicians at their wits' end, of philosophers who shrugged their shoulders, wrinkled their brows, laid a finger on the lip. Petrarch ended his account with these words: 'Is it possible that posterity can believe these things? For we, who have seen them, can hardly believe them.'

CHAPTER THREE

The Mystery of Syphilis

One of the most controversial problems in medical history is how and why the bacterial infection soon known as syphilis suddenly emerged in Europe at the end of the fifteenth century. Syphilis is now primarily a venereal disease, spreading from one participant to the other during sexual intercourse. But it can also be acquired in other ways, for example by the transplacental route, by a person with an open lesion in the mouth sharing a drinking vessel with a syphilitic, by the use of hypodermic needles in common, by tending an affected person without wearing protective gloves, or by a pathologist's carelessness when performing an autopsy. After the initial infection an incubation period follows which can be ten to ninety days but commonly two to four weeks, before the first sign of disease appears. This takes the form of an ulcer, known as a chancre, which is a local tissue reaction at the site of contact. Obviously the chancre will generally develop on or near the genital organs, but will occur at the site of infection, lip or finger for instance, when the disease has been acquired by means other than sexual intercourse. The chancre, even if untreated, will disappear spontaneously within three to eight weeks, leaving a very thin and inconspicuous scar. Sometimes the chancre is quite large but often little more than a rather hard pimple. This is why the primary stage of syphilis is so dangerous. The syphilitic is capable of infecting other people but the small initial ulcer and the consequent scar may be so trivial as to escape notice. About a quarter of all patients seen in the clinics say they have not noticed the primary lesion.

Six to eight weeks after the appearance of the chancre, the patient will usually enter the secondary stage but the symptoms may be delayed for a year or even more. The secondary stage is a general tissue reaction to infection, much like any reaction to bacterial invasion. There is a feeling of discomfort, headache, perhaps a sore throat, a mild fever and, in about 75 per cent of cases, a skin rash. The rash is important because it can take a number of different forms. Syphilis has been called 'the great mimic' because it can be mistaken for so many other diseases. This is particularly true of the rash which sometimes bears a resemblance to measles, or to smallpox or to any skin eruption. As a rule the secondary stage does not last for long and the patient then enters the early latent stage, in which he or she appears entirely free of all signs and symptoms, although sometimes the rash will reappear for a week or so and then disappear again. During both the secondary and early latent stages the patient is highly infectious. The most dangerous time is during the early latent stage for the patient can infect others but appears quite free from disease.

After about two years the late latent stage develops. There are no signs or symptoms and the patient is often not able to pass on the infection. It cannot be said that he or she is cured, because blood tests will reveal the presence of syphilis in the body tissues, but the disease is quiescent and may remain so for the rest of the patient's life span, death occurring from some unrelated cause.

The latent stage may last for years without any incident while the syphilitic lives in a fool's paradise, believing that there is no longer any danger. In reality the disease has only settled into a very prolonged chronic phase. From three to ten or even twenty years after the primary infection, the signs of tertiary syphilis may appear. There are many manifestations, for syphilis can attack almost every system in the body. The typical lesion of tertiary syphilis, the gumma, can appear anywhere: in the bones, the heart, the throat, the skin. Some people believe that the swelling on the side of Henry VIII's nose, in the portrait by Holbein, is a gumma.

Due to the development of antibiotic therapy, tertiary syphilis as distinct from the primary and secondary stages, had become a rarity in the Western world by the late twentieth century. In the past it had shown itself by changes in the blood vessels, resulting in weakening and ballooning of the walls, which led to death by rupture of the aorta or one of the vessels in the brain. The nervous system could be affected, causing the illness known as tabes dorsalis when the sufferer gradually became paralysed and incontinent. Or the brain itself might be damaged, giving rise to horrible personality changes and sometimes ending in general paralysis and insanity (GPI) in which the victim was converted into a helpless maniac. This terminal stage was often preceded by a phase in which the sufferer conceived ideas or schemes which were superficially rational but bizarre or grandiose. Conan Doyle tells the story of a young farmer who surprised his neighbours by taking a very rosy view of his prospects at a time when his farm was rapidly running downhill owing to an agricultural depression. He proposed to give up orthodox cropping and plant the whole area with rhododendrons to corner the market. His scheme would have been quite sensible had there been any market to corner. Most untreated patients died within five years of showing the first signs of GPI but a number never became frankly insane or helpless. The disease process in their brains changed their pattern of behaviour but they were able to carry on more or less normal lives and died from some other illness, perhaps having ruined themselves by foolish speculation or terrorized their families by violence.

One of the more terrible attributes of syphilis is that it can be transmitted from parent to child via the placental blood supply. If the mother is in the active or early latent stages, her child will probably die while still unborn but death does not usually occur until the fourth month of pregnancy at the earliest. Thus it can be stated that a history of repeated miscarriages *before* the fourth month of pregnancy does not suggest syphilis but that repeated miscarriages *after* the fourth month are strongly suggestive. As the mother passes through the later stages, the child will have a better chance of being born alive and, when and if the disease has spontaneously cured itself or been cured, normal healthy children may be born. But syphilis rarely produces a 'typical pattern' and healthy children may alternate with diseased children at any time in a syphilitic family.

The diseased children pass through the same stages as the parent. But because the disease process is affecting a growing individual some special signs are often, though not always, present. These include bone defects, impaired sight and hearing, and deformed teeth. The well-known 'Hutchinson's Triad', first described by Jonathan Hutchinson of the London Hospital in 1861, consists of deafness, impaired vision, and notched peg-shaped teeth. The deafness is caused by damage to the auditory nerve and persists or worsens throughout life. The particular defect of vision is known as interstitial keratitis, first appearing as a diffuse haziness near the centre of one cornea, occurring most commonly between the ages of five and fifteen. The haziness spreads over the cornea and the other eye is attacked two or three months later. The child goes blind, or almost blind, but a surprising improvement occurs within a year or eighteen months. Patches of haze often remain for life, so vision may never be entirely normal. For some reason unknown, almost twice as many male children are affected as female. They suffer eye pain in strong light and often develop a habit of lowering the eyelids and eyebrows as though frowning.

Most of what has been said above concerns syphilis as it might have appeared, if untreated, in recent times. It does not necessarily follow that exactly the same clinical picture was observed by physicians when the infection first made its appearance in Europe at the end of the fifteenth century.

According to contemporary writers, from 1495 onwards something which seemed to be a new disease swept over Europe. Thence it spread to India, China, Japan and eventually to the rest of the world. Early medical historians accepted the theory that the disease originated in the army of Charles VIII of France who, having launched an invasion of Italy in the autumn of 1494, attacked Naples in February 1495, or that the disease started in Naples and was transmitted to the French army. This army of about thirty thousand men was not, in fact, composed of Frenchmen only, but also of mercenaries from Germany, Switzerland, England, Hungary, Poland and Spain. The great number of sick forced Charles to withdraw and abandon his attempted conquest of northern Italy. This, at least, is fact and provides an example of how disease can affect the course of history. The classical story, or perhaps legend, continues that the remnant of his army dispersed to their homelands, thus spreading the infection to the many parts of Europe from which they came. Shortly afterwards the disease became known by names which varied according to the supposed country of origin. We hear of the 'French', 'Neapolitan' and 'Polish' disease. Some years later it became known in China as 'Canton disease' and in Japan as the 'Chinese disease'. Englishmen knew it as 'the French pox' or 'the great pox'. In France it was commonly known as '*la grosse vérole*'. The French also named it 'the Spanish disease' and this brings us to the earliest theory of the origin of syphilis.

Christopher Columbus first saw the New World, probably one of the Bahama Islands, on 12 October 1492. Between October and January he visited Cuba and Haiti. In the latter month he set sail for Europe, landing at Palos, the port from which he had set out, on 15 March 1493. He brought with him ten natives of the West Indies, of whom one died soon after landing, and a crew of forty-four men. The crew were disbanded and some are said to have joined the troops of Gonzalo de Cordoba who marched with Charles VIII to Naples. Columbus travelled with his nine natives to Seville, left three there, and took the remaining six on to Barcelona. At the end of April the six natives, all males, were shown naked to the Spanish Court. They are described as brown and comely, resembling Asians more than Africans. There is no mention of any visible disease.

Twenty-five years later, in 1518, a book printed in Venice first mentioned the theory that 'a Spanish disease' had been imported from America (or the West Indies) by seamen in the 1492–3 expedition led by Columbus. This theory was supported and popularized by Gonzalo Fernandez de Oviedo y Valdes, who had been a page at the Spanish Court and claimed to have seen the 'Indians' shown by Columbus. Oviedo made several voyages to the West Indies and reported that he had found evidence of the new disease among the natives. In 1539 Rodrigo Ruiz Diaz de Isla, a physician, published a description of 'the West Indian disease' or *bubas*, and claimed to have treated at least one, if not more, of Columbus's crew at Barcelona. We are justified in presuming that men of his crew accompanied Columbus when he showed the Indians to the court in that city.

The first theory therefore supposes that syphilis was introduced into Europe from the West Indies by ship in 1493. Many medical historians support this opinion. The evidence in favour is that a new disease of great virulence undoubtedly did appear in Europe at about the time that Columbus returned. Another fact sometimes cited is that one of the earliest and more popular treatments was by holy wood or guaiacum, a resin obtained from two evergreen trees, *Guaiacum officinale* and *Guaiacum sanctum*, which are indigenous to South America and the West Indies. Guaiacum was introduced as a treatment in 1508, that is ten years before the first known mention of West Indian origin. This is, of course, a point in favour of the theory. But opponents of the theory maintain that the useless guaiacum was imported not because it was a traditional native remedy, but deliberately to support the West Indian origin. Also against the theory must be set the fact that there is no evidence whatever of disease in the imported Amerindians or among the forty-four seamen who returned with Columbus. It may, too, be of some significance that the Columban or American theory did not achieve credence until over a quarter of a century after his return and the supposed first appearance of the disease. There is, of course, always the possibility that new facts may have come to light in later expeditions to the West Indies.

The second theory maintains that syphilis originated in Africa and was introduced into Spain and Portugal by the importation of slaves. In 1442 a Portuguese expedition led by Prince Henry the Navigator explored the Atlantic coast of Africa and anchored in the Bight of Benin. One of the captains, Autam Goncalves, captured a few Moors and took them as prisoners on board his ship. Prince Henry ordered Goncalves to return them. He did so and was rewarded with gold dust and ten native Africans. These fetched a large price in Portugal, which led to a quite extensive trade in black slaves from Africa to Portugal and Spain. The descendants of many of these slaves became Christians. In 1502 King Ferdinand ordered that Christian slaves be shipped to the West Indies. So many were sent that the governor of Haiti became alarmed by the increasing number of Africans on the island and in the following year asked that the trade should cease.

This second theory depends upon the existence of an African disease known as yaws, the bacteriological appearance of which is virtually indistinguishable from syphilis. Unlike syphilis, it is chiefly transmitted by non-venereal contact, being particularly common among children who play together naked. For this reason true yaws is only found in hot climates, where it appears as a most unpleasant skin eruption. There is a good deal of argument on the question of whether yaws and syphilis are or are not different manifestations of the same disease. Some people believe that if the tropical yaws is introduced into a cold climate, where the inhabitants are normally fully clothed, the infection will take the form of ordinary syphilis carried mainly by venereal contact. This theory is attractive because it could explain the behaviour of syphilis during the first years of its European existence. But obvious skin disease was undoubtedly sometimes confused with true leprosy, which aroused particular horror among all humans, partly because of the terrible destruction of tissues and partly because of the widely held belief that a leper had been visited with divine punishment for unforgivable sin. It has been sensibly argued that the six Amerindians brought back by Columbus and shown naked to the Court cannot have been diseased, for someone must surely have noticed a gross skin lesion. The same objection can be applied to the African slave theory. In view of the general fear of skin disease, traders would not have shipped slaves suffering from yaws.

An extension of the African theory of origin places the introduction of syphilis to Europe at a much earlier date. Equatorial Africans found their way to Egypt, Arabia, Greece and Rome and they may have brought yaws with them. This implies that syphilis is a very old European disease and that something unknown caused a great increase in virulence and infectivity at the end of the fifteenth century. Some historians hold that leprosy, often said to have been brought back from the Levant by crusaders, was in fact syphilis. It is undoubtedly true that leprosy disappeared from Europe (or from European medical literature) before syphilis became rampant. It is also true that both infections can produce horrible skin eruptions, which contemporary doctors might find difficulty in differentiating.

The objection to any theory of an ancient origin depends on the fact that syphilis often causes permanent and visible changes in the bones which are now recognizable by pathologists. No skeletal remains that have been radiocarbon dated to before the beginning of the sixteenth century have ever been found in Europe with reliable evidence of syphilitic damage. Such is not the case with bones, particularly skulls, unearthed in Europe after sixteenth-century or later burial. The evidence regarding South American and West Indian burials is controversial and, although pre-Columban bones with apparently syphilitic lesions have been found, the number is too small to postulate with any certainty that the disease is of American origin.

So we had better leave the argument as to origin unanswered. We can be sure that contemporary physicians believed that a new disease of great virulence spread rapidly over Europe in the 1490s. They possessed none of our modern aids to diagnosis and their descriptions are not always as clear as we could wish, but they were capable of honest observation. It is also possible that a modern doctor might not have recognized this mysterious disease as syphilis had he made only a superficial examination without blood tests or the help of a bacteriologist.

In 1519 Ulrich von Hutten published an account of the disease in Germany. According to him, it first appeared there in 1497, spread widely, and produced 'disgusting sores'. After about seven years the disease underwent a change which was not caused by any kind of treatment. He said that the acute, obvious skin lesions became less common and, because the person no longer appeared revolting, the risk of infection became greater. Von Hutten made the important observation that, at the time of writing in 1519, transmission seemed to be only by venereal contact. Diaz de Isla in his description of 1539 described the stages as they are known today but added a terminal illness of fever, emaciation, persistent diarrhoea, jaundice, abdominal distension, delirium, coma and death.

The most important early work on syphilis is that of Girolamo Fracastoro in 1546. In 1530 he published at Verona a long poem entitled *Syphilis sive Morbus Gallicus* (*Syphilis or the French Disease*) in which he gave the disease its modern name, derived from an imaginary shepherd

Syphilus, although the term did not come into common use until the end of the eighteenth century. In his book of 1546 published at Venice and entitled *De Contagione et Contagiosis Morbis,* by which he really means *About Infection and Infectious Diseases,* he described syphilis as commencing with small ulcers on the genital organs followed by a pustular skin rash which usually began on the scalp. These pustules ulcerated to such a depth that bone might be exposed. The patient also suffered from a 'pernicious catarrh' which eroded the palate, uvula and pharynx. Sometimes the lips or the eyes were entirely eaten away. Later swellings or 'gummata' appeared, accompanied by violent pains in the muscles, lassitude and emaciation. Fracastoro thought that the infection had changed its character in the last twenty years (i.e. since 1526) for it seemed to him that many sufferers showed fewer pustules and more gummata than before.

This new disease did not spread with the same speed as bubonic plague. Even if we take 1493 as the date of first appearance of a syphilis-like disease in Europe, there was a lapse of three years before its invasion of England in 1496. Poland was infected in 1499, Russia and Scandinavia in 1500 and Canton in 1505. Some countries escaped infection until much later: Japan in 1569 and Iceland in 1753, while the Faroe Islands were free until 1845. An interesting puzzle is the infection of India in 1498. At first sight this would be an impossibly early date but, in fact, it provides proof that, wherever the origin of European syphilis may have been, Europe itself played a role in infecting much of the world. An expedition of four ships and 160 men led by Vasco da Gama left Lisbon in July 1497, rounded the Cape of Good Hope and sailed north and east, landing at Calicut on the Malabar River on 20 May 1498. The crews carried syphilis with them.

The disease was far more contagious in the opening phase of its European history than it is today. Figures are unreliable but about a third of the citizens of Paris are said to have been infected by the opening years of the sixteenth century. The scholar Erasmus wrote in 1519 that any nobleman who had not contracted syphilis was considered *ignobilis et rusticans,* i.e. 'a country bumpkin'. Very interesting confirmation of the early virulence and later recession is supplied by Sir Thomas More, surely a reliable witness. In 1529 he wrote the tract *Supplication of Souls in Purgatory* in answer to a demand for the suppression of monastic hospitals. This contains the sentence: 'And then of the french pockes thirty years ago went there about five against one that beggeth with them now.' That is, five patients attended the hospitals on account of syphilis in 1499 for every one attending in 1529.

But why was syphilis so contagious in the sixteenth century? If the disease was indeed imported from the New World, then it would have had the impact of any infection introduced to a completely unaccustomed community. There can have been no immunity, absolute or relative, maternal or acquired by a previous attack. Thus the illness would tend to be more severe and the chances of infection higher at its first appearance. But we must also recognize the possibility that European syphilis derived from yaws. This would account for the gross skin lesions and also for an added risk of contagion, infection by direct contact, by means other than sexual intercourse. One such simple means of contact has been unaccountably overlooked by historians of syphilis. The common method of greeting in Tudor times was not the handshake but the kiss. The kiss was used by both sexes and by all classes, more usually than not from mouth to mouth.

So the more common method of transmission may have been innocent, that is non-venereal. Infection was passed from one individual to another by mouth-to-mouth contact or by drinking from a shared vessel. In such cases the primary chancre would have appeared upon the lips or tongue and, in those days of neglected personal hygiene, must often have passed unnoticed or have been mistaken for the 'cold sore' of impetigo. For instance, Cardinal Wolsey was accused of infecting Henry VIII by 'breathing and rowning in his ear'. He may have done so, but equally the Cardinal may have been suffering from a cold sore on his lip. There must, of course, have been many cases of venereal infection, but we need not search for immoral relationships or juicy scandals when investigating the syphilis of the early sixteenth century. There is an equal or even greater chance that transmission was by innocent contact.

Another reason for the wide spread of syphilis is that the tertiary stage of nervous or arterial involvement was not yet recognized as being associated with the earlier phases. Gross cutaneous manifestations were not always present and the minor lesions of the early stages – the primary chancre and the secondary rash – could be mistaken for trivial disorders and, in any case, soon disappeared without treatment. There is some confirmation for this supposition in the dates at which certain terms were first used. The *Oxford English Dictionary* gives the following: Pox 1476, Great Pox 1503, Small Pox 1518. 'The Pox', preceding the introduction of syphilis, is another name for any kind of skin eruption. 'Great Pox', introduced seven years after England was first infected, is definitely the common name for the cutaneous signs of syphilis. 'Small Pox', 1518, cannot be a specific name for the infectious disease known as 'smallpox' because that was known long before 1518 and was no doubt lumped with other rashes under the old nurse's diagnosis 'the poor child's got the pox and fever'. In fact 'Small Pox' almost certainly meant what the name implies, a lesser form of the 'Great Pox', applied to the secondary rash which often resembled any other kind of 'small pox', for instance measles. Thus it is reasonable to suppose that many infected people went through life untreated and without even realizing that they suffered from syphilis.

As for the historical effects of this disease, they have been devastating. The tale of suffering and misery is multi-faceted. Magnificent specimens of mankind such as the South Pacific islanders have been destroyed en masse. Brilliant statesmen in positions of power have become drooling idiots; artists, painters and poets have been ruined. Francis I of France, Pope Alexander Borgia, Benvenuto Cellini and Toulouse-Lautrec, Winston's father Randolph Churchill, these are just a few names drawn at random from hundreds of victims. Millions of lesser men and women have suffered equally. Millions more have suffered indirectly, as we can well see in the case of Ivan the Terrible. There is no doubt that he was a syphilitic, for during the period of Soviet rule his remains were exhumed from their resting place in the Moscow Kremlin and found to show typical lesions in the bones.

Ivan, Grand Duke of Muscovy and first Tsar of All the Russians, was born on 25 August 1530, and ascended the Grand-Ducal throne when he was three years old, on the death of his father Vassili III in December 1533. Outwardly Ivan was a typical Russian prince of his time, spending his youth in hunting, womanizing, drinking, robbing merchants and terrorizing the unfortunate peasantry. But there was a little more to him, for beneath the surface lay a serious scholar who preferred the company of lower-born but educated clerks to that of illiterate nobles. He chose one of the former, Alexei Ardatchev, as his most intimate friend and adviser. On 16 January 1547 Ivan was crowned Tsar, the first Muscovite ruler to be so styled formally, basing the claim on his descent from Vladimir, grandson of the Byzantine Caesar, Constantine Monomakh. Two weeks later he married a pious and humane woman, Anastasia Zakharina Koshkina.

In the same year a fire destroyed the greater part of Moscow. The Metropolitan, Archbishop Makary, took this catastrophe as an opportunity of impressing on Ivan the sinful follies of his youth, urging him to reform. Now opened a reign which promised to be one of the most enlightened in the history of Russia. Ivan established some kind of legal code, banished the most oppressive nobles, partially reformed the all-powerful Church and founded schools in Moscow and the larger cities. Although neither a brave man nor a good general, Ivan inspired his troops with a crusading spirit, captured Kazan from the infidel Tartar horde, and extended his empire down the Volga to Astrakhan. In 1558 he turned westward against the Teutonic Knights and by the summer of 1560 had reached Riga on the border of Prussia.

By our standards Ivan was no doubt a cruel despot even during those early years. By contemporary Russian and, indeed, European standards he ruled wisely and humanely from 1551 to 1560. He played a vigorous part in the deliberations of his council, but allowed freedom of speech and opinion. He received petitions from all classes of his subjects. Legend has it that, for the first and the last time in Russian history, the poorest man in the country could gain access to his sovereign.

In October 1552 Anastasia gave birth to a son, Dmitri, who died when six months old. Nine months later she bore another son, Ivan, and a third, Fedor, in 1558. Probably Tsar Ivan had been infected with syphilis during his womanizing years before marriage. We surmise – it is only surmise – that the infant Dmitri died of congenital syphilis. Giles Fletcher in his *The Russe Commonwealth* described Fedor, who survived Ivan the Terrible as 'of mean stature, somewhat low and gross, of a sallow complexion, and inclining to the dropsy, hawk nosed, unsteady in his pace by reason of some weakness in his limbs, heavy and inactive, yet commonly smiling almost to laughter. For quality otherwise simple and slow witted.' Although no certain diagnosis can be made on such slight evidence, the above suggests that Fedor may also have suffered from congenital syphilis.

Anastasia died in July 1560. Ivan was genuinely broken-hearted and drowned his grief in a prolonged drunken debauch which started immediately after her funeral. His brain conceived the fantasy that his friend Alexei Ardatchev and his wise adviser, the monk Sylvester, had contrived Anastasia's death by witchcraft. He spared their lives but dismissed and imprisoned them both. He then put to death Ardatchev's brother, a successful soldier, together with his twelve-year-old son. Next, he condemned to death his friend Maria Magdalena and her five children. On 21 August 1561 Ivan married a rich Circassian princess, but this did not stop him making a proposal of marriage to Queen Elizabeth I of England in 1563. In the same year he led a large army to invade Lithuania. He captured the important trading city of Polotsk and seemed to have the whole country at his mercy. Then his martial mood passed and he returned to his debauch in Moscow, where his new Tsaritsa had given birth to a son, Vassili, who lived for five weeks.

Towards the end of 1564 there occurred the first ludicrous incident which clearly shows that Ivan now suffered from cerebral syphilis (GPI). Early in the morning of 3 December a number of sleighs gathered in the Kremlin Square. Servants loaded them with gold, silver and jewels from the palace. The Tsar, the Tsaritsa and their two sons boarded one of the sleighs. Then the cavalcade drove off, leaving no forwarding address. Later in the day Ivan sent a message back home: 'Unable to brook the treachery by which I was surrounded, I have forsaken the state and taken my way whither God shall direct.' His bewildered nobles and bishops set out in search. They found him in the small village of Alexandrov, a hundred miles north-west of Moscow, and besought him to return. Ivan consented, making conditions that he was free to execute any 'traitors' he so desired, to live in a house outside the Kremlin, and to have a personal guard of a thousand men, the '*oprichniki*'. He returned to Moscow on 2 February 1565 and the executions started two days later. The *oprichniki* were enlarged to number over six thousand bandits and the new house outside the Kremlin became a strange monastery with Ivan as abbot. Three hundred of the *oprichniki* served as monks, clad in black cassocks over their sables and cloth of gold. The day started with early matins at four in the morning and ended at eight in the evening with vespers, Ivan praying with such fervour that his forehead was permanently bruised by his prostrations. These bouts of prayer were relieved by visits to the torture chamber, conveniently situated in the cellars.

The remainder of Ivan's reign is a sickening tale of tortures and floggings, of burnings and boilings, of all manner of hideous deaths. The dreadful vengeance that he exacted on the city of Novgorod for an alleged conspiracy, where for five weeks thousands were flogged to death, roasted over slow fires, or pushed under the ice, or the executions at Moscow on 25 July 1570 when Ivan and his son Ivan themselves helped in the ghastly work, when Prince Viskavati was hanged from a gallows and sliced to death with knives while Ivan raped the widow and his son raped the eldest daughter – these are but two of the recorded episodes in a reign of terror which lasted from 1565 until 1584. Ivan's madness culminated in the slaughter of his own son and heir, the Tsarevitch Ivan, whom he stabbed to death with his steel-pointed staff in a fit of murderous rage on 19 November 1581.

Disappointed in his hope of marrying Elizabeth of England, Ivan made overtures to her cousin Lady Mary Hastings and, when she declined the offer, announced his willingness to marry any kinswoman of the Queen. Despite the fact that he was already married, Ivan seems to have been obsessed with the fantasy of a royal union with England. Elizabeth, probably bearing in mind the fortunes of the Russian Company which had been founded under the patronage of Ivan in 1553, caused the envoy to assure him that any one of a dozen of her kinswomen would be happy to marry him. Fortunately for some unknown girl, Ivan died on 15 March 1584 before the project went any further. His last days were horrible, a time of sleeplessness, terror and insanity, surrounded by soothsayers, his only relaxation the fondling of his jewels and discoursing on their curative powers. The immediate cause of death was an apoplectic fit while setting the board for a game of chess.

Thousands of his subjects perished because Ivan suffered from syphilis but, in the long term, the effect of his disease may have been even greater. It is debatable whether the whole pattern of Russian Tsardom would have developed in a different fashion, but there might have been, in this first of the Tsars, an exemplar of enlightened rule rather than of cruel despotism. Ivan's murder of his son probably saved the country from a no less bloody reign, for Ivan the Terrible had trained him in cruelty and lust. But the murder left the throne to inheritance by a congenital idiot, Fedor. Incapable of ruling, he was first under the tutelage of Boris Godunov and then displaced by him. Chaos descended on Russia after the death of Boris in April 1605 and no semblance of unity was achieved until the election of the first Romanov in 1613.

That Ivan was syphilitic is certain but the case of his near contemporary Henry VIII of England is controversial. Many writers have emphatically denied that Henry suffered from syphilis. That he suffered from something is agreed but the various authorities differ on the nature of the illness. Gout, varicose veins, osteomyelitis of the femur, one or more injuries suffered in tournaments, scurvy – all these have been suggested as possible causes for the character change which became evident in Henry's forties. In view of all these differing opinions it seems reasonable to re-examine the evidence for, whatever the nature of the illness, there is no doubt that its effect upon the king profoundly influenced the future history of the English nation.

First, let it be said that there is no reason why Henry should not have suffered from all the disabilities so far mentioned. A sixteenth-century man who lived to the age of fifty-six must have counted himself lucky if he suffered from only one chronic illness, for most were untreatable in those days. Henry took part in the rough sports of the time, in which he is known to have had two accidents and suffered concussion. He ate and drank enormously, becoming monstrously obese in his later years, so it would not be surprising if he developed varicose veins. Gout and scurvy, both disorders associated with diet, were common and Henry's mode of life would certainly have encouraged the former. But none of this can be adduced as proof that he did not also suffer from syphilis.

Henry was born in 1491, at least two years before syphilis erupted in Europe. While that fact makes it pointless to examine his ancestry, the question of his progeny is altogether relevant. The first of his six wives, Katherine of Aragon, mother of Queen Mary, gave birth to a male infant who died within a few days, and had at least three stillborn children all in the seventh or eighth month of pregnancy. Anne Boleyn, mother of Queen Elizabeth I, miscarried at six months, at three-and-a-half months, and of a foetus of unknown age. Jane Seymour had one son, King Edward VI, born in 1537, and is unlikely to have had another pregnancy in her seventeen months of wedded life. The fourth marriage, with Anne of Cleves, was never consummated. There is no history of any pregnancy in the cases of Catherine Howard, wedded to Henry from 1540 to 1542, or Catherine Parr who was left his widow in 1547, after four years of marriage.

Henry had at least four children. The one known illegitimate boy, Henry Fitzroy, Earl of Richmond, died at age seventeen from a lung infection, possibly tuberculosis. Nothing else is known of his health. Elizabeth I died at the great age of sixty-nine. She is reported to have been short-sighted and may have had reason to believe she could not bear children. 'The Queen of Scots is lighter of a fair son and I am but a barren stock' was her remark on hearing of the birth of a Stuart heir north of the Border. Mary Tudor died aged forty-two. She was very short-sighted, spoke with the kind of loud voice used by a deaf person, and is reported to have had 'a nose rather low and wide' which discharged foul-smelling pus, of which her husband Philip II complained. The one legitimate son, Edward VI, died in 1553 aged fifteen. He was never a healthy child and the cause of death remains rather mysterious. Just over a year before, in April 1552, he fell ill of 'mesels and smallpockes which breaking kindly from him was thought would prove a means to cleanse his body from such unhealthful humours as occasion long sickness and death'. There is little or no doubt that from the beginning of 1553 he became increasingly ill with pulmonary tuberculosis (consumption) but a skin eruption developed in the last fortnight of his life, his nails fell off and the top joints of his fingers and toes became necrotic. There was a widely held opinion that he had been poisoned.

Every single incident in the above history can be fitted to an illness other than syphilis. But the evidence is cumulative. Katherine of Aragon's three stillborn children, all dying later than the fourth month of pregnancy, Anne Boleyn's miscarriage at six months, Edward's skin rash in 1552 followed in little over a year by death from something sounding like a combination of tuberculosis and congenital syphilis producing syphilitic dactylitis, all are suggestive. Then we have Elizabeth's and Mary's short sight, Mary's presumed deafness, the flattened bridge of her nose and a foul, purulent discharge – any of these could result from congenital syphilis. Finally we have the evidence of Henry's last two marriages. If, as historians hold, his marriage policy was dictated by the desire to found a strong Tudor line, then the inference is that Henry became sterile or impotent in his late forties. This is a very strong argument in favour of syphilis.

As for Henry himself, he was described in his youth by the Venetian Pasquiligo as being: 'The handsomest potentate I ever set eyes on, above the usual height with an extremely fine calf to his leg, his complexion fair and bright, with auburn hair combed straight and short in the French fashion, and a round face so very beautiful that it would become a pretty woman, his throat being rather long and thick.' The nineteen-year-old boy had everything: physical beauty, a magnificent presence, charm, a good brain. He was perhaps the finest specimen of manhood ever to wear a crown. He revelled in all sports, in dancing and music, but his chancellor Wolsey makes it plain that Henry also attended to his business of ruling, held strong opinions, and was not easily overborne.

In February 1514, when he was twenty-three years old, he fell sick of the smallpox but he developed no pustules and made a seemingly uneventful and complete recovery. Perhaps we are justified in questioning the diagnosis, just as we questioned the nature of his son's skin rash in 1552. In 1521 Henry had his first attack of malaria, a common enough disease in sixteenth-century England, from which he suffered intermittently for the rest of his life. Three years later, in March 1524, he met with an accident while jousting with the Duke of Suffolk, but seems not to have sustained a severe injury. Henry started to suffer from headaches in 1527 and in 1527–8 he developed the notorious ulcer on his thigh (or thighs) which plagued him for the rest of his days.

In 1527, the crucial year, Henry was aged thirty-six. Until then he ruled wisely and with moderation. More than one dangerous riot, for instance the 'Evil May Day' of 1517, was suppressed firmly, but without cruelty by the standards of the time. During these years Henry laid the foundations of English naval administration, built ships, founded Trinity House, improved harbours, established shipyards and storehouses. In 1521, aided by 'all the learned men of England', he wrote the scholarly counterblast to Martin Luther which earned him from Pope Leo X the title Defender of the Faith, used by his successors on the throne to this day. Henry encouraged Thomas More in his largely unavailing efforts to provide a clean water supply and sewerage. Since the Black Death medicine had ceased to be the Church's prerogative with the result that quacks and illiterate practitioners flourished. An Act of 1512 sought to regulate medical practice by requiring examination for proficiency, conducted by the bishop of the diocese and such experts as he might appoint. The Act led to the institution of the College of Physicians in 1518. Henry, himself a skilled amateur physician, played his part in these reforms.

From 1527 his character started to change, until the brilliant young man gave place to a morose and bitter tyrant. Part of the change is undoubtedly due to the worries of his divorce from Katherine, for the arguments lasted no less than six years. The first definite sign of imbalance comes in 1531, when Henry permitted enactment of the new and frightful punishment of boiling to death. At least three people were executed by this means. The Act was repealed within a few months of Henry's death by the advisers of Edward VI. In 1533 came the first 'Treason Act' by which any person who cast a slander on Henry's marriage with Anne Boleyn or who tried to prejudice the succession of its issue was guilty of treason and faced with death by the barbaric method of hanging and quartering while still alive.

Henry's reign of terror began in 1534 with an indiscriminate slaughter of Lollards, Lutherans, Anabaptists and Catholics. This was followed in 1535 by the cruel execution of the prior of the Charterhouse and all his monks, and the beheading of the saintly Thomas More and Bishop John Fisher. On 17 January 1536 Henry suffered a severe injury while jousting and lay unconscious for over two hours, not fully recovering until 4 February. This accident forms the basis for the contention that Henry was essentially 'punch drunk', but it occurred nine years after the character change became evident. Concussion of the brain could certainly have exacerbated his trouble and, from now on, we must regard Henry's behaviour as definitely abnormal. His treatment of Anne Boleyn was savage. Head of the Church in England, he could easily have divorced her but he preferred to put her to death and to declare her daughter a bastard. The suppression of the abbeys in 1538–40 was marked by the hanging of any abbot or monk who dared to resist or delay his submission. The unnecessary vandalism, in which so much of the medieval art of England was wantonly destroyed, would surely not have been countenanced by the brilliant, cultured young scholar who mounted the throne in 1509.

During these repressive years, Henry suffered from continual headaches and insomnia, from sore throats, and from the ulcer or fistula in his leg. In May 1538, at the age of forty-seven, he is reported to have been 'sometime without speaking, black in the face and in great danger'. The French ambassador Castillon, who recorded the incident, associated the attack with closure of the fistula in the leg. For this reason it has been suggested that Henry suffered a pulmonary embolism, blockage of the pulmonary artery by a blood clot from a varicose vein. The loss of speech is more in favour of an apoplectic fit.

In 1539 came the Statute of Six Articles, a remarkable piece of legislation directed against any who challenged Henry's position as 'Head of the Church in England', rendering a Protestant liable to be burned as a heretic and a Roman Catholic to be hanged as a traitor. Henry's vacillating policy as to the extent of religious reform was probably influenced by the changing opinions of his wives and their 'parties'. There is no doubt that Henry's chagrin over the ugliness of Anne of Cleves, introduced to him by the reforming party, led directly to the fall of Thomas Cromwell, endangered Henry's firm friend and supporter Archbishop Cranmer, and resulted in a renewed persecution of Protestants. The impression given is that Henry started out with the intention of reforming what was now his own Church and then took fright at the possible consequences to his soul on the Day of Judgement. There is here the suggestion of a split mind, one part trying to present itself as a loyal son of Holy Mother Church, the other part intent on bending that Church to his own will.

Henry never lost his grip on affairs of state. In fact, after the fall and death of Wolsey in 1529, he tended towards an absolute rather than a constitutional monarchy. Only three years before his death he led his army in person during the war with France and actively superintended measures to combat the threatened invasion of England. Although prematurely aged, white-haired, monstrously obese, he never decayed into a mental and physical wreck. Nor did Henry die as Ivan died, terrified and gibbering. The accounts of his death vary and the actual cause is obscure, but he died peacefully holding the hand of Archbishop Cranmer, the only friend who remained devoted to the last.

There is nothing indisputably diagnostic of syphilis in Henry's case history, but much that is suspicious, as has been detailed above. A modern medical student is taught to look for the simple things before turning to the 'small print'. If examining a fifteen-year-old child suffering from a temperature, abdominal pain, and tenderness in the right flank with some degree of muscular rigidity, he or she should exclude acute appendicitis before considering a rarer type of illness. Further, the student should always try to fit the signs and symptoms into one clinical entity before deciding that the patient must be suffering from two or more separate complaints. The history of Henry VIII should be considered in a similar manner. The king undoubtedly suffered from several minor complaints but his medical history, the obstetric history of his queens, the suspicious death of his son Edward, the disabilities of his daughter Mary, even the short-sightedness of Elizabeth, all these must be balanced in the diagnosis. All can be separately explained by invoking a number of different ailments but, if taken together, the evidence is more than just suggestive. Syphilis was a very common infection in the early sixteenth century and there is no good reason to believe that Henry escaped it.

Whatever the nature of Henry's ailment, or combination of ailments, it exerted a profound effect upon the future of England. His failure to produce a healthy male line was the beginning of the end of the strong Tudor dynasty. There were no grandchildren, legitimate or illegitimate. The firm, efficient rule of the Tudors gave way to the attempted absolutism of the weaker Stuarts and plunged the country into a civil war.

After Henry's death the nine-year-old Edward came to the throne under the guardianship of his mother's family, the Seymours. With Seymour patronage, Edward became the champion of Protestants. Henry's despoliation of monastic property was continued even more ruthlessly, the bulk of monastic lands, treasure and revenues being grabbed by greedy nobles. There was still considerable affection for the Old Faith. The fanatical iconoclasm of Edward's reign did not endear Protestantism to the ordinary Englishman. Had Edward's successor and half-sister Mary behaved with moderation she might well have succeeded in restoring the Roman Catholic Church, perhaps not to its former power, but lastingly as the official English religion. There is no doubt that Mary persisted in her persecution despite warnings from her Catholic husband Philip II of Spain. Had she quietly burned half a dozen rabid Protestants a year, she might have been honoured as a defender of the pure faith against heresy. But Mary, almost certainly mentally abnormal, would not listen to reason. She caused over three hundred simple men and women to die at the stake in a little over three years and thereby ensured that the great majority of her subjects would regard Roman Catholicism as more evil than paganism. The settlement under Elizabeth I came too late and religious toleration was unthinkable for many years to come.

The effect of Mary's persecution is evident even today. It is still difficult to unravel the truth of many events in the sixteenth and seventeenth centuries because the account given by a Protestant writer will often differ materially from that of a Catholic. Nowhere have those distant fires smouldered on longer than in Northern Ireland. The Marian persecution also altered the attitude of the English to suffering. Like their North American cousins they have always honoured valour but, unlike some other peoples, have never taken kindly to the idea that there is anything particularly noble in the voluntary bearing of pain. Might this be one of the reasons why the merciful science of anaesthesia found its first practitioners in America and Britain? The agony of the sixteenth-century martyrs aroused not only anger and pity but also disgust. These tortures were borne voluntarily, for the sufferer would have been spared by a simple recantation, in most cases involving nothing more than a reversion to doctrines accepted in earlier life. For the great majority of English people, the medieval concept of a glorious martyrdom perished in the fires of Smithfield.

In conclusion let us turn to the efforts made towards preventing and curing syphilis. The earliest known treatment was by purgatives and semi-magic antidotes to poisoning. The specific drug guaiacum remained a popular remedy until the end of the sixteenth century, although it was attacked by Paracelsus, one of the more revolutionary physicians. These treatments must have been quite ineffective. A more efficient, though more dangerous, medicament was found in mercury.

Mercury, in the form of the ore cinnabar, had been used for the treatment of skin diseases by the Arabian school of doctors and an ointment containing metallic mercury was prescribed by Theodoric of Lucca in the thirteenth century. This early use of mercury has been adduced as evidence that syphilis is an ancient disease in Europe, while the lack of any mention of mercury treatment (which is difficult to hide) has suggested to some historians that Henry VIII cannot have suffered from syphilis. Neither argument is particularly convincing. Mercury seems to have been tried in any severe and intractable skin disease. In Henry's case mercury would not have been used unless there was manifest skin involvement, of which there is no evidence.

It is probably because of evident skin lesions that Giorgio Sommariva of Verona tried mercury for the treatment of syphilis in 1496. He was not a doctor but some years later the physician Jacopo Berengario da Carpi achieved fame in Italy for his success with mercury. Benvenuto Cellini was one of his patients. The method became known as 'salivation' because near-poisoning with metallic mercury and its salts produced immense amounts of saliva. This form of treatment by oral administration, ointments and vapour baths remained a fairly effective but extremely unpleasant and dangerous medication for over three centuries. Many attempts were made to find other specifics but the only one of any lasting value was potassium iodide, introduced in the 1840s and effective in the later stages of the disease. So much harm resulted from quacks who claimed success with secret remedies that in 1917 treatment of syphilis by unqualified persons was made a criminal offence in Britain.

Rational treatment of a disease is impossible unless the cause is known. The cause of syphilis was not fully understood until the twentieth century. In 1905 F.R. Schaudinn and P.E. Hoffmann discovered the causative organism to which they gave the name *Spirochaeta pallida*. The name has since been changed to *Treponema pallidum*, the various sub-species of which are now known to be the cause not only of the venereal and non-venereal types of syphilis but of the related yaws, pinta and bejel. Hideyo

Noguchi isolated the bacterium from brains of patients suffering from the late manifestation, general paralysis of the insane, and so proved the link, half suspected for a century. In 1906–7 the Wassermann test was developed which showed the presence of syphilis even when latent. In 1909 Paul Ehrlich of Frankfurt succeeded, after many experiments, in producing the first 'systemic antiseptic', one which could be injected into the bloodstream and kill bacteria without harming the body tissues. This, the famous '606', was an organic arsenic compound which Erhlich called his 'magic bullet' in the belief that it would prove lethal to a wide range of bacteria. In fact he was wrong for it was only effective against the important group of spirochaetes or treponemes. Prescribed under the name 'salvarsan' this drug became widely used in the treatment of syphilis but produced quite serious side-effects and was replaced by neosalvarsan shortly before the First World War. These arsenical preparations proved their worth when venereal disease became rampant in the special conditions of warfare. The Second World War saw the introduction of penicillin, the first of the antibiotic group of drugs, which was successfully used by John Mahoney in 1943 to treat not only syphilis but the second of the ancient venereal infections, gonorrhoea.

Prevention is far more important than treatment in a disease of this nature. The enemy of prevention is secrecy. By the early years of the twentieth century the Scandinavian countries had been actively and sensibly tackling the problem for nearly a hundred years. But in Victorian Britain, and many other countries, prostitution and venereal disease were taboo subjects, having no official existence. On 1 November 1913 the British government set up a Royal Commission to explore and recommend action. The Commission reported in February 1916 at a time when venereal disease had enormously increased. Briefly, they recommended that local authorities be empowered to provide free diagnosis and treatment. One of their recommendations permitted residents outside the authority's area to seek advice and treatment, a sensible means of preserving anonymity. They could devise no way of combining notification with anonymity and decided the latter to be essential. The most important part of the report dealt with proper education in place of secrecy.

Action soon followed the report. Clinics, attached to voluntary and municipal hospitals, came into operation in 1917. Many local authorities posted the address of the nearest clinic in public lavatories, a common-sense method of advertisement. The most notable reform came in 1925 when local authorities were empowered to undertake a programme of education. Since education of this kind can be achieved only by public discussion and open acceptance that there is something to be discussed, the social taboo which overlaid the whole subject had at last been removed. Frank recognition of the public danger combined with anonymity of the individual removed much both of fear and of stigma and helped to transform the patient from a sinner into an unfortunate.

The Second World War saw a world-wide increase in the number of cases and the British government took firm action. Social workers not only made people aware of treatment facilities but traced contacts and persuaded them to be Wassermann tested. At the same time notification and compulsory treatment of syphilitics found to have infected three or more contacts was introduced. These measures, combined with effective penicillin treatment, greatly reduced the number of cases. The regulations ended in 1947 but social work continued so efficiently that syphilis had apparently been defeated by 1956 and many clinics closed for lack of patients. Similar measures, and treatment with penicillin in particular, achieved excellent results on almost a global scale.

Within ten years the greater part of this good work had been rendered nugatory. The number of cases of primary and secondary syphilis had again risen in accordance with a pattern that applied to Britain and the United States among other countries. This tragedy was caused partly by the emergence of a penicillin-resistant strain of organism, partly by introduction of a more virulent type, but chiefly by the laxer moral code and sheer carelessness of young people in the 'permissive' 1960s. Today another disease, largely transmitted by sexual intercourse, tends to divert attention from syphilis, not only in the Western world but far beyond. This will be considered in the Conclusion.

CHAPTER FOUR

Smallpox, or the Conqueror Conquered

We must now consider a little more deeply those infections which have developed in the early centres of civilization and have been transferred from one centre to another, sometimes with devastating results. These diseases have become tamed in their original habitat by acquired resistance of the human to the infecting organism but have returned to their ancient virulence when accidentally transmitted to unaccustomed communities by immigrants such as explorers, missionaries or traders.

Much of this chapter will be devoted to the history of smallpox and its prevention. Smallpox, caused by a virus, is one of a group of infections once known as 'childish diseases' of which measles was another leading example. They are diseases of the crowd and cannot have persisted in a society of small, scattered settlements. Their origin as pathogens causing disease in humans must lie in the earliest large concentrations of population, because the causative organism can only produce the disease by direct transfer from one actively infected person to another who has not been infected. In this respect they differ from diseases such as typhus and bubonic plague, infections of the louse and of the rat or flea respectively, which can be transferred to the human, but do not depend on the human host for their existence.

An attack of an acute infection, such as are smallpox and measles, will confer resistance or actual immunity to a second attack for a period of time or perhaps for life. A person who is immune can neither acquire the infection nor transmit it to a person who is not immune, because the disease can only be transmitted or acquired when active. Such an infection is never totally absent from the community but will be preserved by sporadic cases and small outbreaks. When in this state the particular disease is spoken of as 'endemic' in the community. Continuance of the disease always requires a reservoir of uninfected and non-immune people and they will always be at risk. A single 'endemic' case may then infect a number of unprotected individuals until there is an 'epidemic' of varying numerical severity. At the end of the epidemic, the number of totally immune or partially protected people will be at a maximum, and the disease will retreat into the endemic state. Then the number of susceptible people will increase and the process repeats itself. This will determine the age group most susceptible to infection. For instance, if a major epidemic has not occurred for twenty years, then children and adolescents will be at greatest risk.

Measles commonly confers a life-long immunity but is so easily transmitted that in the early part of the twentieth century doctors expected a severe epidemic about every five years, the great majority of patients being young children. Thus the larger part of the European adult population had already suffered from measles in childhood and so were immune. Many more adults were partially protected by a degree of resistance inherited from immune parents and so were unlikely to experience the full severity of the infection. The latter 'maternal resistance' also applied to susceptible children. This is why measles tended to be regarded as the typical 'childish disease' in Europe and why measles behaved in so unusual a manner when accidentally introduced to a totally unprotected community in the South Pacific Islands.

In 1872 epidemic measles appeared among a largely unprotected community in South Africa, spreading to Mauritius in 1873–4 and Australia in 1874. On 10 October 1874 the British government formally annexed the Fiji Group of islands. Later that year King Cakobau of Fiji with his family and royal suite visited Australia to experience the delights of civilization. Measles was one of the civilized delights they experienced. The party left Sydney for Fiji on the cruiser HMS *Dido*, arriving home on 15 January 1875. One or two of the party landed while still seriously ill with something resembling a very severe attack of measles. Within a little over three months at least one-fifth and probably more nearly a quarter of the Fijian population had died. The total number of deaths in the Fiji Group alone is estimated at over forty thousand. The illness spread throughout the South Pacific causing similar mortalities and creating panic wherever it appeared. A contemporary writer, William Squire, recorded that many died from sheer terror, others from seeking to relieve the burning skin rash by immersing their bodies in the sea. He believed that 'the epidemic only ceased when every person had been attacked'. In other words all ages, and not children only, had been at risk. No one really knows how many died of measles, because Europeans introduced other unaccustomed and lethal infections, tuberculosis and syphilis among them. It is widely believed that the magnificent physique of the natives has been ruined and their number reduced to about one-tenth of the population living in the South Pacific Islands less than a hundred and fifty years ago.

The story of measles in North America is also instructive. In this land of wide open spaces and scattered communities, repeatedly refreshed by immigrants from Britain and France, introduction from the European centre of infection produced a pattern quite different from the rapid, explosive pandemic in the South Pacific. The first recorded outbreaks of measles were in Canada in 1635 and 1687. Boston was attacked in 1657 and again in 1687, the latter outbreak being probably derived from the Canadian epidemic rather than from Europe. Further epidemics occurred in Boston in 1713, 1729, 1739 and, more severely, in 1740. The long sea voyage of the eighteenth-century sailing ships militated against transmission from Europe. If the report that South Carolina, Pennsylvania, New York and Connecticut were not attacked until 1747 is correct, it would seem that 'American' measles was now developing. Boston appears as the main centre of a severe epidemic in 1772, in which some hundreds of children are reported to have died in the district of Charlestown, Massachusetts. Six years later a similar lethal epidemic ravaged New York and Philadelphia, which suggests that the infection was now settling into the class of 'childish diseases' but producing an illness of greater severity than in Europe at the same date. From the East Coast measles rode in the covered wagons to the Mississippi Valley, Kentucky and Ohio.

Although some of the above statements may be regarded as questionable, because differentiation between measles and other rash-producing diseases was not exact, the broad pattern is of great importance in the history of infection. It well illustrates, first, how a pool of infection is formed and, second, what happens when one pool converges on another pool which does not contain the particular infection. The American pattern can be little different from those which developed in the earliest centres of civilization. The course taken by measles in North America was not dictated by any change in the infecting virus but by growth and cohesion of the population. In the beginning scattered communities were separately infected, and the small community might develop a resistance sufficient to prevent persistence of the causative virus so that no fresh epidemic could develop until a new invasion came from outside. If the new invasion came within a few years, then the illness would appear only among children. If invasion was delayed for twenty or more years, then adults, too, would be at risk. As the distance between communities decreased and intercommunication became quicker, so the chance of infection increased and the age of the susceptible group fell. Thus measles became a nationally rather than a locally endemic illness. There can be little doubt that a similar merging of any disease from an exotic pool will produce exceptional virulence initially, followed by reversion to its previous state.

When we turn to the highly controversial history of smallpox, we must remember not only that an unaccustomed introduction can produce a more lethal type of illness in a new community, but that an old infection can be refreshed by introduction of a new strain of causative organism. Some historians believe that smallpox was a member of the Mediterranean pool of diseases as early as the fifth century BC. The illness commonly leaves scars known as pock-marks and no depiction of a pock-mark has been found on any Greek or Roman representation of the human features. Such absence may be artistic licence rather than proof of non-existence. A second school of thought proposes that India is the original pool of infection and argues that the Indian goddess Shitala has been invoked as protection against smallpox since time immemorial. There is a suggestion that the Indian disease and a method of prevention were exported to China. The earliest definite and recognizable description is that of Ko Hung, a Chinese physician who lived from AD 265 to 313. Whether of Indian or Chinese origin, smallpox could have travelled the ancient Silk Road from the East, reaching Europe before AD 581 when Gregory of Tours described an undoubted epidemic in France. By then it had almost certainly been introduced into Japan by Buddhist missionaries travelling from Korea. Smallpox and measles were a central feature of the Japanese 'age of plagues' covering the period from 750 to 1000. About 980 there is a mention from Japan of special buildings to isolate smallpox patients and an interesting form of treatment with hangings of red cloth. An Englishman, John of Gaddesden, recommended red drapes for the same purpose in 1314. This 'red treatment' persisted in folk medicine for many centuries and achieved a semi-scientific status in 1893 when the Danish pioneer of light therapy, Niels Ryberg Finsen, used red light produced by a screen which excluded ultra-violet rays. In no case was 'red treatment' of any value but it is of interest as an example of the Doctrine of Signatures or 'like cures like', since smallpox produces a confluent rash of crimson colour.

The most authoritative early account of smallpox is by the Persian physician commonly known as Rhazes, about AD 900. Part of his achievement was to differentiate more clearly between this disease and measles. Smallpox certainly existed in Europe, Asia and Africa from the tenth century onwards but the severity of the European disease varied. It seems to have been neither so widely spread nor so lethal as it was to become in the seventeenth and eighteenth centuries. Some contemporary writers regarded measles as the more dangerous infection and it is quite possible that the term 'smallpox' was used for a number of illnesses, measles included, which are characterized by a rash. Smallpox itself existed in three forms: *Variola major* or true virulent smallpox; *Variola minor*, a mild form known as alastrim; and *Variola vaccinae*, the disease primarily of cattle known as Cowpox. As all three are caused by variants of the same virus, an attack of one will protect against attack by either of the other two, although the immunity may not be life-long. The balance of evidence suggests that the mild form alastrim was the more common in Europe until the seventeenth century.

The true or virulent form of smallpox played a large part in the Spanish conquest of Mexico and it seems certain that the existence of the mild alastrim in Europe was also responsible for the comparative ease with which a very small Spanish force defeated an entire nation. On 18 November 1518 Hernando Cortez sailed from the Spanish colony of Cuba with an army of eight hundred mixed Spaniards and Amerindians. He landed on the coast of Yucatan to receive friendly messages and presents from the Aztec Emperor Montezuma (or Moctezuma) of Mexico. Continuing his voyage, Cortez founded the city of Vera Cruz, ensured the loyalty of his hesitant troops by burning the ships so that they had no means of returning to Cuba, and marched inland to Tlascala. Here he encountered a hostile force but, after a hard-fought battle, concluded a treaty with the Tlascalans and set out for the Aztec capital Tenochtitlan (Mexico City) with a reinforcement of about a thousand Tlascalan 'friendlies'.

The city, a large community of some three hundred thousand inhabitants, stood isolated in a great lake and was approached by three stone-built causeways, one of them six miles long. Cortez maintained friendly relations with Montezuma for some time but they deteriorated after an attack on Vera Cruz apparently instigated by the Emperor. Cortez imprisoned him, fined him a large amount of gold and forced him to acknowledge the overlordship of Spain. Six months later, in May 1520, Cortez learned that a second Spanish-Amerindian army under Panfilo de Narvaez was striking inland from the coast with the intention of restoring Montezuma to power. Leaving one of his officers, Pedro de Alvarado, in charge of the capital, Cortez intercepted Narvaez and defeated him in a surprise night attack. Then came news that Alvarado was fighting off an insurrection in the city. Cortez hastened back, arriving on 24 June 1520 to find Montezuma dead, Alvarado besieged with a tiny remnant of the army, and the Aztec people in general revolt. Cortez fought his way out of the city with great difficulty after a heroic struggle in which he lost almost half his remaining men, and took refuge with the more or less friendly Tlascalans. By the end of 1520 Cortez had received a few Spanish reinforcements, recruited an army of ten thousand Tlascalans, and built a flotilla of small ships. He ordered a canal to be dug and succeeded in bringing his boats to the lake surrounding the capital, to which he laid siege in April 1521. Cortez himself commanded his task force of boats carrying three hundred men. He defeated a superior force in canoes and made landings on the causeways but suffered a reverse with many casualties in his first attempt on the city. However, the city fell to him, after a stubborn defence, on 13 August 1521. When the Spaniards entered, they found houses filled with dead. The inhabitants had not died from wounds or starvation but from disease.

When Panfilo de Narvaez left Cuba in May 1520 on his voyage to Mexico, he took with him a number of Africans, probably the same Christian slaves (or their children) who had been shipped to the West Indies by order of King Ferdinand. Some of them fell ill and at least one was landed on the American mainland while still sick. He infected others and the disease spread very rapidly among the Amerindian population who called it 'the great leprosy'. The description bears no resemblance to leprosy and the very rapid spread with an immediate skin rash does not favour yaws or syphilis. From the subsequent story, there can be little doubt that the infection was a lethal form of smallpox.

The illness was certainly more fatal than the smallpox known in sixteenth-century Europe. It must have assumed an epidemic form among the native Tlascalans and been carried by them to the capital in the first abortive attempt at capture during the early summer of 1521. When Cortez entered the city in August he found that approximately half the inhabitants had died. Within six months hardly a single village in the known regions of New Spain remained uninfected. It has been estimated that almost half the Aztec population perished in this first epidemic.

A second epidemic, known to have been a fresh introduction by Spanish ships, carried on the devastation in 1531. Three further visitations in 1545, 1564 and 1576 reduced the native population of New Spain from a much-disputed ten to twenty-five million before the conquest to perhaps fewer than two million by the early seventeenth century. Dreadful as this mortality sounds, another area of Spanish conquest seems to have suffered even worse. Over much the same period the Inca population of Peru diminished from some seven million to approximately half a million. Smallpox is undoubtedly the chief culprit but the Spaniards also introduced mumps and measles which caused many deaths. There is no evidence at all that any of these infections existed in the area before the coming of the Spanish Conquistadores. But the appalling mortality had another effect. The Amerindians in general came to regard resistance as hopeless. Invaders who were able to cause death on this scale could not be mere mortals but vengeful gods. The natives of South America were not alone. The aboriginal tribes of south-eastern Australia may well have felt similarly when, in the last years of the eighteenth century, they too were more than decimated by sudden exposure to the smallpox accompanying the first stage of British colonization.

The reason for the supposed divinity of the Conquistadores is not that they wore armour capable of turning an Aztec weapon or that they used gunpowder to outshoot a native arrow. The overriding reason for regarding them as superhuman is that they themselves appeared immune to the terrible punishment they inflicted upon the Amerindians. The initial epidemic among the Aztecs in the summer of 1521 may have been caused by a chance case of the lethal *Variola major* introduced by an African slave or it may be that the milder form *Variola minor* or alastrim underwent a change to the major type when introduced to an entirely unaccustomed and unprotected people. In either case, the Spaniards came from a far continent in which the milder form was a common disease and therefore they had at the very least some resistance to infection. Whatever the explanation may be, there is no doubt that smallpox, and the relative immunity of the Spaniards to smallpox, played as great a part, if not a greater part, in the destruction of the Aztec race as did the superiority of Spanish arms. Thereafter Mexico remained one of the reservoirs of virulent smallpox. As late as 1947 a traveller from Mexico introduced a limited epidemic into New York.

Smallpox produced only a comparatively mild illness in Europe during the whole of the sixteenth century. In the seventeenth century it started to change to a more lethal type. The reason for the change is not known, but may well have been refreshment of the virus by re-introduction from Spanish America. In 1629 the first Bills of Mortality for London listed smallpox under its name, the number of deaths averaging not more than a thousand a year in a population of between three and four hundred thousand. The figure started to rise steeply in the last years of the century. From being a relatively innocuous but common disease of childhood smallpox gradually became the most lethal illness of the young. At the beginning of the eighteenth century smallpox destroyed more European children than any other infection except, perhaps, infantile diarrhoea. In one English provincial town of fewer than 5,000 inhabitants, 589 children died of smallpox between 1769 and 1774. Of these 466 were under three years and only one over ten. During a similar period in Berlin, 98 per cent of deaths from smallpox were children under twelve and in London 85 per cent were under five. Deaths of young people on this kind of scale must have produced a check on the increase of population but numerical evidence is unreliable in the absence of census figures.

Efforts first to control then to defeat such a killer as this must be as important in world history as the effects of the disease itself, so let us examine how they came about. Even the most ignorant of witch-doctors must have observed that some diseases are by nature chronic and some acute, that a person may fall victim to one disease quite frequently, that another disease may attack him only once in his lifetime, but not kill him. Thus the phenomenon of acquired immunity, though not expressed in that term, has been common knowledge for centuries. Reason would suggest that, if a dangerous disease does not strike an individual more than once, a mild attack of that disease is highly desirable. Since it was also known that such a disease somehow passed from one person to another, it would also be reasonable (but not invariably correct) to expect that an uninfected individual would benefit if placed in contact with the mildest possible case available. An example is found in the diary kept by John Evelyn. On 13 September 1685 Evelyn travelled to Portsmouth with his friend Samuel Pepys, stopping at Bagshot on the way. Evelyn recorded:

I went and made a visit to Mrs Graham, wife of James Graham Esq. Her eldest son was now sick there of the small pox, but in a likely way to recovery, and other of her children ran about and among the infected, which she said she let them do on purpose that they might whilst still young pass that fatal disease she fancied they were to undergo one time or other, and that this would be for the best, the severity of this cruell disease so lately in my poor family confirming much of what she affirmed.

This practice was combined with the Doctrine of Signatures or 'like cures like' to produce the method of protection known as variolation: implantation of tissue or secretion from an infected person into the subject to be protected. The Chinese are believed to have learned the first method from India and practised a form of variolation from the tenth century AD onwards. They removed scales from the drying pustules on a patient suffering from mild smallpox, ground them to powder, and blew a few grains into the nostrils of persons who had not developed the illness. There is no definite evidence of any such method being practised in Europe.

It is possible, though by no means certain, that variolation, using matter from a smallpox pustule, had been practised in Asia Minor for a long time. The first certain attempt was about 1710 when a Greek or Italian physician, Giacomo Pylarini of Smyrna in the Ottoman Empire, removed some of the thick liquid from a pustule and rubbed it into a cut which he had made on the arm of a person he wished to protect. So far as is known this is the first occasion on which the method of 'inoculation' was used. In 1713 another physician, Emanuel Timoni of Constantinople, performed a small series with apparent success and wrote an account to Dr John Woodward in London. Woodward published his findings in *Philosophical Transactions*, the Journal of the Royal Society. His paper aroused some interest but little practical experiment. In 1717 Lady Mary Wortley Montagu, wife of the British Ambassador in Constantinople, had her infant sons inoculated. She returned to England shortly before one of many epidemics caused a number of deaths in 1721, and had her five-year-old daughter inoculated in the presence of several London physicians who were impressed by the mildness of the subsequent illness. This success and the status of Lady Mary stimulated interest. King George I decided to have his grandchildren inoculated but took precautions. Six prisoners under sentence of death in Newgate Prison volunteered to be 'guinea pigs' on promise of reprieve. A trial was next made on eleven charity school children of varying ages. So mild were the following attacks that two royal grandchildren received treatment.

Royal approval made inoculation fashionable in Europe and a number of leading physicians commended the practice. But a good deal of opposition developed when it became clear that the method was by no means always successful. The ensuing protecting attack of smallpox did not always take a mild form, two or three deaths occurring in every hundred inoculations. Further, many intelligent people rightly suspected that variolation, even though it might protect the individual, spread the disease more widely by multiplying the foci of infection. For these reasons inoculation fell into disrepute and was rarely used in Europe after 1728.

The story took a different turn in the North American colonies, first infected with smallpox by British settlers in Maryland during the mid-seventeenth century. The disease slowly spread to Virginia, Carolina and New England. It never became so prevalent as in Europe because of the lesser density of population, but was one of the major killers and aroused proportional fear. The sixth American epidemic, possibly connected with that in England, developed at Boston, Massachusetts, in April 1721. The famous minister Cotton Mather, a Fellow of the Royal Society, had read of Timoni's experiments and suggested that a trial of inoculation be made by the medical profession. Initially only one doctor, Zabdiel Boylston, showed any interest. He first inoculated his six-year-old son and two Negro slaves on 26 June 1721. The experiment was successful and, in the course of the summer, he inoculated 244 people in all. Unfortunately six of his subjects died and the report that he had used actual smallpox matter aroused hostility. In September Boylston was accused of spreading infection and narrowly escaped lynching. Although forced by public opinion to desist, Boylston lived to see general acceptance of variolation in America before he died in 1766.

General acceptance depended upon a much lowered death rate. In 1738 a severe epidemic ravaged the town of Charleston, South Carolina. Using an 'improved method' Dr James Kilpatrick carried out a programme of mass variolation and claimed that a high mortality had thereby been prevented. In 1736 Benjamin Franklin had lost his only legitimate son from smallpox and he subsequently became one of Kilpatrick's most fervent supporters. Probably Franklin influenced George Washington who urged inoculation on his troops and set up special hospitals for the purpose.

Dr Kilpatrick came from Charleston to London in 1743 where he wrote an account of the 1738 epidemic and emphasized the success of his new method. Earlier practitioners believed inoculation would be successful only if the pustular exudate 'lymph' was implanted deeply into the fatty layer underlying the skin. Kilpatrick used a shallow scratch in the skin itself. The lymph, taken from the mildest available case, was then rubbed into the scratch. This method tended to produce a local rather than a general infection and was therefore safer although perhaps not as certain. Kilpatrick's enthusiasm combined with an increase in the severity and incidence of smallpox to bring back the popularity of variolation in Europe during the 1750s.

Inoculators were specialists in their art and often not medically qualified. Some of the better-known are Robert Sutton and his son Daniel, Jan IngenHousz and Thomas Dimsdale. The Suttons developed the important advance of 'removes' or 'passaging'. They inoculated lymph from the mildest possible case into a number of recipients, selected the mildest of those showing signs of local infection (reaction), inoculated lymph from this subject into another group, selected the mildest and so on. IngenHousz, called to inoculate the Royal Court of Vienna in 1768, used two hundred subjects before the Royal recipients, probably ten or more removes. In the same year Thomas Dimsdale inoculated Catherine the Great, Empress of Russia, after passaging the lymph through several hundred servants. He received a truly imperial fee and there is still a descendant bearing the title of Baron Dimsdale to commemorate his success. The Suttons were probably also the first to use 'Airing Houses', premises where inoculated persons stayed under supervision until danger of spreading infection had passed. These houses were obviously essential to avoid the accusation that variolation increased the risk of transmitting smallpox to the community.

Such precautions added to the expense of variolation and for this reason many medical historians believe that only the more wealthy classes could afford protection. The evidence provided by England shows this view to be partly incorrect. Records suggest that, although variolation was very rarely used for the protection of the poorer classes in towns and especially in London, it was frequently used in country districts, the fees being charged to the parish. Here is an extract from the churchwardens' accounts of a tiny village named Fitzhead in Somerset:

May ye 21st 1769. It is this day agreed upon by the churchwardens and overseers and the other inhabitants of the said Parish of

Fitzhead that all poor children that have been chargeable to the said parish, at a parish meeting held this day or a Vestry for that purpose held, shall be inoculated by the parish expence, as witness our hands John Comer, John Arscott, Jno Holcombe, William Toogood.
1769 Paid for inoculating of the parish 01.15.00
1789 Paid Dr Comer his bill for inoculating 27 poor people 05.08.00
1796 Paid Mr Sully for inocklating 34 children 08.10.00
1798 Towards Inocklating Stook and Stone's children 00.15.00
1798 Paid for inocklating Wm Crewse three children 00.07.06

Another village, Swallowfield in Berkshire, was a little larger. Many of the village women acted as wet nurses for the Foundling Hospital in London. In 1767–8 there was much smallpox in the district and prospective employers demanded that the children, now aged seven or a little more, should be inoculated before apprenticeship. Mrs Juliana Dodd, an Inspector of Wet Nurses for the Foundling Hospital, wrote: 'I have now but eighteen children under my inspection but mention'd twenty to the surgeons for inoculation, intending to make up that number by having two that are already apprenticed inoculated at my expence, having promised it to their masters at the time of their being apprenticed.' Mrs Dodd enclosed two letters from practitioners giving their terms. The first wrote: 'The lowest price for servants as indoor patients is three guineas each. Yet in consideration of the number proposed, and being children of the poor, he is ready to receive them under his care at his house near Reading and to find all necessaries, washing excepted, at two guineas each.' The second practitioner was somewhat cheaper: 'The lowest terms to inoculate twenty poor children and find them in every thing necessary will be twenty guineas, if charitably bestowed. All must be taken at once and the children sent decently clean. If any be afflicted with any complaint or disorder, that complaint will be cured before they are inoculated.' Mrs Dodd added that there would be some additional expense to have the children 'aired', which means that they must be kept in quarantine. If inoculation of the poor was practised to this extent throughout the country and was successful, smallpox must have been a dying disease in the last quarter of the eighteenth century.

Edward Jenner's introduction of vaccination in 1798 has tended to overshadow the value of variolation as a means of protection. For centuries there had been a folk tradition that cowhands and dairymaids never contracted smallpox. Cowpox is not common but, if introduced into a herd, may infect a number of beasts. It usually takes the form of a local ulcer on the udder and will affect the cow's general health and milk production if untreated. The lesion is very contagious. A person who milks the cow is liable to develop a cowpox pustule or ulcer on the hand or wrist but the risk of human-to-human spread is slight. Only very rarely is the local skin lesion followed by a generalized illness, although there is sometimes a low fever and malaise. Transmission is by direct contact, that is matter from the ulcer must impinge on a scratch or wound in the skin before the human can acquire the disease.

There are probably many unknown instances of farm workers deliberately allowing themselves to be infected with cowpox but only two have entered the literature. In 1774 a farmer named Benjamin Jesty of Yetminster in Dorset took matter from a cowpox lesion and rubbed it into scratches made with a darning needle on the arms of his wife and two sons. None of them acquired smallpox although there was a considerable epidemic in the district. The sons are said to have been inoculated with smallpox fifteen years later with no effect, local or general. In 1791 a German named Plett performed a very similar experiment.

As for Jenner, born at Berkeley in Gloucestershire on 17 May 1749, he was a house pupil of the great surgeon John Hunter at St George's Hospital in London. There is little doubt that Hunter fired his pupil with enthusiasm for 'the experimental approach'. The cowpox story first came to Jenner's notice in the 1770s when he was serving his apprenticeship with a surgeon at Sodbury. Jenner returned to practise in Berkeley and, contrary to the popular story, investigated the effect of cowpox for nearly twenty years before making his first human experiment. On 14 May 1796 he took lymph from a cowpox pustule on the wrist of a dairymaid named Sarah Nelmes and inserted it into two superficial incisions, each about three-quarters of an inch long, made in the arms of a boy, James Phipps. Jenner thus described his progress:

> On the 7th day he complained of uneasiness in the Axilla, and on the 9th he became a little chilly, lost his appetite and had a slight headache. During the whole of this day he was perceptibly indisposed and had rather a restless night, but, on the day following, he was perfectly well. The appearance and progress of the incisions to a state of maturation were pretty much the same as when produced in a similar manner by variolous matter.

On the first of July following, this boy was inoculated with matter immediately taken from a smallpox pustule. Several punctures and slight incisions were made in both his arms, and the matter was well rubb'd into them, but no disease followed.

Jenner was not satisfied with one success but decided to defer publication until he had a series. Unfortunately cowpox disappeared from the neighbourhood of Berkeley and did not return for two years. He then 'vaccinated' twenty-three subjects, before proceeding to inoculate them with smallpox after a lapse of some weeks. In every case variolation produced nothing more than a slight local reaction. Not until then, in 1798, did Jenner publish his great classic, a seventy-five page pamphlet entitled *An Inquiry into the Causes and Effects of the Variolae Vaccinae, a Disease, Discovered in some of the Western Counties of England, particularly Gloucestershire, and known by the Name of Cow Pox.* Jenner had carefully thought out his subject and had conducted experiments as opportunity offered over a number of years. He did not put his theory to the crucial test of human experiment until he believed that no harm would result. He did not rush into print. Even with a volume of evidence, an assured result, and although frustrated by absence of cowpox for two years, he resisted the temptation to publish his findings until the results were proved beyond question. Edward Jenner was a true scientist.

Within five years translations of Jenner's pamphlet had appeared in all the major European languages, but despite his careful preparation, his *Inquiry* had a mixed reception and aroused prolonged opposition. The 'inoculators' obviously attacked Jenner's 'vaccination' because its general adoption would end their lucrative trade. His method became a favoured subject for cartoonists. Clergy thundered from their pulpits against the iniquity of transferring an animal disease to Man. The protests of those who objected that other and worse infections might be transmitted from cattle to the human were more rational. This last criticism, combined with a rather natural distaste for inoculation with matter from a sick cow, induced early vaccinators to adopt an arm-to-arm technique whenever possible. It became customary to perform one inoculation with cowpox from the animal and then to set up a chain by vaccinating from one human to another, just as the inoculators had used the system of 'removes'. The method proved successful and disposed of the objection to 'animal matter' but added considerably to the danger of transmitting other human infections such as syphilis. Arm-to-arm inoculation also caused the great vaccination controversy.

By the end of 1801 about a hundred thousand vaccinations had been performed in England and the method was coming into world-wide use. It now became difficult to supply sufficient cowpox lymph and to ensure its activity when sent over long distances. Many different methods were tried. In 1803 the King of Spain decided to introduce vaccination into his American colonies. Twenty-two children who had never suffered from smallpox were enlisted and two of them were vaccinated. On the voyage, two fresh children were vaccinated from the preceding pair every ten days and so the active vaccine arrived at the port of Caracas in Venezuela. Here the expedition split into two, one party going to South America where over fifty thousand people were vaccinated in Peru alone. A second ship picked up twenty-six fresh children and carried the chain round the Horn to the Philippines, Macao and Canton. From there British and American missionaries took vaccine into the Chinese interior.

The highly infected Indian sub-continent received vaccine in 1802 after several abortive attempts. The lymph originally came from Jenner in Berkeley but travelled via London, Vienna, Turkey, Baghdad and the port of Bussora on the Persian Gulf. The lymph lost potency and only one vaccination 'took' on its arrival in Bombay. This single case provided enough for a new series distributed to Madras and Ceylon.

Thus the original 'Jenner Strain' travelled to Asia but a second strain became more widely distributed. Dr William Woodville of the London Smallpox and Inoculation Hospital found two cows suffering from cowpox at a dairy in Gray's Inn Lane on 20 January 1799. He immediately vaccinated seven subjects at the Smallpox Hospital and then inoculated all seven with matter from a smallpox pustule, three of them after an interval of only five days. From the original seven he 'vaccinated' a first series of two hundred and then from the latter a second series of three hundred persons. Woodville reported: 'In several instances the cowpox has proved a very severe disease. In three or four cases out of five hundred, the patient has been in considerable danger and one child actually died.'

Jenner was furious. He had purposely delayed test smallpox inoculation of vaccinated subjects for over a month in his own trials. He believed that Woodville's strain of vaccine had become contaminated with smallpox virus, so producing a dangerous illness. But Jenner practised in a rural area, while Woodville not only worked in the metropolis, the chief centre of British smallpox, but in a hospital founded for the purpose of inoculation and segregation. The demand for vaccine was such that few questions were asked. Woodville's strain became disseminated world-wide and is reckoned to have been passaged through at least two thousand removes before 1836. The North American strain probably derives from Woodville because he supplied the Vaccination Hospital in Bath from which Dr Haygarth sent lymph to Professor Benjamin Waterhouse of Boston in 1800.

All vaccinations were performed by the arm-to-arm method until 1881. Continued passage through the human resulted in over-attenuation of the virus and increased the risk of transmitting such human infections as erysipelas, tuberculosis and syphilis. In England the government instituted an Animal Vaccination Establishment in which calves were deliberately infected with cowpox and lymph distributed. This lymph proved very uncertain but the quality improved after it was found that glycerin prolonged preservation. The first 'glycerinated calf's lymph' was sent out in 1895, provision being made to supply 'humanized lymph' to those who objected to inoculation with animal matter.

Opposition to vaccination persisted throughout the nineteenth and early twentieth centuries. In Britain it came chiefly from the uneducated class and largely centred on threatened compulsion. But, curiously, the lower strata of society favoured variolation. An epidemic in 1837–40 caused about thirty-five thousand deaths, almost entirely among infants and young children of the urban working class. Thomas Wakley MP, editor of *The Lancet*, laid the blame squarely upon variolation, arguing that the epidemic would not have occurred had the practice been prohibited. The British Parliament accepted his view and passed an Act making inoculation with smallpox a felony.

Vaccination therefore became the only method of protection and was made compulsory for infants at the ratepayers' expense in 1853. Unfortunately no machinery to enforce the law existed and there was much evasion. About half the children born in British towns were vaccinated, the number being considerably smaller in most rural districts. The critical period is 1870–3, the most important years in the history of vaccination. Compulsory vaccination had been introduced by the more authoritarian European states, one of the first being Bavaria in 1807. Compulsion became general throughout Germany and army conscripts were always revaccinated. France did not introduce compulsory vaccination for either civilians or the armed forces. A general European pandemic of smallpox started in 1869. The Franco-Prussian War broke out in 1870. During the war 4,835 cases of smallpox occurred in the German armies with 278 deaths. Among French prisoners of war held by Germany, there were 14,178 cases with 1,963 deaths. The total of French prisoners seems to have been lost but they must have been many fewer in number than the whole German army.

French refugees are blamed for introducing infection to England though any human communication between Britain and the Continent could have done so. The resultant epidemic caused 44,079 deaths, nearly a quarter occurring in the London slum areas. Average mortality was 148 per 100,000 of the population compared with an estimated 400–500 per 100,000 before the days of vaccination. This epidemic greatly increased demand for infant vaccination. In the peak year 1871, 821,856 children were born in England and Wales of whom 93 per cent were vaccinated. Special Officers were now appointed to ensure that all children received treatment. Compulsion aroused opposition with the result that about 20 per cent of children escaped between 1871 and 1888, the figure rising to nearly 30 per cent in 1897. The government then introduced a 'conscience clause' which permitted exemption after satisfying two Justices of the Peace or one Stipendiary Magistrate. Probably because such exemption involved considerable trouble the number of infants vaccinated rose in the next ten years. Compulsion ended on 5 July 1948.

Accurate figures for the incidence of non-fatal smallpox in Britain are not available until 1899 when compulsory notification of cases was introduced. By then incidence had greatly decreased and the fall continued. From 1911 until 1921 annual notifications varied from a high of 315 to a low of 7, deaths ranging between 30 and 2. Then came an extraordinary incident. Notifications greatly increased in the years 1922–32 with a peak of 14,767 in 1927. But deaths were not on the same scale, for only 47 people died in the peak year. In April 1928, while this mild form was still prevalent, a ship from India brought true virulent smallpox to Liverpool, causing 35 cases with 11 deaths. This epidemic of the major type was easily contained by vaccination of all contacts and rigid segregation. No new cases occurred after the end of May. The epidemic of the minor form could not be contained because many people suffered so slight an illness that they did not even call in a doctor. Incidence must have been much higher than recorded in the notifications and the epidemic did not die out until the end of 1934. This is obviously an example of the *Variola minor* or alastrim prevalent in the sixteenth century, but whether it developed because of partial protection by vaccination or was imported from America is an open question.

The widespread success of vaccination first suggested an attempt to defeat disease on a global scale. In 1851 an international conference in Paris undertook the standardization of quarantine regulations which had varied from country to country. This resulted in the first organization for World Health, the Office International d'Hygiène Publique, established in Paris in 1907. The League of Nations carried on and enlarged the scope of the work in 1923. In 1946 an International Health Conference, held in New York, absorbed the Paris Office and the League to form the World Health Organization on 7 April 1948. WHO attacked a multitude of problems, including tuberculosis, malaria and venereal disease, and embarked on a massive programme of vaccination. The programme has been immensely successful, the last countries to be declared free of infection being Bangladesh, Somalia and Ethiopia. By 1979 WHO was able to declare that, except for certain laboratory specimens, the whole world was now free from the smallpox virus. Provided strict surveillance is maintained, this terrible killer should never imperil humanity again.

But who defeated smallpox, Edward Jenner or William Woodville? What were the twentieth-century vaccinators really using in their world-wide battle, cowpox or an attenuated strain of smallpox virus? These issues have been much discussed. One attack of virulent smallpox seems to have conferred life-long protection from another. Judging by the relative freedom of the Spaniards in the lethal Aztec epidemics, the milder alastrim of the sixteenth century must have conferred a considerable resistance if not actual immunity. Jenner claimed that his vaccination with cowpox gave life-long immunity from smallpox but experience must have shown that he was incorrect, for the Germans made revaccination compulsory every seven years and vaccinated all conscripts to the armed services whether they had already been vaccinated or not. Most doctors advised renewal every five or seven years and insisted on revaccination if a person came in contact with a case of smallpox. Until very recently, any traveller to a known smallpox area was advised to undergo revaccination. All this can be put in one sentence – no one was sure that cowpox gave life-long protection against smallpox.

Why, then, did vaccination succeed in defeating smallpox? A very distinguished epidemiologist, Dr Arthur Gale, has probably given us the correct answer in a small book published shortly after his tragically early death in 1956. Having given full credit to Jenner, he discussed Woodville's work, as described above, and continued:

> It is impossible to trace all the ramifications of the early history of vaccine lymph and it is difficult to interpret even so good an account of experiments as that of Woodville. One can only make a guess at what happened in London after 1799. The most plausible guess seems to me to be that the bringing together of cowpox and smallpox virus did in some way produce a modified smallpox virus which by an empirical process of selection on the part of the vaccinators gradually became safer and safer. The virus was kept going by arm to arm vaccination right up to 1881 when glycerinated calf lymph began to be substituted for it. Arm to arm vaccination was not finally prohibited until 1898. Modern work on viruses lends some support to this theory, in that, in the laboratory, the *vaccinia* virus resembles the smallpox virus rather more than the cowpox virus, though the cowpox has a similar antigenic structure.

Gale does not state the origin of the cowpox lymph used to vaccinate calves and so provide fresh supplies after 1881. As cowpox is uncommon and supplies of humanized lymph would have been freely available, it seems probable that the chain continued and the attenuated strain of mixed cowpox-smallpox virus remained in use until the end of the story, but that is only supposition.

Nothing of this takes away from the enormous debt that the world owes to Edward Jenner. He did not know the cause of disease but his work must be recognized as the starting point of all attempts to combat infection by immunization. In 1880, after he discovered the existence of the disease-producing micro-organisms which he named Germs, Louis Pasteur resumed where Jenner had been forced by lack of knowledge to leave off. Pasteur's successful production of a rabies vaccine (that word itself commemorates Jenner's work with cowpox) focused attention on the methods by which the body naturally protects itself against infection. From Pasteur's work developed not only the protective vaccines, but also the antitoxins used successfully in treating developed disease. Diphtheria antitoxin serum, first used in 1891, reduced the death rate from that infection in London isolation hospitals from 63 per cent of diagnosed cases in 1894 to 12 per cent in 1910.

Jenner's work and the train of events which he initiated have changed the pattern of infectious disease. He also, although quite unwittingly, effected a social revolution. Vaccination induced official action in a number of countries, where for the first time in history governments became actively involved in sustained attempts to eradicate disease on a national scale. Individual freedom of choice yielded to the interests of the community. National attempts combined into a great international campaign. There has been much opposition, sometimes for reasons that must command respect, but there can now be no doubt that large-scale compulsory vaccination somehow displaced smallpox from its position as a common endemic disease to the status of an increasingly rare exotic infection and finally ensured its extinction. Nor can the most widely divergent opinions on the merit or demerit of vaccination affect the indisputable fact that its compulsory application was the first massive endeavour to vanquish disease. As such, the prevention and eventual conquest of smallpox is a landmark in social history.

CHAPTER FIVE

General Napoleon and General Typhus

Napoleon Bonaparte is a towering personality. But the Napoleonic adventure is as much the story of his armies as of the man himself. These armies, born of a nation devastated by revolution, emerged as the greatest fighting force since the Roman Army and subjugated the whole of Europe except Britain. The fate of Napoleon cannot be divorced from that of his soldiers, nor can the fate of his soldiers be divorced from that of Napoleon. The emperor's victorious career was ended by the destruction of his Grand Army, which had itself become the victim of his own vaulting ambition. Having known almost unbroken success for nearly twenty years, the army was brought to ruin in the late summer of 1812, partly through Napoleon's failing judgement and partly by sickness. A number of diseases attacked his army during the 1812 campaign, the primary and most destructive of them being an epidemic of the campaign disease known as typhus or gaol fever.

Typhus fever is a disease of dirt. The causative organism, *Rickettsia prowazekii*, belongs to a class lying midway between the relatively large bacteria, which produce diseases such as syphilis and tuberculosis and can be seen under an ordinary laboratory microscope, and the viruses which produce infections such as smallpox and measles and are so minute that they can be identified only with an electron microscope. The organism is carried by lice. Lice are often found on animals, in the cracks and crannies of old buildings, or infesting unwashed human bodies and the seams of their dirty clothing. It is not the bite but the excrement and crushed body of the louse which transfers the organism.

Typhus acquired the name gaol fever because of its association with poverty and dirt. Since fevers were supposed to be caused by bad smells, this is the reason why judges ceremonially bear small nosegays of sweet-scented flowers. The infection originated in the filthy prisons and spread from the felon in the dock to the judge upon the bench. Three notable 'assize epidemics' occurred in the sixteenth century but these epidemics may have been late incidents in the history of typhus. The origin of the disease remains obscure. One theory holds that it originated in the East as an infection of lice and rats but subsequently became an infection of lice and men. Cyprus and the Levant have been suggested as the first focus of spread to Europe, the earliest certain outbreak being in the Spanish armies of Ferdinand and Isabella in 1489–90. Another theory maintains that typhus is a much older European disease, referred to as 'famine sickness' in the records.

There is no doubt that typhus has been associated with the special conditions of warfare for centuries. Campaign conditions entail that a number of people are herded closely together, wearing the same clothes for long periods and lacking means of ensuring bodily cleanliness. Lice will multiply rapidly in those circumstances and, since typhus is a lethal disease, the sickness and death rate may have a profound effect on the fortunes of war. A remarkable example is the relatively small and localized epidemic which inflicted a mortality of no less than 50 per cent on a French army besieging Naples in July 1528, thus making a decisive contribution to the final submission of Pope Clement VII to Charles V of Spain. Typhus also forced the armies of Maximilian II to break off the campaign against the Turks in 1566. Soldiers carried typhus across Europe during the Thirty Years War of 1618–48 and it seems that the infection became firmly established during this period.

Typhus fever remained endemic in the whole of Europe from the seventeenth to the early twentieth century but it was only in conditions of warfare, famine or extreme poverty that major outbreaks occurred. The United States was not infected until early in the nineteenth century, causing a great epidemic at Philadelphia in 1837. But the story of typhus is complicated by the existence of more than one form of the disease. 'True' typhus fever, characterized by high fever, delirium, a crisis and a blotchy rash, is very dangerous. Other less serious variants are Rocky Mountain Spotted Fever, Brill's Disease (now proved to be a recrudescence of epidemic typhus and renamed Brill-Zinsser Disease) and (questionably) Trench Fever. This last variant, the prevalent illness of the First World War, is carried by lice but caused by an organism, which in 1961 was removed from the genus *Rickettsia* and given the name *Rochelima*. All armies engaged in the European trenches became lousy, living in conditions of filth and deprivation unknown since the Middle Ages, yet the non-fatal trench fever seems to have replaced true typhus on the Western Front, infecting both German and Allied troops. True typhus did not occur among them although it wrought havoc among the Serbian, Austrian and Russian armies of the Balkan and Eastern Fronts. The Russians were particularly badly affected. After the revolution of 1917 and the Civil War that followed, famine and disease devastated the whole country. Approximately twenty million cases of true typhus occurred in European Russia alone between 1917 and 1921, causing from 2.5 to 3 million deaths.

The mode of transmission of typhus by an infected body louse was first described in 1911. The Brazilian H. da Roche Lima isolated the causative organism in 1916 and named it after the American Howard Taylor Ricketts and the Pole S.J.M. von Prowazek, both of whom had died while investigating the disease. In the Second World War improvements in hygiene, the use of persistent insecticides, the much-maligned DDT in particular, and a vaccine first prepared by Herald Cox in 1937 reduced the danger of typhus to such an extent that only 104 cases occurred in the US armed services with not a single death. Since the late 1940s broad spectrum antibiotics have also become available as an even more important means of combating the disease. None the less a certain mystery still surrounds the infection, for it seems that very special conditions are necessary before it will flourish in a virulent form even when there is gross infestation with lice. Typhus seems to require concomitant malnutrition and sordid living before it will produce a lethal epidemic. But the disease still exists and causes deaths in areas such as the Andes, the Himalayas and parts of Africa, so we must hope that a world-wide standard sufficiently high to deter infection can be instituted and maintained.

The fall of Napoleon was not inevitable. Given time, patience and a certain measure of luck, he could have extended his empire to the East, consolidated his administration of the conquered lands, and forced Britain into impotent isolation, impregnable upon the seas but helpless to intervene on the Euro-Asian land mass. Ill-luck and impatience were chiefly responsible for the defeat of Napoleon's army.

Napoleon had reached the height of his power and his glory in the spring of 1812. His empire spread from the frontiers of Russia and Austria to the coasts of the North Sea, the Atlantic and the Mediterranean. Three of his brothers wore crowns, Joseph as King of Spain, Louis as King of Holland and Jerome as King of Westphalia. One sister was Grand Duchess of Tuscany, another was the Princess Borghese, while a third had married his marshal Joachim Murat who now sat on the throne of Naples. Eugène, son of Napoleon's first wife, Josephine de Beauharnais, acted as Viceroy of Italy. Napoleon himself, having divorced Josephine in 1809, had contracted a brilliant marriage with the Archduchess Marie Louise, great-niece of Marie Antoinette and daughter of Francis, last Holy Roman Emperor and first Emperor of Austria. To this union had been born on 20 March 1811 his first legitimate child and heir, who had immediately been accorded the title King of Rome.

All this family splendour and imperial prestige ended at the sea coasts. No means had been found to cross the narrow Channel, only twenty miles wide – less than a day's land march – which separates France from England. The Royal Navy barred the way. Further, the insolent British had recently managed to establish a base in Portugal and, having entrenched themselves behind the strongly fortified lines of Torres Vedras, demonstrated the possibility of maintaining and supplying an army by sea. But Britain was still vulnerable by land. A large part of her trade and the bulk of her wealth derived from India, then administered by the Honourable East India Company. Britain needed Indian money to carry on the war. The French navy could not intercept and capture the armed merchant ships of 'John Company' which bore the riches of India to Britain. But the taking of India itself would not only deny her that wealth but also immeasurably harm her prestige. The overland route to India would be long and hard, but the prize which lay at the end of the road would be worth almost any sacrifice.

Napoleon had already tried the southern route across the Mediterranean, through Egypt and Arabia to the Indian Ocean. That adventure ended at Aboukir Bay on 1 August 1798, when Horatio Nelson inflicted a heavy defeat on the French Navy, transforming the Mediterranean into a British lake. The French army, cut off in Egypt and Palestine, was ravaged by sickness and only succeeded in returning to Europe with great difficulty. Aboukir proved that seaborne invasion was too dangerous to be practical. The conquest of India and the East could be attained only with the help of Russia or after her defeat and submission.

On 25 June 1807, ten days after winning a military victory over the Russians, Napoleon met Tsar Alexander I at Tilsit and early in July concluded a treaty of everlasting friendship. Six months later Napoleon outlined his plan for a combined Franco-Russian invasion of India through Turkey and Persia. The moment was propitious. Napoleon had beaten every enemy by land and at that time the British had not yet secured a base in Portugal. He had sufficient forces at command. Backed by supplies and some military aid from Russia, the campaign might prove no worse than a long and difficult route march.

The abnormal psychological make-up engendered by absolutism is seldom conducive to easy negotiation. Given a cooperative France, Alexander had everything to gain by helping Napoleon and simultaneously extending his realms to the Dardanelles, the Balkans and the China Sea. Given a cooperative Russia, Napoleon could have stabilized his European conquests, fed his peoples from the wide cornfields of eastern Europe, tapped the wealth of India, fortified his coasts and contemptuously resigned the empty dominion of the seas to the British Navy. The scheme held a fair chance of success and, if successful, must have resulted in an impregnable Franco-Russian domination of the whole of the Euro-Asian continent. But the essential trust and cooperation were lacking. The potential victors fell out over division of the spoils even before the spoils had been won. Alexander demanded Constantinople and the Dardanelles as a minimum payment for Russia's help. Napoleon, looking forward to the reconquest of the Mediterranean and the Straits of Gibraltar, refused to envisage a solid Russian entrenchment on his eastern flank. The all too short propitious moment was wasted in sterile argument. In May 1808 Napoleon found himself faced with a Spanish insurrection. In August a British expeditionary force defeated Marshal Jean Junot at Vimiero in Portugal and the opening shots of the Peninsular War had been fired. Napoleon, forced to acknowledge that he had a full-scale war in Europe on his hands, transferred the bulk of his Grand Army to Spain. Meanwhile Russia became entangled in a war with the Ottoman Empire which engaged her for the next four years. The projected Grand Alliance was tacitly abandoned.

The two emperors concluded their conference of September–October 1808 at Erfurt in Germany, outwardly in an amicable fashion. But one major problem remained unresolved. In 1807 Napoleon had created the Grand Duchy of Warsaw, which Alexander saw as a preliminary to detaching Poland from Russia and restoring an independent Polish state. At Erfurt Alexander promised Napoleon his support in the event of war with Austria, but he did nothing to prevent the war and made no move when it broke out in April 1809. His primary interest had now become the foiling of French ambitions in Poland. The question became acute in February 1810 when Alexander formally insisted that 'the kingdom of Poland shall never be restored'. Napoleon wrote in the margin of the dispatch 'Divinity alone can speak as Russia proposes'.

Another and more intimate disagreement had caused friction between the emperors. Napoleon's first marriage to Josephine was childless, yet she had borne children by her previous marriage with Beauharnais. Napoleon suspected that he could not father children, a suspicion widely shared in France. His doubts were resolved in 1807 when his mistress Eléonore Denuelle bore him a son, and another illegitimate child from Maria Walewska followed. Napoleon now asked Tsar Alexander for the hand of Anna, his fifteen-year-old sister, but was implacably resisted by the powerful Dowager Empress of Russia, who not only hated the French alliance but had heard and believed the rumour of his impotence. In 1810 Napoleon abruptly ended this negotiation by making a formal offer of marriage with Archduchess Marie Louise Habsburg of Austria. The offer was immediately accepted.

This dramatic *volte-face* was a symptom rather than the cause of the breach between Russia and France. Ever since the agreement at Tilsit, Alexander had faced the hostility of his nobles who derived a large part of their wealth from the sale of timber to maritime countries, especially Britain. Napoleon's Continental System of trade, reinforced by the British blockade of Europe, cut off that source of income. In December 1810 Alexander, who until now had acquiesced in the System, issued an Imperial ukase imposing a high tariff on French goods and opening Russian ports to neutral shipping. As Britain controlled the seas, this was equivalent to permitting unrestricted trade with the principal enemy of France. Russia had opted out of the Continental System and out of the French alliance.

It now seems obvious that in 1810–11 Napoleon should have consolidated his empire by clearing his threatened western flank. The British, though strongly entrenched within their fortified lines, could not muster a force of more than thirty thousand men. There can be little doubt that Napoleon, by attacking with overwhelming numbers, could have driven the British from Europe. But such a campaign would have been long, costly and inglorious. A military dictator, if he is to survive, must repay his people's sacrifices with dramatic successes. To the east there lay the possibility of a brilliant series of dashing battles and, at the end, the gilded cupolas and barbaric splendours of Moscow.

Beyond Moscow the road led to the gorgeous East. Napoleon was a narcissist and something of an exhibitionist – even the simple uniform he wore as Emperor was in contrast to the gold-bedizened and multicoloured uniforms of his staff officers. He commissioned the Italian artist Antonio Canova to sculpt a statue of his body, naked except for the classical figleaf. He designed his own gem-encrusted coronation robes. When in Egypt he considered conversion to the Muslim faith and donned the flowing garb of an Arab chief. Perhaps it was the jewelled turbans, the diamond aigrettes and the opportunity of wearing exotic ceremonial robes which drew Napoleon towards India, as much or even more than the chance of dealing a humiliating blow to England.

So Napoleon committed the grievous mistake of sacrificing reality for a dream. In January 1812 he denuded Spain of many seasoned troops to reinforce his eastern armies. He commonly spoke of his proposed campaign as 'the Polish War'. France was to appear as the saviour of a Poland enslaved by Russia. He proclaimed to his troops: 'the peace which we shall conclude will terminate the fatal influence which Russia for fifty years has exercised in Europe'. He told his Ambassador to Russia, Armand de Caulaincourt, 'I have come to finish once and for all with the colossus of the barbarian North'. But early in 1812 he privately revealed his true ambition to the Comte de Narbonne in the words: 'Alexander [the Great] was as far as I am from Moscow when he marched to the Ganges.' Narbonne thought the scheme to be half-way between Bedlam and the Pantheon.

From August 1811 onwards Napoleon was fully engaged in making preparations on an enormous scale for the invasion of Russia. In March 1812 he induced Prussia and Austria to sign agreements providing troops for his adventure. In April he made the obvious move of offering a peace treaty with Britain but met with no success. On the other side, Tsar Alexander wisely secured his southern and northern flanks by ending the Turkish war and by inducing the Prince Royal of Sweden to bring his country over to Russia's side in return for promised aid against Norway.

Napoleon's armies began to assemble in cantonments strategically sited on a line stretching from northern Germany to Italy, and in June 1812 started their concentration in East Prussia. The immense force numbered in all 368,000 infantry, 80,000 cavalry, 1,100 guns and a reserve of 100,000 men. During the campaign reinforcements brought the total number of troops engaged to well over 600,000. The Russian armies numbered slightly less than a quarter of a million which meant that Napoleon had an overwhelming majority for the first time in his career.

Legend has it that almost the whole of Napoleon's enormous army was destroyed on the retreat from Moscow. The legend is incorrect. A much larger number of men perished on the outward march through Poland and west Russia than on the retreat. Excluding the flanking forces, mainly German and Austrian, Napoleon's central or task army numbered about 265,000 men. Only 90,000 of these reached Moscow.

At first all went well. The summer of 1812 was unusually hot and dry so the men could march quickly over easy roads and the slower-moving supply columns, sent on ahead, could maintain their position. Food was therefore abundant and close at hand. The health of the troops remained uniformly good. Military hospitals had already been established at Magdeburg, Erfurt, Posen and Berlin but there was little demand for their services. On 24 June 1812 the army encamped on the west bank of the River Niemen, the boundary between Prussia and Poland. Here Napoleon inspected his army in dazzling review. Then the troops marched down to the river and crossed over by narrow pontoons erected by the bridge-building engineers. Four days later the army reached Vilna where Napoleon slept in the room vacated by the retreating Alexander a week earlier.

Napoleon had thought of almost everything but had forgotten that Poland was filthily dirty. The miserable peasants were unwashed, with foul matted hair, lousy and flea-ridden. Their insanitary hovels abounded with insects of all kinds. The abnormally hot, dry weather had affected the wells, water was scarce and polluted by organic matter. The enemy now menaced the front lines, so the supply trains had to move back to the rear of the fighting regiments. Poland's rudimentary roads were either soft with loose dust or rutted and hardened after the spring rains and hot sun, causing the wagons to lag behind and food to be scarce in the leading columns. The huge army – much too large for coherent command – lacked efficient discipline. Only the best units were accustomed to long, ordered marches and moved in a compact military formation but the greater part of the army dissolved into straggling undisciplined bands. Despite stringent orders and harsh punishments, this multitude of stragglers was forced by hunger to pillage the cottages, livestock and fields of the Polish peasants, their nominal allies. The Poles can hardly be blamed if they did not greet the French as their liberators from the Russian tyrant. The supplies, the auxiliary troops, the guerrilla fighters, upon which Napoleon had counted, failed to materialize. Instead, the eternal pillaging by his half-starved armies aroused a sullen fury which was to recoil upon his soldiers during the retreat.

If the war of liberation had already been lost, so had the chance of an easy victory over Russia. Nearly twenty thousand horses, twice the number that might be expected to fall in a single major battle, died from lack of water and forage on the road to Vilna. Men also suffered. Hunger and polluted water produced the common campaign diseases of dysentery and enteric fevers. New hospitals were hastily established at Danzig, Konigsberg and Thorn but they were unable to cope with the mob of returning sick. Then, just after the successful crossing of the Niemen, a few cases of a new and disastrous malady appeared. Men developed a high temperature and a blotchy pink rash and their faces assumed a bluish tinge. Many died quickly. Typhus fever now held the army in its unrelenting grip.

Typhus had been endemic in Poland and Russia for many years. There is no real evidence that the Napoleonic armies had encountered it before 1812 and they had certainly never suffered a major epidemic. Their medical and sanitary arrangements, brilliantly organized under the great military surgeon Baron D.J. Larrey, were the finest in the world but could not possibly cope with disease on the scale which now developed. Any preventive method proved useless because the cause of infection was unknown. Lack of water and insufficient changes of clothing made bodily cleanliness impossible. Fear of Russian attacks and Polish reprisals caused men to sleep together in large groups. The lice of infested hovels clung to the seams of clothing, deposited their excrement, were crushed and released the organisms of typhus fever which entered the slightest wound, even those made by scratching the site of irritation. By the time of the battle of Ostrovna in the third week of July, over eighty thousand men had perished from sickness or were too ill for duty. Disease alone had robbed Napoleon's central force of nearly a fifth of its effective strength within a month. His army was about a hundred and fifty miles from the Prussian frontier and Moscow was three hundred miles away.

There had, of course, been wastage from battle casualties as well as from disease, though not upon the same scale. The Russians had no overall strategic plan and their two armies, one led by Barclay de Tolly and the other by Prince Bagration, acted independently. De Tolly just succeeded in eluding Napoleon at Vilna, while Jerome Bonaparte and Marshal Davout failed to entrap Bagration. Fierce battles were fought by

Murat at Ostrovna and by Davout at Moghilev but the Russians still managed to disengage with most of their forces intact. Napoleon believed that the two armies would join to make a stand at Vitebsk and this, in fact, had been their original plan. On 27 July Napoleon established contact with de Tolly's army but, on the same day, de Tolly learned that Bagration had decided to retreat to Smolensk. During the night de Tolly succeeded in slipping away while Napoleon was still preparing for battle.

De Tolly's successful withdrawal had the effect of alarming the more cautious of the French generals. On 28 July Louis Berthier, Joachim Murat and Eugène de Beauharnais sought a conference with Napoleon. They sensed that the failure of the Russians to stand and fight was drawing the French army into a most dangerous situation. They told Napoleon that wastage of troops through sickness and desertion from less reliable units had reduced the effective fighting strength to little more than half and that the difficulty of provisioning even this depleted number in a hostile countryside had become formidable. They implored Napoleon to halt the advance. Having listened to their arguments he agreed to announce the end of the campaign of 1812. Then the urgent need for a spectacular victory caused him to change his mind. Two days later Napoleon reversed his decision and told the generals: 'The very danger pushes us on to Moscow. The die is cast. Victory will justify and save us.'

So the sick, half-starved army struggled on. Just over two weeks later, on 17 August, they came in sight of Smolensk and the River Dnieper where the two Russian armies had joined and it seemed that they would at last make a stand. Napoleon, determined to destroy his elusive enemy, did not hurry to press the attack. He ordered a frontal bombardment of Smolensk and a feigned assault, while sending Junot across the Dnieper to outflank the city and cut the Russian line of retreat. De Tolly learned of the danger in time, fired the city and hastily withdrew. On 19 August Junot brought the Russians to battle at Valutino, ten miles north-east of Smolensk, but he failed to encircle the army and lost over six thousand men.

At Smolensk, two hundred miles from Moscow, a decisive choice had to be made, either to turn back or go forward. The option of turning back would have meant acknowledging humiliating defeat. That of driving on, whatever the cost, may well have seemed the only way to realize Napoleon's eastern dream. However, it has been suggested that he could have settled for a third and more prudent course of action, by simply halting at Smolensk and giving his army time to recover.

Napoleon had acquired a considerable knowledge of public health measures and understood their importance. He showed great interest in Edward Jenner's discovery of vaccination. He had his own son vaccinated when eight weeks old and encouraged a campaign for vaccination of children and army recruits. No one as yet appreciated the relationship between lice and typhus fever but lousiness had been regarded as a sign of dirty habits for centuries. Samuel Pepys cannot be accounted the most cleanly of men, but lousiness was unusual enough to be recorded in his diary on 23 January 1669: 'when all comes to all she [his wife] finds that I am lousy having found in my head and body above twenty lice little and great, which I wonder at, being more than I have had I believe these twenty years.' Pepys changed all his clothes and cut his hair short 'so shall be rid of them'. This simple treatment was as well known to Napoleon and his doctors as to Pepys.

Smolensk had been partially destroyed by fire but Napoleon's efficient engineers could have improvised shelter. The supply line to Germany and France was open and could be kept open. A winter of rest, good rations, ample water, medical care and sanitary control might have restored the broken army, allowed time for reinforcement of men and commissariat, and enabled Napoleon to consolidate his position in Poland and launch an overwhelming attack on Russia in the summer of 1813. Such was the opinion of J.R. de Kerckhove, one of the army surgeons, who later wrote that if Napoleon had been content to play this waiting game, his campaign might have been successful and his domination of central and eastern Europe permanently established.

Apart from Napoleon's character, there are still two reasons why this sensible third course did not appeal to him. First, his army had encountered formidable difficulties in the Peninsular War. In July Wellington had gained a resounding victory over General Marmont at Salamanca and had entered Madrid in August. Napoleon could not foresee that these successes would end, if only temporarily, in Wellington's costly and dispiriting winter retreat to Ciudad Rodrigo. The second and more potent reason is that Napoleon had convinced himself that the capture of Moscow must force Alexander to capitulate. He decided to make Smolensk an advanced base for concentration of reserve troops and supplies, and establish similar bases at Minsk and Vilna. Having thus secured the road back to the frontier, he felt free to push on as quickly as possible to Moscow. He resumed the march on 25 August. His striking force had now been reduced to 160,000 men; by 5 September 30,000 more fell victims of typhus.

On 30 August Alexander appointed the veteran Prince Michael Kutusov commander-in-chief of the Russian armies. Kutusov had led the Russian division at Austerlitz in 1805 where he acquired a healthy respect for Napoleon as an opponent and gained some knowledge of his strategical methods. He continued the policy of giving ground, slowly withdrawing as the French advanced. On 5 September the Russians came to the banks of the Moscow River, fifty miles to the south-west of the city. Kutusov would have preferred to continue a planned slow retreat, relying on the wide barren spaces of Russia and the imminent bitter cold of winter to destroy the French, but realized that national pride demanded at least a token defence of the ancient capital. Karl von Clausewitz, the eminent Prussian strategist and military historian, summed up the position thus: 'Kutusov, it is certain, would not have fought at Borodino where he obviously did not expect to win. But the voice of the Court, the Army, all of Russia, forced his hand.'

Kutusov did not risk the whole of his command. The Russian forces engaged at Borodino numbered 120,000 men, but 10,000 of these were raw, hastily trained militia. Opposing them were 130,000 seasoned French troops with 600 guns. The Russian artillery was slightly superior in number and weight. Kutusov entrenched his infantry on a slope above the Moscow River, centring them on the village of Borodino, and prepared redoubts for his cannon. There, for two days, the Russian army awaited battle.

The engagement which followed bore some resemblance to Waterloo, probably for similar reasons. Napoleon was a sick man at Waterloo, unable to give undivided attention to the battle. The same is true of Borodino. He was in great pain from an acute attack of cystitis, inflammation of the bladder. He also suffered from a heavy feverish cold. The two days' delay in attacking may have resulted from his indisposition but the question also arises of how far was Napoleon in charge of the actual battle and to what extent, if any, did his illness affect the issue. He disregarded Davout's advice to attempt an encircling movement by turning the Russian left wing, which seems a sensible method of destroying an entrenched army. The excuse has been made that Napoleon had already experienced the Russians' agility in disengaging when threatened on the flank. Whatever the reason, the French mounted massive cavalry attacks upon the well-defended Russian centre, the same disastrous tactics which Marshal Ney employed against the unbroken British line at Waterloo.

Battle was joined at dawn on 7 September. The French cavalry charged repeatedly but the Russians succeeded in re-forming the line and were not driven from their entrenched position until the evening. At the height of the engagement, when it seemed a spectacular Russian defeat was in reach, Davout urged Napoleon to throw in his most trusted Imperial Guard. Napoleon refused: 'If I throw in the Guard, with what shall I fight tomorrow?' he asked. Whether by foresight or by chance, the decision to withhold his best troops prevented absolute disaster two months later.

Both sides suffered heavy casualties, the Russians losing about fifty thousand men and the French just over half that number. Obviously the French loss was the more serious, since they were operating in hostile country with little opportunity for reinforcement. But at least it was victory of a kind, though meaningless in the long term. The Russians retired, retaining freedom to manoeuvre and with the certainty of receiving ample supplies and fresh troops. Kutusov plainly appreciated the situation. He had fought this token battle for Moscow and withdrawn in good order. Now disease, the winter cold and hunger would effectively do his work for him. On 13 September he held a council of war and said to his officers: 'The salvation of Russia is in her army. Is it better to risk the loss of the army and of Moscow by accepting battle, or to give up Moscow without a battle?' His reasoning was accepted and the army retreated through Moscow in a south-easterly direction towards the town of Ryazan.

So the French marched unopposed into Moscow on 14 September and typhus marched with them. They had already lost ten thousand men from sickness in the past week. Of over 300,000 who had formed and reinforced Napoleon's task force, only 90,000 reached Moscow. Seven out of ten had fallen on the way. But the tattered remnant at last saw the gilded and multicoloured domes shining before them. All the church bells were ringing. Napoleon expected to be met by a humble deputation of leading citizens offering him the keys of the city, but the gates remained shut. That primitive but effective weapon, the battering-ram which had been dragged across the length of Poland, was brought forward. The gates were battered down and the army entered to find empty streets and silent houses. Within a few hours fires broke out in several districts.

The true story of these fires will probably never be known. The population of early nineteenth-century Moscow numbered about 300,000. For some days the governor, Count Rostopchin, had been organizing the evacuation of the city and only about 50,000 people remained at the time of Napoleon's entry. Immense quantities of stores and valuables had also been removed. In the last phase of the evacuation, Rostopchin released prisoners from the city gaols. Legend has it that he released them on the condition that they remained in the city to harass the French by pillaging and arson. Rostopchin's action in sending all the fire engines out of the city suggests that the fires were deliberate rather than that they were caused by drunken French soldiers.

Napoleon, overjoyed that Moscow had been won, clung to his opinion that Alexander must now sue for peace. His judgement here was at fault. Alexander could not submit. He had been warned by his sister that the capture of Moscow would stiffen national feeling against the French to such an extent that peace negotiations might endanger his life. Alexander well knew, with the example of the assassination of his father Tsar Paul in mind, that he was not safe from even his intimate advisers. The late French ambassador to Russia, de Caulaincourt, tried to convince Napoleon that Alexander neither would nor could accept defeat and refused to act as an intermediary. On 4 October Napoleon sent General Lauriston on a peace mission to St Petersburg.

Kutusov learned of Lauriston's mission and ordered his Cossack patrols to fraternize with the French outposts, thereby lulling Napoleon into a false sense of security and providing a rational basis for his peace fantasy. Kutusov was again playing for time. He knew that nearly three-quarters of Moscow had been destroyed by fire. He was also aware of the sickness that increasingly reduced his enemy. Typhus spread unchecked among the French, the sick finding such shelter as they could in the burnt-out ruins or in improvised hutments. Army morale fell to a low ebb as the idle soldiers, disappointed of the ample supplies they had been promised, spent their time in plundering and drinking such stocks of alcohol as they could find in the city cellars.

The hot dry summer had passed into an unusually warm autumn. De Caulaincourt, the one man in Napoleon's entourage who had experience of a Russian winter, warned him that the wasted, ruined city would be untenable when the cold weather set in. Napoleon, misled by the mild season, replied that de Caulaincourt was exaggerating and must know that a Russian winter could be little worse than a winter at Fontainebleau.

Thus his futile peace parleys combined with a mild October to lead Napoleon into the final mistake of this disastrous campaign. The remnant of his army could only be saved by adopting one of two courses: either to return immediately to Smolensk or march north, join with his Prussian allies, and invest St Petersburg. A bold, successful attempt on the capital might possibly have brought Russia to her knees.

Squadrons of moving cavalry ringed Moscow with the result that the French had lost touch with the main body of the Russian forces. They had retreated to the east, then rapidly marched in a half-circle south and west to cut Napoleon off from the chief centres of supply and arms manufacture at Kaluga and Tula. Murat's army was stationed at Tarutino, south of Moscow. Here, on 18 October, Kutusov launched a surprise attack, inflicting six thousand casualties and forcing Murat to withdraw. This comparatively small engagement warned Napoleon that the Russians had taken the offensive, that his peace bid had failed, and that he was now in danger of encirclement. On 19 October his army at last began the retreat from Moscow.

Fifteen thousand reinforcements had joined the French army during their month's stay in the city, but nearly ten thousand soldiers succumbed to disease and wounds. The army which left Moscow on 19 October amounted to just over ninety-five thousand dirty, half-starved, unhealthy men. They were encumbered with their sick and wounded, six hundred cannon and insufficient horses to draw them, an immense mass of loot including the enormous and quite useless gilded copper cross from the cupola of the Kremlin tower called Ivan Veliki. Napoleon turned south to avoid the already devastated direct route to Smolensk. On 24 October the Russians met him at Malojaroslavetz. A heavy day's fighting ended indecisively. Napoleon, having suffered too many casualties, declined to press the attack next day and Kutusov also lost the opportunity of victory.

The southern route being effectually barred, Napoleon had no option but to turn north, rejoining the Smolensk road at Borodino. The cold had now become intense and snow started to fall heavily on 5 November. Fast-riding bands of Cossacks, aided by guerrillas, rendered foraging almost impossible. No preparations had been made for a winter campaign. De Caulaincourt managed to obtain ice-shoes for the horses of Napoleon's suite, but not a single cavalry or artillery horse was properly shod. This and not the cold is the reason for Napoleon's dispatch of 7 November: 'the cavalry is on foot'.

The army pressed on to the promised food and shelter of Smolensk. Napoleon arrived with the vanguard on 8 November, to find his reserve, under Claude Victor, wasted by typhus fever and the hospitals already crowded with their sick. Discipline had deteriorated to such an extent that rations could no longer be fairly distributed. The greatest blow of all was the lack of food, for the reserves and communication troops had consumed most of the supplies stored against the army's return. Finding no succour in Smolensk, Napoleon evacuated the town on 13 November, leaving over twenty thousand sick in the makeshift hospitals and ruined houses. Next day he found Kutusov barring the road leading west.

The Russians, now entrenched at Krasnoi, expected that the depleted French army would try to avoid battle but the men had straggled to such an extent that Napoleon decided his only hope was to give them time to concentrate. He therefore ordered the Imperial Guard to attack. These valiant troops, preserved so carefully at Borodino, now prevented complete and humiliating defeat. Kutusov, hurled back by their fury, could not reform to attack. Leaving Ney to fight a magnificent rearguard action, Napoleon pushed on to his next supply base at Minsk. On 22 November he received the appalling news that Minsk had already fallen to the enemy.

Two days later he learned that the Russians had destroyed his bridgehead over the River Beresina. The pontoon bridges had already been abandoned for lack of transport. The position now seemed hopeless, for Napoleon's flanking armies, also in retreat, had been heavily defeated by Prince Wittgenstein in the north and by Admiral Tchitchagov in the south. The Russian pincers were closing in from either side and Kutusov's army blocked the way to the west. The French were saved by their brilliant engineer General Jean Baptiste Eblé. While a small force made a feigned crossing of the river to the south of Studianka, misleading Tchitchagov into believing that the whole army intended to make the attempt, Eblé improvised two bridges on the north side of the town. But, despite the heroism of the rearguard, only fifty thousand men succeeded in continuing the retreat.

The army now began to degenerate into an undisciplined rabble. On 29 November Napoleon wrote: 'Food, food, food – without it there are no horrors that this undisciplined mass will not commit at Vilna. Perhaps the army will not rally before the Niemen. There must be no foreign agents in Vilna. The army is not a good sight today.' Fifteen thousand men died on the road between the Beresina and Vilna. But there was worse in store.

The starving vanguard reached Vilna on 8 December, having marched through thickly falling snow driven by a bitter north-east wind. Only twenty thousand sick and disheartened men comprised the effective force. The rest were stragglers, stumbling along as best they could, starving and frozen, harried by Cossack patrols. Just twenty men remained of Ney's Third Corps, who had fought so valiantly in the rearguard. The town of Vilna offered no relief. Already starving, it was crowded with sick, and typhus fever had spread throughout the surrounding countryside. Men suffering from typhus, dysentery and pneumonia lay on rotten straw soaked with their own excrement, without medical attention or means of warmth, so hungry that they gnawed leather and even human flesh. By the end of December over twenty-five thousand sick and frost-bitten men had struggled into the town. Fewer than three thousand of these were alive in June 1813.

On 5 December Napoleon had received news from Paris of his rumoured death and of a conspiracy led by General François de Malet. Next day, at Smorgoni to the west of Vilna, he decided on a hasty return to France before the full extent of the disaster could be understood. He drafted a bulletin for dispatch in the usual manner, giving a frank account of the horrors experienced during the retreat but not mentioning the breakdown of supply arrangements and laying blame entirely on the atrocious weather. Napoleon then set out, first by chaise, later on horseback. After a furious ride across the whole of Germany and eastern France, he arrived at the Tuileries in Paris on the night of 18 December, anticipating his catastrophic bulletin by two days. He handled a dangerous, indeed a desperate, situation with supreme skill, from the understatement of his report to the Senate on 20 December – 'My army has had some losses, but this was due to the premature rigour of the season' – to his successful mobilization of 470,000 fresh troops by the autumn of 1813. This, perhaps the most remarkable episode of Napoleon's astonishing career, bears witness to his tenacity and speed of action when faced with a threat to his power.

He could save himself but he could not save his army. Murat, left in command, proved a broken reed. He refused to make a stand at Vilna and on 10 December abandoned the last guns, the remaining baggage and the army's treasury to the Russians. On 12 December Berthier sent a private report ahead to Napoleon that the army no longer existed, and that even the Imperial Guard, now reduced to five hundred men, had lost all semblance of a military formation. Ney, still stubbornly fighting a rearguard action, crossed the Niemen on 14 December. When the last stragglers had shuffled over to the German bank, there remained fewer than forty thousand of the brilliant Grand Army which Napoleon had reviewed on 24 June. It is said that only a thousand of those who returned were ever again fit for duty. So ended Napoleon's dream fantasy, the conquest of Russia and of India. There were, of course, other causes of defeat besides typhus fever. Cold, hunger, the Russians, all helped to destroy the army – and so did Napoleon Bonaparte himself.

Napoleon was born by a precipitate labour on 15 August 1769. At the age of twenty-six in 1795 he was only five feet six inches tall, with a square face, a strangely sallow complexion, a well-formed nose, grey eyes and dark brown hair. His most striking physical characteristic at this time was excessive thinness. Although well muscled and fairly powerful, he looked a runt of a man. He had a lively, rather impressive expression provided his interest had been aroused, but at other times often looked so miserable that people thought he must be in actual pain. He took little care of his person in early life. His long ill-powdered hair hung over his collar, his clothes and boots were shabby and his hands dirty. Napoleon had been a bookish youth, intelligent, eager to learn, a brilliant mathematician. He had shown little interest in sex during adolescence.

Napoleon's swift and dazzling rise to supreme power depended on a combination of controlled imagination, unusual intelligence tempered by downright common sense, and an acute perception of the correct moment for any course of action. His magnificent brain seemed as if divided into separate compartments which he could open and close at will. Thus, he dictated orders and plans to a number of secretaries, turning from one subject to another as he walked between their desks. His notorious anger was a weapon calculated to inspire fear and was entirely under his control. He lived for power and knew that power largely comes from the master's ability to instil fear: 'Abroad and at home I reign only through the fear I inspire.' Later in his career, he was to imagine himself as his own ideal of a gloomy, cold-blooded, inaccessible tyrant, but he never achieved that character for, although formidable, he remained fascinating. Talkative, gregarious, possessed of great charm which, like his anger, could be switched on and off at a moment's notice, he aroused a genuine love and devotion among those who came in contact with him. Even his enemies were impressed. The ship's company of HMS *Bellerophon* which took him to St Helena agreed that 'if the people of England knew him as well as we do, they would not hurt a hair of his head'. His veterans worshipped him, for his fantastic memory enabled him to call any one of them by name – and it was the duty of his aide-de-camp to prompt that memory should it fail.

Napoleon also achieved his success by a phenomenal capacity for hard work. Pressure of work caused him to neglect his natural body requirements. He slept for only three hours each night and developed the ability, not uncommon among hard-pressed administrators, of falling deeply asleep for short periods at intervals during the day. Anthelme Brillat-Savarin dismissed Napoleon as 'an undiscerning eater'. He bolted his food, often taking only twelve minutes over dinner, and ate when business permitted rather than at set hours. Despite this unhealthy regimen, Napoleon seems to have kept remarkably fit during his earlier years in power.

He had certain disabilities which became more troublesome as he aged. The story of infertility, half believed by himself, came to a happy end with the birth of his bastard sons. The rumour of epilepsy possibly has a firmer foundation. As a lad at Brienne he fell unconscious to the ground, but this was probably nothing more than a faint. During the near-disaster of Brumaire in November 1799, when he was physically menaced by members of the Five Hundred, friends dragged him to safety in an almost unconscious state. This, although it has been cited as evidence, was probably reaction to a totally unexpected crisis. But three attacks bearing some resemblance to epileptic fits are recorded between January 1803 and September 1805.

The suggestion has also been made that Napoleon suffered from syphilis. This story is based on some urinary trouble during the Consulate of 1802–4. Napoleon himself wrote that the opinion of his doctor, Alexis Boyer, caused him to 'conceive strange suspicions of Josephine, for I was quite sure of myself'. But his urinary symptoms (which we have already noticed at the battle of Borodino) are more suggestive of small stones, 'gravel', in the bladder. There is nothing here to support a diagnosis of syphilis.

The most serious of Napoleon's illnesses to be diagnosable with any certainty is migraine, the distressingly painful 'sick headache' which is only too common among highly strung people who work under great pressure. The first report of migraine comes towards the end of the Italian campaign in 1796 and he suffered from similar attacks at times of stress throughout his life. Another symptom of Napoleon's highly strung temperament is his itching skin. This must have been a dermatitis of nervous origin but may well have been induced by the true 'itch' or scabies which he contracted at Toulon in December 1793.

Two other disabilities, neither serious in itself, profoundly affected Napoleon's later career. Napoleon was certainly a man of 'irregular habits', which resulted in constipation, and the straining at stool, a natural sequel of constipation, rendered him liable to prolapsed haemorrhoids, generally known as piles. The first mention of this very common and very painful ailment is in 1797, when he was twenty-eight years old. Five years later, in 1802, irregular eating habits produced another painful condition, equally common among those who live at high pressure and without due care. Fauvelet de Bourrienne, Napoleon's chief secretary, recorded that his master began to suffer from abdominal pain early in 1802. He would quite often lean against the right arm of his chair, unbutton his waistcoat and exclaim 'Oh what a pain I feel!' This is possibly gall-stone colic or simple indigestion but the later history suggests that bane of the harassed financier, a peptic ulcer.

In 1805 Napoleon, crowned Emperor on 2 December 1804, was thirty-six years of age. From now on he started to deteriorate, both physically and mentally. This fairly rapid change was noticed by all those in close contact with him. He began to fill out, developing a paunch. His thin face became rounded and his neck thickened. The long straggling hair receded from his forehead, grew sparser and finer in texture. His skin was softer and his hands, once long and 'beautiful' (although dirty), were covered with fatty tissue and so gave the appearance of being small and pudgy. The lean, haggard Corsican Ogre of the James Gillray caricatures changed into the better-known stocky little Napoleon of school history-book pictures.

This physical deterioration was accompanied by a marked alteration in temperament and mentality. Basically, he lost self-discipline. From 1806 onward his rule became more absolute and his ministers little better than yes-men. Denis Decrès, Minister of Marine, declared: 'The Emperor is mad and will destroy us all.' In 1807 Prince Metternich observed that 'there has recently been a total change in the methods of Napoleon. He seems to think that he has reached a point where moderation is a useless obstacle.' His temper was not under the same control as before. His rages were less frequent but he could no longer switch them on and off at will. He lost the common sense which had nearly always guided his actions and now allowed his fantasies to take charge of his plans. Hand-in-hand with lust for power and dream-fantasies there went an unwonted impatience. But the body refused to obey the dictates of the mind. His magnificent vitality slackened and he lost the old capacity for prolonged constructive work. By the age of forty Napoleon had changed into a lethargic and hesitant but irritable man.

What was the cause of this dramatic change? Many reasons have been suggested but not one wholly explains the facts. His obesity and lethargy suggest a physical rather than a mental cause. Thyroid deficiency, myxoedema, might produce changes of this kind, but portraits of Napoleon's features do not favour the diagnosis. Fröhlich's Syndrome, deficient secretion of the pituitary gland at the base of the brain, has been suggested, but it is unlikely that a person suffering from this disorder would be capable of siring children. Neither of these theories takes into account the three 'fits' or epileptiform convulsions reported in 1803–5. These are unlikely to have been true epilepsy but may be associated with his known migraine. Ordinary migraine can occasionally develop into the syndrome now called 'complicated migraine' in which fits or paralyses or disturbances of speech may occur. These severe symptoms result from spasm of the cerebral arteries which, though transient, can lead to brain damage. If this is the case, Napoleon's lethargy resulted from minor brain damage and his obesity was consequent on the lethargy. The damage must have been only minor, for it is evident that Napoleon could react violently and swiftly when faced with a direct challenge to his power, nor is there evidence that he showed any of the grosser signs of severe brain damage.

Whatever the cause may have been, and it is certainly unwise to be dogmatic on this point, the new Napoleon lacked the quickness and decision of the old. Nevertheless he successfully recruited a new army of 470,000 between December 1812 and July 1813. His army was superior in numbers to that of the Allies, but was poorer in quality since it mainly comprised raw recruits, the type always more susceptible to campaign diseases than seasoned veterans. On the way back from Moscow the retreating French and pursuing Russians had infected Germany with typhus fever. All central and eastern Europe suffered an epidemic in the autumn and winter of 1813–14. Thousands of Napoleon's new army succumbed until, by the late autumn of 1813, fewer than half remained fit for service.

Towards the end of August 1813 the French had seemed on the point of inflicting decisive defeat upon the Allies at Dresden. After two days of bitter fighting, during which Napoleon directed the battle in person, the Allied armies were forced to retreat, leaving the French poised for an annihilating stroke on the next day. But now one of Napoleon's comparatively minor disabilities attacked him and helped to change the course of history. On the evening of the second day, he was exhausted, soaked to the skin and famished with hunger. He ate hurriedly and ravenously. During the night of 27/28 August abdominal pain and vomiting became so severe that he was forced to return to the rear, leaving Marshal Mortier, Marshal Laurent de St Cyr and General Dominique Vandamme to resume battle next day. The defeat of Vandamme prevented a rout of the Allies.

Two months later, on 17 October, a similar attack of abdominal pain and vomiting prostrated Napoleon during the decisive battle of Leipzig, but in this case probably did not affect the issue. By November the French had been driven back across the Rhine. Prussians under Prince Blücher, Austrians under Prince Schwarzenberg and Russians under Tsar Alexander gave chase and poured along the roads to Paris. Wellington was fighting his way up from the Pyrenees. The days of the Napoleonic Empire were numbered. At this critical, hopeless time something of Napoleon's old magic returned. Wellington said of the campaign of 1813–14: 'the study of it has given me a greater idea of his genius than any other . . . but he wanted patience'. On 6 April 1814 the Marshals insisted on unconditional abdication and on 11 April Napoleon made a declaration renouncing the thrones of France and Italy.

There followed an attempt at suicide, probably by means of strychnine, on the night of 12 April. Then came the terrible journey through southern France, when the fallen Emperor narrowly escaped lynching at Avignon and saw himself hanged in effigy at Orgon, and his departure into exile as monarch of Elba. Here he seems to have been reasonably happy, administering his tiny kingdom, exercising his toy army, no doubt supported by his dreams and his plans. Then came the dramatic, almost insanely adventurous return to France. On 1 March 1815 Napoleon landed at Antibes and started on his triumphant progress through Mouans-Sartoux, Grasse, Digne, Grenoble and Lyons back to Paris.

The ill-health which had now dogged him for ten years almost brought the adventure to an end before it had really started. The returning hero rode triumphantly on horseback at the head of an impressive cavalcade from Antibes to Grasse. Here the haemorrhoids, which had troubled him on and off since 1797, became excruciatingly painful. Even to walk was agonizing, to ride unthinkable. Napoleon commanded a carriage to be brought forward and for a time found some comfort, but the rough road and the jolting wheels made relief only temporary. A sick and deposed monarch lolling on cushions is very different from a returning conqueror prancing on his war-horse. But the attack passed fairly quickly and Napoleon found himself able to continue the march after two days. Had the bout been more prolonged, his triumphant progress might well have ended at Grasse.

These same troublesome piles, together with Napoleon's somnolence and lethargy, largely account for what the French still call the enigma of Waterloo. Of all the armies which Napoleon recruited, that which fought at Waterloo was the one most needing inspiring and coherent command. They were a 'scratch lot', unaccustomed to their leaders, hastily enrolled during the Hundred Days. But these troops cannot be blamed for the disaster of Waterloo. Napoleon lost the battle of 18 June by losing his opportunity on the previous day. On the evening of the 16th the strategic position looked most favourable for the French army. Considering the poor quality of his troops, this fact itself testifies to Napoleon's skill as a military leader.

Napoleon, commanding about 124,000 men, faced a Prussian army of 120,000 under Prince Blücher and a mixed British-Dutch-German-Belgian force of 100,000 under the Duke of Wellington. Napoleon's admirable plan was to operate with two wings and a large reserve. Headquarters having been established at Charleroi, he ordered one wing under Marshal Ney to hold Wellington on the Brussels road while the other, under General Grouchy, engaged the Prussians. These were still about ten miles to the east of the nearest point where they could make contact with their British allies and so face Napoleon with numerical superiority. On 16 June Ney duly attacked Wellington at Quatre Bras, while Grouchy and Napoleon defeated and partially routed the Prussians at Ligny. Neither battle was decisive, but the opportunities for the following day were immense. Napoleon with his reserve could either complete the rout of the Prussians on his right flank or take an easy swing to the left and smash Wellington. But, as the military historian Becke has written: 'it was in these twelve hours from 9 p.m. on the 16th to 9 a.m. on the 17th that the campaign was lost.'

Napoleon had been in the saddle for the whole day of 16 June. This obese, prematurely aged man of forty-six was completely worn out. Worse still, his piles had once more become agonizingly painful. He remained sleepless, in pain, throughout the night of 16/17 June. Whether Larrey did or did not administer opium will probably never be known for sure, but Napoleon stayed in his bed until eight in the morning. He did not resume active command until eleven, when he ordered Grouchy to pursue the Prussians. By this time contact had been lost and Napoleon made the mistake of ordering pursuit to the east, whereas Blücher had retired to the north. At the same time Napoleon ordered the Guard to support Ney at Quatre Bras. Wellington, having learned of Blücher's retreat to the north, moved his army back up the Brussels road to parallel the Prussians and to establish a defensive position on the high ground before the village of Waterloo. For some time the British were entangled in the narrow village street and single bridge of Genappe, an easy target for Ney. Meanwhile Grouchy, feeling his way east and south, was every moment increasing his distance from the coming battle.

On 17 June the sun rises at about 3.45 GMT. Over four hours of daylight were wasted before Napoleon awoke from his uneasy sleep, over seven hours before he was able to assume control of strategy. It is certain that he had the opportunity of inflicting decisive defeat and it is certain that he lost the chance. The young Napoleon would never have missed the opportunity offered but would have risen triumphantly to the occasion, exhaustion or no exhaustion, pain or no pain. The lethargic, impatient, pain-ridden Napoleon of June 1815 was no longer capable of the effort required. To the medical historian Saturday 17 June is the fatal day and the Sunday of Waterloo itself comes as something of an anticlimax. Napoleon was still in no fit state to exercise control of the battle, yet despite his ill-health and the mistakes made by Ney he very nearly defeated Wellington at Waterloo. If we accept the victor's own opinion – 'It was the most desperate business I ever was in. I never took so much trouble about any battle and never was so near being beat' – then Napoleon's ill-health may well have provided the necessary weight to tip the balance.

Six years later, on 5 May 1821, the deposed Emperor died on the island of St Helena. The second period of exile had been a time of hopeless frustration, of petty quarrelling, of sulky seclusion. Undoubtedly the Governor, Sir Hudson Lowe, lacked the tact and intelligence to handle so difficult a prisoner as Napoleon, but the legend of the 'Martyrdom of St Helena' has no basis of fact. Political necessity prompted the British to present the island as something in the nature of a health resort. Conversely, similar considerations encouraged Napoleon's sympathizers to depict it as more akin to Devil's Island. Even Pope Pius VII, whom Napoleon had arrested and exiled, made a plea for his release on the ground 'that the craggy island of St Helena is mortally injurious to health and the poor exile is dying by inches'.

A form of liver disease, an acute infective hepatitis, was endemic on St Helena. Napoleon may have fallen sick of it but, if so, he quickly recovered. His terminal illness lasted six months. Much has been written about it and many theories have been advanced. In fact the history is quite clear. During his last days he suffered from 'tarry stools' and 'coffee-grounds vomit', both of which are caused by digested or semi-digested blood. The treatment given to him does not seem very sensible. One of the last drugs administered was a large dose of calomel, which can have done not the slightest good and may have actually hastened death. The post-mortem reports vary as to the condition of Napoleon's liver, but all mention a large 'scirrhous growth' of the stomach. This, taken together with the tarry stools, coffee-grounds vomit and the obstinate hiccups described by General Bertrand, make the cause of death certain. Napoleon died of a cancer which had invaded the stomach wall, piercing an aperture of sufficient size to admit a finger. The cancer had eroded a blood vessel and the immediate cause of death was exhaustion from haemorrhage and peritonitis, both secondary to perforation of the stomach wall by the malignant growth.

Although the cause of death is plain, a number of allegations were made. Among these is poisoning, a very common allegation when the deaths of prominent persons are under consideration. Napoleon ordered in his Will that his head be shaved and locks of hair distributed to various friends and followers. Some excitement was caused in 1960 by the report that traces of arsenic had been found in samples of his hair. Poisoning by arsenic cannot have been the immediate cause of death. Arsenic is, however, a known carcinogen and, if taken inadvertently or purposely administered for any length of time, might have been the causative agent. It is conceivable but unlikely.

Napoleon died nearly six years after Waterloo and lost Waterloo three years after the Moscow campaign. His disastrous fall began and became inevitable when his own health and judgement began to fail. His Grand Army was destroyed by his own impatience and by the ill-luck of encountering typhus fever. His empire never recovered from the destruction of that army. On 29 November 1812, during the crossing of the River Beresina, Marshal Ney wrote to his wife: 'General Famine and General Winter, rather than the Russian bullets, have conquered the Grand Army.' This is the accepted opinion but, to tell the whole truth, we must add the names of General Typhus and General Napoleon.

CHAPTER SIX

Cholera and Sanitary Reform

There is an important group of diseases, known as enteric fevers, which are caused by human excrement contaminating food or drinking water with the relevant bacteria. These include typhoid, paratyphoid and dysentery. To them must be added cholera, often known as Asiatic cholera to differentiate it from infantile cholera, better called infantile diarrhoea. Until recently these afflictions, together with typhus fever, were often classed as campaign diseases, that is illnesses which were particularly prevalent in the special conditions of warfare.

Before the Battle of Crecy in 1346 the French rudely spoke of the English invading force as the breechless or bare-bottomed army because they so often squatted to defaecate. It would be impossible now to decide which disorder had attacked them but typhoid or dysentery seem the most likely. Until the twentieth century endemic enteric diseases of this group, together with typhus fever and eventually the exotic Asiatic cholera, killed many more soldiers than any weapon. In the grossly mismanaged Crimean War of 1854–6 ('the army was destroyed by its military leaders and saved by a civilian woman') out of 97,000 British troops dispatched to the theatre of war, 2,700 were killed in action, 1,800 died of wounds, and 17,600 died of disease. Cholera was rampant in the British forces and, during the winter months, scurvy (Vitamin C deficiency) also caused a number of deaths. In the American Civil War of 1861–5 the Northern Armies lost 93,443 men killed on the battlefield or later dying from their wounds. The toll from disease amounted to almost exactly double at 186,216, the deaths of 81,360 being ascribed to typhoid and dysentery. Again, cholera was partially responsible for the high mortality. Accurate figures are not available for the Confederates but it is believed that typhoid caused even more deaths than in the North.

The Boer War of 1899–1901 is also of considerable medical interest. British military commanders have been less noted for intelligence than for their refusal to accept civilian advice, but the Boer War generals must surely have been unusually wooden-headed. The organisms causing typhoid and bacillary dysentery had already been discovered and measures for prevention, including anti-typhoid inoculation, were available. Long before 1899 typhoid had been recognized as primarily a water-borne disease and it was well-known that contaminated water could be rendered harmless by boiling or filtration. About 400,000 troops in all were engaged in South Africa, the field army numbering 200,000 at any one time. From February 1900 until the end of 1901, 6,425 British soldiers died in battle or from wounds. The Boers used the high-velocity Mauser rifle which either killed outright or inflicted a clean and fast-healing wound. The terrain was largely uncultivated, not highly populated, and so relatively free from the organisms which cause human disease such as wound sepsis. Despite this comparative freedom from pathogenic organisms, 42,741 men fell sick of typhoid fever alone and the total who died from all forms of disease amounted to 11,237, nearly double the deaths from enemy action. There is no doubt whatsoever that the armed forces themselves introduced infection and that the incidence of typhoid and the number of deaths from enteric disease could have been greatly reduced had proper water discipline and sanitary measures been ordered by the high command.

This may appear a severe and unfair judgement, so let us see what happened only four years later in the Russo-Japanese War of 1904–5. The Russians did not issue exact figures but claimed that of 709,587 men engaged, less than one in a hundred suffered from illness. The report may be an underestimate but observers remarked that the health of the troops remained excellent throughout the Russian débâcle. The Japanese lost 58,357 men from enemy action and 21,802 from disease, thus reversing the previously recorded battle casualty/sickness ratio. Of the Japanese who died from sickness, 5,877 died from typhoid fever and dysentery. These water-borne diseases were as prevalent, if not more prevalent, in Manchuria as in South Africa. The enormous improvement in the sick rate largely depended on forbidding troops to drink unboiled water, providing constant supplies of hot water for making tea, provision of latrine areas, and, so far as possible, never billeting men in villages.

We can understand that the common soldiers on active service suffered badly from these infections but it is more surprising to find that even royal commanders were affected. Of English monarchs who led their armies in person, William the Conqueror died in 1087 from a ruptured ulcer in the bowel, a late result of typhoid fever. Edward I died of dysentery in 1307 as did the hero of Agincourt, Henry V, in 1422. Edward the Black Prince, heir to Edward III, died of the same disease, and may thereby have changed the course of English history, for his weak young son came to the throne during the land and labour crisis following the Black Death, one of the more difficult periods in social development. King John's romantic death in 1216 from 'a surfeit of peaches and new cider' is likely to have been the plebeian effect of resultant diarrhoea violent enough to rupture a bowel already weakened by typhoid fever. The demise in 1135 of the second royal glutton, Henry I, was undoubtedly from another of the enteric group, food poisoning: 'He ate voraciously of a lamprey, which he was accustomed to delight in more than anything else, and paid no attention to his physicians when they forbade it him.' It is said that a man who helped embalm the body fell ill and died in great pain a few days later.

In rather more recent times, Albert the Prince Consort, husband of Queen Victoria, died of typhoid in 1861 (although the diagnosis is now challenged). His son, Edward VII, very nearly lost his life from the same disease ten years later, and Edward's nephew, Tsar Nicholas II, fell seriously ill of typhoid fever in 1900. His mother, Maria Feodorovna, complimented him on his strength of mind when the physician reported to her that Nicholas had refused to eat a mutton cutlet until it had been minced, a precaution commonly adopted in the recovery stage of typhoid fever.

The early story of this group of diseases is impossible to disentangle because they were commonly lumped together under the term 'continuing fevers'. Many physicians suspected that the group contained more than one disease but many more thought the appreciable differences to be variations in behaviour of the same type of illness. In the late summer and autumn of 1839 William Budd, a doctor in North Tawton, Devon, had under his care the inhabitants of several cottages notorious for the number of 'fever cases' they produced. Budd studied the problem and concluded that he was dealing not with one but with two types of disease. He found that, although both were characterized by fever and a blotchy pink rash, one tended to be acute, killing within days, and the other chronic, sometimes causing months of sickness. It is not clear whether Budd himself named the two infections, because he did not publish his findings until 1873, by which time credit for the differentiation had already been attached to Sir William Jenner in Britain (1849) and to William Wood Gerhard of Philadelphia (1837). The acute disease was named 'typhus fever' and the more chronic one was called 'typhoid' because it resembled typhus in some respects without being identical.

Continuing his observations, Budd found that the majority of his typhoid patients came from a single group of cottages which all drew their water from the same shallow well. In view of the unmistakable bowel symptoms, he concluded that the excreta of the sick individuals must be leaking from the earth privy which served the cottages into the well from which the cottagers drew their water. After one or two inconclusive experiments, he treated the privy with massive doses of chloride of lime. The number of typhoid cases gradually dwindled and finally reached a low which might be expected in any village community of the time. Local historians who search old parish registers often find a pattern of deaths obviously from small localized epidemics affecting all age groups and occurring at any time of the year. Sometimes it is possible to trace the names of the dead to a group of families living in close proximity and even to identify the disused well from which they drew the water.

The village system of drawing water from a surface supply, streams or shallow wells, and disposing of human excreta by spreading over the fields had worked quite satisfactorily for centuries without producing unbearable living conditions and persisted in the remoter country districts almost down to the present day, until the thatched hovel with its unreliable well and earth privy became the desirable residence ripe for conversion. But during the eighteenth century living conditions of the labouring class started to be changed by the industrialization which first developed in the relatively small country of Britain. Here the population of England and Wales rose from 8.9 to 17.9 millions between 1801 and 1851. The problem caused was greater than even this increase suggests. As the Industrial Revolution quickened, there developed a swiftly accelerating movement from country to town. It is for this reason that our primary consideration will be the problems and the solution of the problems as they affected Britain.

As in all European countries, the life and economy of Britain had been sustained by agriculture for centuries. Now the villages and small market cities of a farming community burst their bounds and sprawled over the countryside until, in many districts, the intervening fields disappeared and individual hamlets lost identity to become parish names in one coalescent mass. Unfortunately for the health of the public, landlords, speculative builders and the inhabitants themselves regarded these new towns simply as enlarged villages, which they were not. As the towns expanded and spread over the fields, so the difficulty of waste disposal intensified. The temptation to pour excremental waste into the river could not be resisted.

This river also supplied much of the drinking water. A swiftly flowing stream carried most of the waste away from the town and its water supply. A tidal river, such as the Thames in London or the Avon in Bristol, returned a large part of the noxious material on the incoming flow and so increased the risk of pollution. Use of steam power diminished an already inadequate water supply and mills used the river as a convenient waste pipe for their effluent. By 1830 no large manufacturing town in England possessed water entirely safe to drink and rivers in these areas had become so polluted that fish could no longer survive.

More and more houses had to be built as the country people continued to pour into the town. The new houses must be close to the mill, for neither master nor worker desired that time be wasted on travelling. Contractors used any available land to the best advantage, cramming a maximum number of dwellings into a minimum of space. Speed was essential since the mill could not start work until the operatives were housed, so builders did not waste time on digging out foundations, building weight-supporting walls and erecting tower blocks. They built skimpily of readily available material, back to back in rows or narrow courts. These new houses were serviced on the same principle as the village dwelling, one house or part house to a family, with a shared water supply and outside privy, often no more than a single earth closet for each court or row of houses.

As time went on and the number of factories increased, building could no longer keep pace with the influx into manufacturing towns nor was there any more available land close to the existing mills. Taking in lodgers and sub-letting became the rule. Few families occupied more than a single room and a two-roomed cottage might contain as many as twenty people. Cleanliness, privacy, decency, proper sanitation and clean water supply were all impossible in conditions such as this. The uncleaned privies, in daily use by dozens of people, overflowed and filled the courts with a morass of excrement which permeated the soil to contaminate the shallow wells from which the inhabitants drew a scanty supply of water.

We should rid our minds of the common fallacy that all this sordidness was entirely new. All the major evils of the industrial town already existed in the rural village. Underfed families lived in overcrowded hovels, women and young children worked in the fields, labourers toiled from dawn to dusk for a starvation wage. A child of seven scaring crows on a bleak hillside in midwinter does not command the same sympathy as a child of that age labouring in a mill. We remember the overseer's strap but forget the farmer's whip. We are not so horrified by the picture of a pregnant woman engaged in the back-breaking task of hand weeding a cornfield as we are by that of her sister harnessed to a coal-truck underground. The modern city-dweller's Cloud-cuckoo-land of a rural Arcady, a Merrie England that never existed, has blinded us to the fact that every evil of the industrial town originated in the agricultural village and resulted from the transfer not of people only but of their manner of living. This way of life did not become intolerably dangerous in the countryside because communities were small, cottages widely separated, and work performed in the open air. The disaster of epidemic illness became inevitable when the community was cramped for space, houses lay cheek by jowl and factory hands worked close together for long hours in an enclosed atmosphere.

The cholera which was to cause huge mortalities in communities such as this and to become a world-wide pestilence during the early nineteenth century had never before been endemic in Europe. Even in India, where cholera probably formed part of the ancient disease pool, it seems to have been confined to a quite small area for centuries. It is, like typhoid, one of the water-borne infections and there is reason to believe that the Hindu ritual of river bathing, while probably encouraging human-to-human spread, also limited the range of distribution because the illness is typically a short one, often not more than a few hours. Older reports of cholera by Europeans in India cannot be regarded as trustworthy because of its similarity to the much more widely prevalent bacterial dysentery, but the true disease was certainly existent in Madras during the years 1770–90. In June 1814 it appeared among native troops on a march of many hundred miles from Trichinopoly, a district of Madras, to Jaunpur or Jawalpur, both towns in the United Provinces, the latter standing on the River Ganges. In 1817 cholera broke out with great violence over the whole Ganges delta, which became notorious as a focus. Medical men in the area stated that it had not been seen in the delta before 1817 and considered it a new disease. Their opinion is now regarded with some doubt. A possible explanation is that cholera was endemic in Central India, then largely unexplored by Europeans, and made its way down river to the coast, carried by troop movements and river shipping.

Cholera was on the move at the beginning of the nineteenth century. In 1817–18 came the first known export from India, eastward to China and the Philippines, south to Mauritius and Reunion, north-west to Persia and Turkey. By 1823 a pandemic covered the whole of China, Japan and Asiatic Russia. Then, for some unknown reason, the advance halted for three years, only to recommence in 1826. This may or may not have been a new export from India which followed the same route to Persia and the Caspian Sea area, from where it travelled to Europe. The first English cases appeared at Sunderland in October 1831. The whole of the British Isles had been invaded by the winter of 1832/3 and most of Europe by the end of 1833, Italy remaining free until 1835. Quebec and New York received cholera by ship in 1832 and the disease spread slowly south through North America to Mexico and beyond. This slow advance is typical and we cannot improve upon John Snow's account of a later pandemic in 1849:

> There are certain circumstances connected with the progress of cholera which may be stated in a general way. It travels along the great tracks of human intercourse, never going faster than people travel, and generally much more slowly. In extending to a fresh island or continent, it always appears first at a seaport. It never attacks the crews of ships going from a country free from cholera to one where the disease is prevailing, till they have entered a port, or had intercourse with the shore. Its exact progress from town to town cannot always be traced, but it has never appeared except where there has been ample opportunity for it to be conveyed by human intercourse.

This slow, relentless progress, which of course also characterized the first waves of 1817–32, aroused a peculiar horror fed by rumour and superstition. There was a widespread return to the medieval idea of Divine Punishment. Cholera is an agonizingly painful illness, producing intolerable vomiting and diarrhoea until the gut is entirely emptied and the whole body dehydrated. Dehydration brings on terrible cramps of the limbs and often of the abdominal muscles, while attempts to empty the already empty stomach cause continual retching and hiccupping. A cholera patient is a pitiful sight, whether he or she lives or dies, but the most terrifying aspect of the illness is its sudden onset and the speed of development. Heinrich Heine wrote a letter on 9 April 1832 describing a scene in Paris of which this is a much edited version. On 29 March a masked ball had been in progress, the 'chahut' in full swing. Suddenly the merriest of the harlequins collapsed, cold in his limbs and, underneath his mask, violet-blue in the face. Laughter died out, dancing ceased, and in a short while carriage-loads of people were hurried from the dance hall to the Hôtel Dieu (the oldest of the Paris hospitals) to die. To prevent a panic among the patients already there, the dead were hastily thrust into rude containers still wearing their dominoes. Soon the public halls were filled with dead bodies sewed in sacks for want of shrouds or coffins. Long lines of hearses stood in queues outside the cemetery of Père Lachaise. The rich gathered up their belongings and fled the city. Among the poor, the suspicion of secret poisoning caused the cry of 'à la lanterne' to be raised again. Six persons were murdered and their naked bodies dragged through the streets in the belief that they were culprits.

The horror of this disease and the rumours which preceded its appearance demanded that action be taken by those in authority and the slow progress gave time to prepare. Britain, closely followed by some of the German states, was the first country to attempt centralized control of 'public health' and enforcement of health regulations upon the whole civilian population. For example, a Board of Health had already been instituted for this object in 1804 when a sea-borne epidemic of yellow fever threatened. However, this was dissolved two years later once the immediate danger had receded and no rules had been implemented. In practice the government could only exert influence through such local authorities as existed. The only ones available were composed of parish officers and justices of the peace, whose primary duty was to implement the Poor Law under the titular control of the Privy Council. The system dated from the reign of Elizabeth I and in the course of time had become so decentralized that every parish was virtually a self-governing unit.

Towards the end of 1830, when it appeared likely that Britain would soon be endangered by cholera, there were some people determined to make good use of the little time that might be left. In January 1831 Charles Greville, Clerk of the Privy Council, asked Dr Walker of St Petersburg for a description of the epidemic already affecting northern Russia. Walker seems to have left the city, for he did not reply until March and then with a second-hand account. Cholera reached the west Baltic coast in early summer and on 17 June Greville sent Dr William Russell and Dr David Barry to investigate and report. Four days later, on 21 June, government established a Central Board of Health under the aegis of the Privy Council.

However, the authorities made a serious mistake by appointing leading members of the medical profession and high officials instead of waiting for the return of Barry and Russell or employing doctors from the East India Company who had first-hand experience of cholera. The Board met almost daily from 21 June until 11 November 1831, preparing 'such Rules and Regulations as they may deem most effectual for the adoption of the most approved method of guarding against the cholera'. The Privy Council received its first recommendations on 29 June. This historic document is the first attempt to influence public health through a centrally directed coordination of local government but was of little value at the time as no member of the Board had yet seen a case of cholera.

The Board advised the establishment of local Boards of Health, consisting of members of the medical profession, clergymen and leading citizens, which would maintain contact with the General Board in London. They provided a few obvious but not inspired directions for dealing with patients and their belongings and promised more detailed instructions and a description of the disease in due course. On 3 September *The Lancet* carried an announcement of the scheme, which was violently attacked by the editor Thomas Wakley.

On 12 October danger became acute with the appearance of cholera in Hamburg, a port of regular communication with the British Isles. The Rules and Regulations, with an additional statement on the nature and treatment of cholera, were published on 20 October. A week later, on 27 October, an army surgeon named James Kell reported the first British death from cholera at Sunderland. Four more deaths were reported before 1 November. The Home Secretary now issued instructions that the regulations published on 20 October must be enforced. The Privy Council decided that a Central Board of Health composed of members who knew something about cholera might be useful, and dismissed the physicians on the pretext that they were too busy to attend the almost perpetual sessions required. The new Board consisted of Dr Russell and Dr Barry, a customs official named Edward Stewart and Sir William Pym of the quarantine service. The Board was full-time and did not confine its meetings to London. Barry left immediately for Sunderland and other members travelled the country encouraging formation of Local Boards, instituting isolation hospitals, and advising on segregation and treatment. By February 1832 the Central Board of Health employed four deputy inspectors-general of hospitals, twenty-one medical officers and seventeen surgeons. At the end of the epidemic these officers were advising 1,200 local Boards of Health in England and Wales and about 400 in Scotland. Cholera caused some twenty-two thousand deaths before the end of May 1832, then started to decline rather rapidly until the epidemic had virtually ceased in December and the Central Board of Health was dissolved. In February Parliament had authorized a Cholera Prevention Act permitting local authorities to provide nurses and medicines, cleanse infected houses, destroy bedding, clothing and other articles, cover drains and cesspools and abate nuisances in general, the cost to be chargeable to the poor-rate.

There had been some rioting in the worst slum areas of industrial towns leading to apprehension that the close-packed, insanitary streets might prove breeding grounds not of disease only but of social unrest. Fear was intensified by the riots preceding the 1832 Reform Act. The government set up a Royal Commission to enquire into the working of the Poor Law, and to make recommendations for ameliorating the lot of the working class. The Commission invited the help of Edwin Chadwick, a lawyer-journalist who had been secretary to Jeremy Bentham, the social reformer and co-founder of the University of London. Chadwick later became secretary and the most active member of the Poor Law Commission.

He is chiefly remembered by the British public as the originator of the hated Union, the central workhouse in which men, women and children, paupers, the sick and the disabled, were herded in prison-like conditions, including segregation of the sexes. The memory is unjust because Chadwick had recommended hospitals for the sick, orphanages for the fatherless, homes for the aged and workhouses for the healthy unemployed, but a parsimonious government bungled the whole scheme and it was further mismanaged by incompetent local authorities interested only in lowering the Poor Rate paid by householders.

In 1836, when the first Registration of Deaths Bill came before Parliament, Chadwick secured addition of a clause requiring registrars to insert the cause of death. He persuaded the first Registrar-General to appoint a statistician named William Farr. In 1838, the first full year of registration, there occurred a major epidemic of typhus fever. About fourteen thousand people fell sick in London, of whom 1,281 died. Many of the manufacturing towns reported similar figures. Some of the better local authorities noticed a relation between the number of typhus deaths and the level of the poor rate. A few took advantage of the Cholera Prevention Act to indict landlords who refused to abate nuisances. The cost of prosecution was charged to the poor rate but auditors refused to allow this as a reasonable expense on the ground that the Act only covered prevention of cholera. The dispute was taken to Chadwick as secretary of the Poor Law Commission. He saw the chance for an investigation with the possible outcome of introducing some of the reforms omitted from his Union scheme.

Chadwick enlisted the help of three doctors. They examined conditions in the worst fever districts and concluded that the high incidence was largely caused by dirty habits and drunkenness but that the poor could do nothing to better themselves while living conditions remained filthy. In August 1839 the House of Lords pressed for an extended enquiry largely undertaken by Chadwick himself with the help of his three medical assistants. They published their findings on 9 July 1842 under the title *Report of an Inquiry into the Sanitary Conditions of the Labouring Population of Great Britain.*

It is virtually impossible to overestimate the importance of this document. On a relatively minor plane it was Chadwick's *Report* that first roused Florence Nightingale's interest in social science and particularly in hospitals, ultimately making her the leading authority on the subject. Chadwick is one of those prophets of whom it can be said that he was honoured save in his own country – though he did receive a belated knighthood. His fame now is world-wide. His report directly stimulated action on public health in the United States. The brilliant American medical historian Fielding Garrison wrote: 'Through Lemuel Shattuck, Chadwick may be said to have started public health activities in the USA and latterly influenced even Billings.' There had been no advance in public hygiene until Shattuck instigated a sanitary survey of Massachusetts in 1849. The survey report stressed the enormous amount of ill-health in American cities consequent upon insanitary conditions and the need for investigation and control. State Boards of Health were instituted which did excellent work but there was no national organization until John Shaw Billings urged the United States Public Health Service in 1889. Chadwick also influenced Max von Pettenkoffer who designed a sewerage system for Munich, did much work on cholera, and was appointed their first Professor of Hygiene in 1859.

Chadwick covered an enormous field. Having examined returns from 533 districts, he produced 'sanitary maps' clearly showing the relationship between infectious disease and overcrowding. He pointed out that disease was propagated by atmospheric pollution resulting from filth, overcrowding, lack of drainage and defective water supply. He proved his point by taking the ages of death from eight districts and showing that average expectation of life was related to class: forty-three years for gentry, thirty for tradesmen and only twenty-two for labourers. The last low figure entailed a very large number of widows and orphans, all of whom must be supported by parish relief. Early loss of the breadwinner, overcrowding and neglect forced children on to the streets to beg, thieve and sell themselves as prostitutes. Disease thinned the ranks of higher age groups leaving a 'young, passionate and dangerous population, easily deceived by anarchist fallacies'. Chadwick's biographer R.A. Lewis wrote that he 'drew his respectable hearers to the edge of the pit and bade them observe the monsters they were breeding beneath their feet'.

The Chadwick report shook government and bourgeoisie out of their complacency. Implementation of the necessary legislation would require heavy expenditure. The government referred the problem to a committee, usually known as the Health of Towns Commission, and a number of semi-official associations recommended action in the larger towns. Liverpool was one of the first to obtain a Sanitary Act in 1846, empowering appointment of a Borough Engineer, an Inspector of Nuisances and a Medical Officer of Health. On 1 January 1847 Liverpool appointed Dr William Henry Duncan to be the first MOH in Britain.

Meanwhile Chadwick turned from broad policy to detail. He had no knowledge of sanitary engineering but set himself to learn and enlisted the help of two efficient advisers. Piped water was coming increasingly into use but the supplying companies were obsessed by the ancient type of main, a bored elm trunk which split under the pressure required. They therefore supplied water under very low pressure by ground-level standpipes usually only for an hour or two on stated days. Thomas Hawksley, one of Chadwick's advisers, proved that flow and pressure could be maintained at no extra cost by using metal piping.

The problem of sewage disposal was solved by Chadwick's second adviser, John Roe. A few sewers already existed to take storm water off the streets but they were simply brick channels with flagstone covers which could be lifted to remove mud and rubbish by hand. Roe demonstrated that it would be economical to replace these 'sewers of deposit' by narrow-bore self-cleaning drains. This type of sewer, circular or oval in section and running in smooth curves, required a constant flow of water for efficient cleansing. If to be used for disposal of human excrement, a sewer of this kind demanded the installation of flushing water closets in place of the dry earth privy.

Self-cleansing sewers carrying noxious waste posed a major difficulty. The ultimate outfall of the sewer could only be into a river, almost certainly the river from which the town drew its drinking water. Chadwick tackled the problem himself and devised the 'arterio-venous system', exchanging rural water for town sewage. Land drainage was coming increasingly into use as more acreage was needed for the growing population and this sub-standard ground required heavy manuring, much of which had been provided by 'night-soil', the term used for the contents of privies. Chadwick proposed to pump water from the land drains into the town and pump liquid town sewage through return pipes on to the land. The term 'sewage farm' still commemorates Chadwick's scheme. This simple exchange of sewage for water proved uneconomic in Britain although it was adopted in a number of other countries.

Now came two disasters. Chadwick was a rather unpleasant, dictatorial man who eventually quarrelled with the Poor Law Commissioners and was dismissed from the secretaryship on 8 July 1847. The threat of another cholera epidemic had been growing since 1845, so the Prime Minister immediately put Chadwick in charge of an enquiry into the sanitary defects of London, thought to be at special risk. He produced a startlingly adverse report which, together with the imminent threat of cholera, terrorized even the British Parliament into embarking on panic legislation. The Public Health Act ('Chadwick Act') was rejected in March 1847 but became law on 31 August 1848.

The Act resurrected the General Board of Health for a term of five years and gave local authorities power to form their own Boards of Health. The General Board would no longer be under the control of the Privy Council; it was responsible to no ministry and had no spokesman in any department. In fact it had no definite duties, and could count on no support except by engendering good will. The Board consisted of two peers and Edwin Chadwick, later joined by a medical adviser, Dr T. Southwood Smith. They held their first full meeting on 21 November 1848.

By this time cholera had appeared in Edinburgh. It reached London in December and infected the whole country by June 1849. The epidemic was much more serious than that of 1831. The ten-year-old Registration of Deaths apparatus collapsed under the strain and the figures are approximate rather than exact. At least fifty thousand and probably more nearly seventy thousand died in England and Wales. London suffered

The Plague of Athens, by the Flemish painter Michael Sweerts (1624–64), whose depiction of the pestilence of 430 BC treats a subject frequently encountered in neo-classical art. (Christie's Images, London, UK/Bridgeman Art Library)

A priest celebrates mass for plague
victims, as pictured in an illuminated
manuscript from the mid-fourteenth
century. (MS Douce 313 f. 394v,
Bodleian Library, University of Oxford)

Tsar Ivan IV, the 'Terrible', ruler of
Russia from 1533 to 1584. (E.T. Archive)

The Cow Pock – or – the Wonderful Effects of the New Inoculation!, by the English caricaturist James Gilray, London 1802. (Private Collection/Bridgeman Art Library)

The Miseries of the French Grand Army in their Retreat from Moscow, bivouacking, 1812, *from a print published by Edward Orme of London in the year following this Napoleonic disaster. (British Library, London, UK/Bridgeman Art Library)*

DEATH'S DISPENSARY.

OPEN TO THE POOR, GRATIS, BY PERMISSION OF THE PARISH.

Death's Dispensary, *a sharp comment on the vital importance of supplies of clean water, from the* Illustrated London News, *1860.*

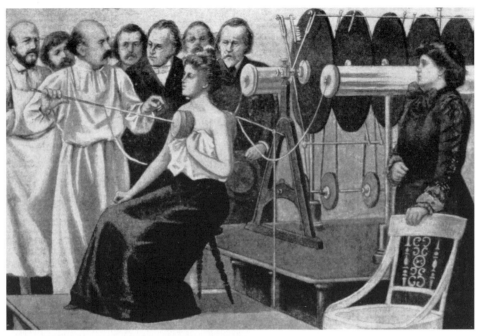

Treatment of tuberculosis according to one of the methods advocated by the unqualified French practitioner, Francisque Crotte, as depicted in the Petit Journal *for 1901. (Private Collection/ Bridgeman Art Library)*

Grigori Rasputin, the 'holy-man', whose hold over the Tsaritsa Alexandra contributed much to the downfall of the Romanov dynasty. (Illustrated London News)

Tsarevitch Alexis, photographed at Friedberg in 1910, together with the sailor Derevenko, the constant companion who was responsible for protecting the haemophiliac heir from life-threatening injury.

Arresting a Witch, *a seventeenth-century scene as portrayed in a much later engraving (based on a picture by Howard Pyle) illustrating 'The Second Generation of Englishmen in America' by Thomas Wentworth Higginson, and published in* Harper's Magazine, *1883. (Private Collection/Bridgeman Art Library)*

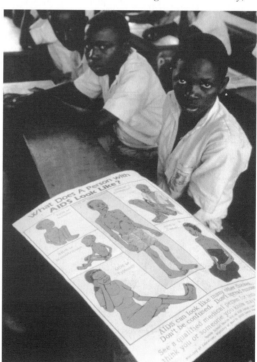

AIDS education in the Jinja district of Uganda, 1990s. (Photographer, Still Pictures)

about fourteen thousand deaths out of at least thirty thousand cases of cholera. The mortality gave the General Board of Health the power denied to them by Parliament. Within three days of their first meeting, sixty-two towns asked for application of the Public Health Act. Local authorities demanded advice on how to implement the vague powers accorded them. The Board secured passage of a Nuisances Removal and Diseases Prevention Bill, which gave power of compulsion but only in times of emergency. Now the General Board could order abatement of nuisances, cleansing of streets, disinfection of houses and provision of isolation hospitals. Chadwick used these powers to recruit a corps of health inspectors, increase the number of Poor Law surgeons and press local authorities to appoint Medical Officers of Health.

The General Board of Health undoubtedly worked hard and did well but it became increasingly unpopular. Chadwick antagonized both medical profession and local authorities by his dictatorial attitude. The medical profession, local authority and public did not understand the reason for insisting on clean water, disposal of sewage and abatement of nuisances in time of epidemic illness. For this the prevalent ideas on the cause of infection were to blame. Microbes, germs or micro-organisms still lay in the future. The majority firmly believed in the theory of miasma – impurity of the air – as the cause of disease. They believed that the impurity arose from cesspits and dungheaps, was carried by movement of the air from person to person to produce the illness which was then carried on the air from the sick to the healthy individual.

The Board's term of office ended in 1853 but the government extended it for another year because of the continuing threat of cholera. On 31 July 1854 a motion to extend the Board's life for another term of five years was defeated by 74 votes to 65. The debate took the form of a venomous attack on Chadwick in which MPs made intemperate and quite unjustified accusations: 'England wanted to be clean but not to be cleaned by Mr Chadwick'. He had been removed from the Poor Law Board 'for his rules of atrocious stringency' (an allusion to the now universally hated Unions). One member announced himself to be 'quite at a loss to know what services this man has rendered to the community'. Next day a leader in *The Times* approved Chadwick's dismissal with the words 'we prefer to take our chance with cholera and the rest than to be bullied into health'.

So Chadwick went. The curious point is that his ideas on clean water and sewage disposal had been completely vindicated by a pamphlet published five years before, in 1849, although the author knew nothing of microbes. John Snow, a London physician better remembered as the first specialist anaesthetist, became interested in cholera in 1832 when he was nineteen years old and working as a surgeon's apprentice in Newcastle-on-Tyne. He concluded that infection was transmitted not by bad air (miasma) but by shared food and unwashed hands. Snow, now in London, followed up his idea during the 1849 epidemic and decided that the hands of a person attending the sick would inevitably become soiled with the cholera evacuations and that, if this person prepared food, there would be great risk to any uninfected person who ate it. Such might account for the massive spread of cholera among the crowded poor, but how did infection reach the houses of the wealthy? Snow thought a likely explanation to be that cholera evacuations somehow got mixed 'with the water used for drinking or culinary purposes either by permeating the ground and getting into wells or by running along channels and sewers into the river from which entire towns are sometimes supplied with water'. Then came the dramatic incident of the Broad Street pump, the only item in Snow's research to have entered folk memory. In 1849 the majority of houses in the Golden Square area of London were not served by piped water but depended on 'pump wells' of which that in Broad Street yielded one of the best supplies. At the end of August cholera caused over six hundred deaths in the district. The outbreak took an explosive form in the Broad Street area, 344 deaths occurring in four days. Snow investigated eighty-nine deaths in Broad Street itself and found that all except ten of the dead lived close to the pump and drew their water from the well. Of the remaining ten, five would have been expected to draw water from another well but preferred the Broad Street supply. Three more were children living in other districts who attended a school served by the pump. Such is the genesis of the story that when the local Vestry asked Snow's advice on the prevention of further outbreaks, he replied: 'Take the handle off the Broad Street pump.' The site of the pump is now covered by a public house named in his honour The John Snow, despite his having been a strict teetotaller.

Snow now traced the pipelines of various water companies and showed convincingly that cholera abounded in districts served by one company but was almost absent in those served by another. He found streets in which the pipes ran side by side, each company supplying different houses in the same street. Cholera was rife in those served by Company A and infrequent in those served by Company B.

John Snow had proved that cholera is a water-borne disease in 1849. He confirmed his findings in the epidemic of 1853–4 when he compared two of the largest water suppliers in London. The water supplied by one company produced a death rate of 315 persons per 10,000 houses, the other a rate of 57 per 10,000. He tentatively advanced the theory that the *materies morbi* of cholera is a living organism. Dr William Budd of North Tawton, mentioned earlier in connection with typhoid fever, had moved to Bristol where he studied the 1849 cholera epidemic and formed the opinion that the causative agent was capable of multiplying in the human intestine and was disseminated by contaminated drinking water. John Snow and William Budd not only proved Chadwick's contention that pure water and efficient disposal of sewage are essential to the health of town dwellers, but came close to anticipating Pasteur's germ theory. From the latter there followed the identification by Robert Koch of the causative organism *Vibrio cholerae* in 1883, although Felix Pouchet had seen and described the vibrio in 1849 when examining the stools of a cholera victim under the microscope – without realizing that he was looking at the cause of the disease.

After the dismissal of Chadwick and his fellow members, the General Board of Health was reconstituted on a year-to-year basis with an Advisory Medical Council containing among others William Farr the statistician and John Simon the Medical Officer of Health for London. Farr and Simon determined to prove whether Chadwick's views on water and sewage were or were not correct. They examined the records of London water companies, comparing the death rates in the areas served, just as Snow had done on a small scale. The results were startling, ranging from a high of 130 to a low of 37 per 10,000. The company with the best record used the method of sand filtration, introduced over twenty years previously by James Simpson.

John Simon presented these results to the Board in May 1856. Parliament again made public health the responsibility of the Privy Council and empowered it to appoint a Medical Officer with the duty of investigating health problems and preparing reports preliminary to legislation. The Privy Council appointed John Simon to this office where he remained until 1876, five years after public health passed into the hands of the Local Government Board.

The two decades of Simon's work as Medical Officer are undoubtedly the most fruitful period in the world history of public health but he and workers in many other countries covered so huge a field that it cannot be dealt with adequately here. Simon possessed in a marked degree the ability to choose men and lead them as a team. He had no permanent assistant staff but was allowed to appoint paid inspectors for specific tasks. The majority of the sixteen doctors specially associated with Simon were young and at first inexperienced. Almost without exception they rose to high rank in their profession. No fewer than eight became Fellows of the Royal Society. Only three failed to attain distinction and two of those were sick men.

They were not office workers. Simon and his team did not depend on reports but visited in person. In times of epidemic illness they tried to visit every town, every street, every infected house. They gathered a mass of information about cholera, smallpox, diphtheria and typhus fever. Infant mortality (death in the first year) then stood at an average of 150 per 1,000 live births and was much higher in the working class and especially high when mothers were in employment. An inspector discovered the frightful truth that excessive mortality was largely caused by drugging the babies with opium. Another inspector, working on deaths from lung disease, produced evidence that many trades put the worker at risk. Others proved that the majority of manual workers suffered from malnutrition, partly because they worked long hours without adequate food, partly because of their wives' lack of domestic education. But polluted water, inefficient sanitation and overcrowding were the major evils. One inspector discovered a mining community where over three hundred families living in single rooms took in lodgers.

By 1866 Simon had gathered an immense body of evidence and the time had come for legislation. He showed himself a skilled diplomat, lobbying Members of Parliament, feeding his own ideas into their minds, flattering them into the self-delusion that they had themselves conceived his plans. In 1871 Parliament established a new department, the Local Government Board, to which the Medical Department of the Privy Council was transferred. Simon the inspired leader became Simon the desk official. He shared the work of drafting 'The Great Public Health Act' of 1875, a remarkable piece of legislation embodying almost all the recommendations made by his team and so wide in its scope that it permitted implementation of most sanitary improvements in Britain during the next sixty years. But the Medical Branch lost ground, becoming increasingly subservient to lay officials. In 1876 Simon found his power so eroded that his usefulness had almost gone. After a last fierce battle with the Treasury he resigned 'with extreme pain' and retired into private life, received a knighthood and died aged eighty-eight in 1904.

Chadwick, Simon, Shattuck, Koch and many others in many lands conditioned the public mind to the need for sanitary reform, showed the way, and made the crowded cities cleaner and more comfortable to live in. But it was the terror-striking cholera which provided the initial and greatest impetus. Unfortunately this disease does not have a history that can be neatly completed by the total eradication described in the case of smallpox. Further visitations of cholera came in 1863 and 1881, the first lasting for eleven and the second for fifteen years. The 1881 pandemic is notable for providing the final proof that cholera is water-borne by a terrible outbreak at Hamburg in Germany. Hamburg was a self-governing city which drew its water supply directly from the River Elbe. Adjoining it lay the town of Altona, part of the Prussian State, where the government had installed a water-filtration plant. Cholera caused a great mortality on the Hamburg side of the street dividing the two cities but spared the Altona side completely. What may be termed the final episode in the emigration of cholera from India in 1817 broke out in 1899 and lasted until 1923 but did not seriously affect Western Europe and the Americas.

Another and unrelated pandemic started in the early 1960s with a new strain of vibrio, given the name of El Tor. First identified in Indonesia, it spread to Asia, Africa and South America. Another variant was detected in India and Bangladesh early in the 1990s. So cholera is still very much with us and there is yet a great deal to be done. Even today we live our own comfortable lives in a world where millions have to fight for survival under conditions of filth and deprivation as bad as any that the Victorian sanitary reformers strove to ameliorate. Indeed, to poverty and pollution we have added our own contribution: an unprecedented level of global movement which serves only to increase our problems in seeking to control cholera and other potentially pandemic diseases.

CHAPTER SEVEN

Gin, Flu and Tuberculosis

Cholera and other water-borne diseases were not the only ills to affect the industrial population. At the time of the Boer War (1899–1901) medical examination of British recruits for South Africa revealed a deplorably low standard of physical fitness. Young men, especially from industrial areas, were found to be undersized, of poor physique, and suffering from a range of deformities and chronic illnesses, many of them preventable. The revelation came as a jolting blow to the pride of a nation which then believed itself divinely created to rule the earth. National arrogance found it impossible to accept that a large proportion of the British people had been turned into chronic invalids by the very processes which made Great Britain the most wealthy and highly civilized nation in the world.

Three of the major evils attending the Industrial Revolution were syphilis, alcohol and respiratory infections, of which last tuberculosis was the greatest scourge. All three of these existed in the agricultural village but each was also exacerbated by the conditions which developed in the industrial town. A close-packed community will obviously encourage promiscuity, entailing risk of transmitting venereal infection, which is much increased by the loss of control engendered by alcohol. Alcoholic drink is a means of escape from reality, harmless and even beneficial in moderation, but one which, like all escapes, tends to be addictive and is harmful in excess. It is easy to become dependent and, in this respect, alcohol resembles any other means of escape, whether smoking tobacco, taking various drugs by mouth and by injection, or deliberately losing oneself in fantasies. Dependence upon any escape, not the means of escape itself, is the cause of disaster. This simple fact is not well understood even today and was certainly not appreciated in the nineteenth century.

Alcohol cannot have been a major social problem while beer remained the staple drink of all classes. The thick, muddy liquid contained much free yeast and had a variable but generally low alcoholic content. It was food rather than drink, adding some desirable vitamins to the diet of the predominantly meat-eating baron as well as to that of the peasant living almost exclusively upon bread.

Alchemists succeeded in distilling the essence or spirit of wine and chemists started to elaborate the method of fractional distillation in the sixteenth century. The small quantities of spirit they produced were medicines rather than drinks. The names *eau-de-vie* and *usquebaugh*, both meaning water of life, remind us that brandy and whisky originated as cordials, preparations alleged to stimulate the heart's action. In London the Company of Distillers received its charter in 1638 but the drinking of distilled spirit did not become popular until after the Battle of Ramillies in 1706. British troops developed a taste for Hollands, a Dutch spirit flavoured with juniper berries. Brandy and whisky were expensive, one being distilled from wine made of grapes and the other from grain or malt. Gin could be spirit of any kind flavoured with juniper (in French *genièvre* which gave gin its name) or even with turpentine. Distillers soon found that any fermentable material yielded a spirit that could be sold to merchants who diluted ('broke') it with water and added flavouring. It was much cheaper to ferment waste grain, vegetables of all kinds, rotten fruit or sawdust and distil the result than to brew good ale. The distillate contained a higher percentage of alcohol than wine or beer and, particularly if sawdust or wood shavings entered the mixture, it was more or less poisonous.

Over five million gallons of unbroken spirit, which had paid duty of 2*d* a gallon, were sold yearly in England during the 1730s. No one can possibly estimate the amount of illicit spirit consumed, for the crude distillation of fermented liquid required only primitive apparatus and little knowledge or skill. In 1736 the Government tried to check gin drinking by imposing higher taxation, but the move caused rioting rather than decreased consumption. One of the more tragic and less obvious effects of heavy drinking is the noticeably increased number of deaths of infants suffering from measles in the mid-eighteenth century. Measles itself rarely caused death; rather death resulted from complications such as pneumonia or ear infections, generally avoidable by good nursing. It is a sad fact that drunken mothers do not make good nurses.

The problem had become so serious by the middle of the century that action was essential. In 1751 the government again raised the tax and prohibited retail sale of less than two gallons by distillers and shopkeepers. This did reduce drinking in the street and the home quite considerably but introduced the notorious 'gin-palace', owned by the distiller or brewer and managed by the publican who retailed the drink.

Gin-palaces acquired a thoroughly bad reputation but, arguably, it may not have been altogether deserved. They did not sell the more poisonous concoctions but gin which had been distilled from a grain liquor. It is for this reason that the series of bad harvests in the years following 1780 did more to check gin-drinking than any legislation. The worst was over by 1790 but heavy drinking persisted among all classes until almost the end of the next century.

No stigma attached to drunkenness. The tough hunting man, the squire and the parson all regarded the dark evenings as a time for enjoying the bottle. There was not much else to do. Music, dancing, reading and writing all require light which was an expensive item only to be provided on special occasions. Talking does not need light and a single candle will reveal cloudiness in the wine. The king and his court, the manor house, the rectory provided no example for the working man to follow. The gin-palace remained the only place of relaxation and good-fellowship open to the illiterate and poverty-stricken mechanic and his family, living among a crowd of similar workers. The failure to provide any alternative to cheap alcohol and to the gin-palace as a place of escape from crowded, comfortless living quarters is the primary reason for heavy drinking in slum areas and industrial towns during the eighteenth and nineteenth centuries.

In 1852 a Swede named Magnus Huss coined the term 'Alcoholism' which he defined as a chronic disease resulting from dependence upon alcohol. Thus he almost instantly turned the problem of drunkenness into a scientific craze throughout much of Europe. Discussion of the virtues and evils of alcohol in the press (then as now!) aroused public interest and in many countries associations were formed to fight 'the demon drink'. For instance in England the Church of England Temperance Society, the Blue Ribbon Army and the Rechabites, among others, preached the virtue of sobriety, induced drunkards 'to sign the pledge' and demanded repressive legislation. Such legislation implied a threat to the liberty of the subject as Dr Magee, Bishop of Peterborough, made plain to the House of Lords in 1872: 'If I must take my choice whether England should be free or sober, I declare, strange as such a declaration may sound coming from one of my profession, that I should say it would be better that England should be free than that England should be compulsorily sober.'

In view of opposition such as this, it is not surprising that the first Licensing Act did not reach the Statute Book until 1904. Alcoholic intake was reduced by social opinion rather than by legislation. Overt drunkenness became unacceptable. As usually occurs, whether it be a fashion in curtain material or in manners, moderation in drinking gradually filtered down from the upper to the lower strata, immensely helped in Britain by muscular Christianity as preached and practised in public schools. By 1895 heavy drinking had quite gone out of fashion at the Universities, to be replaced by chain-smoking of cigarettes, for which we must blame introduction of the White Burley tobacco cultivar by George Webb in 1864, which made the straight-cut, flue-cured Virginian cigarette popular. At first limited by price to the university undergraduate and gilded youth of cities, the firm of W.D. and H.O. Wills brought cigarettes within the workers' budget, so much so that the years 1914–18 may justly be called the Age of the Woodbine. One of the perils of civilization is that most members of the human race will periodically demand escape from reality and as soon as one means of escape goes out of favour, it will be replaced by another, no less addictive or dangerous.

The public attitude towards drinking took a different turn in the United States. The American temperance movement was largely political. Drinking saloons played a major part in corrupt politics and many people thought it would be impossible to clean up local government until the saloon had been abolished. The first State to become 'dry' was Maine in 1851. Others followed and a growing temperance lobby, rather than an abnormally high incidence of alcoholism, prompted the Volstead Act, the eighteenth amendment to the Constitution, which banned all intoxicating liquor throughout the United States from 16 January 1920.

The battle against the evil drinking saloon had produced the innocent drug-store, a curious mixture of pharmacy and refreshment room, where respectable citizens, with their wives and children, could enjoy cooling drinks such as ice-cream sodas. The opposite counter sold a variety of patent medicines with names such as Mrs Pinkham's Vegetable Compound, Colonel Hostetter's Stomach Bitters and Peruna. These famous remedies contained about 20 per cent of absolute alcohol, some herbal flavouring and little else. Sales of 'whisky tonics', always high in the 'dry' states, rose to astronomical figures throughout the country after January 1920. A Supplemental Act of 23 November 1921 imposed drastic regulations on physicians' prescriptions and practically banned the whisky tonics by limiting alcohol content to half of 1 per cent.

There had been little serious opposition during 1920–1 but now the rum barons moved in. America was flooded with the kind of spirit that had almost ruined England in the eighteenth century. The saloon became the speakeasy. The majority of citizens carried a hip flask and dealt with their bootlegger every week just as they dealt with the grocer. Cocaine and heroin, more easily concealed than alcohol, became a national vice. One in every four hundred Americans was a drug addict in the early 1920s. During the late 1920s and early 1930s the United States was synonymous with lawlessness. After thirteen years of gang-fighting and murder, almost amounting to civil war, the prohibition lobby at last gave in and the laws were repealed by the twenty-first amendment to the Constitution on 5 December 1933. The American experiment clearly showed the danger of the single factor or 'pet abomination'. Until a safe, universally acceptable and non-addictive means of escape can be found, it is both hopeless and dangerous to attempt to cure the 'Disease of Addiction' by prohibition of a single agent.

Respiratory diseases, or more correctly diseases that are transmitted by close contact and especially by the breath, will obviously be more prevalent in a close-packed community. It is not so much density of population as occupancy of room space which will determine incidence. When a single individual occupies one room, the infection will be passed only by casual contact with outsiders, but the risk will increase proportionately with the number of persons who occupy and sleep in that room because individuals are continually brought into close contact with one another. Thus the family of eight or more adults and children housed in a single room may increase the risk of infection by as much as eight times and if the family takes in lodgers, as was often the case, then the risk will be still greater.

The common cold must have infected such a family whenever one member introduced it and probably none would have escaped. As the bread-winner worked in an almost equally crowded mill, the chance of introduction from a sufferer outside the family circle was high. Epidemics rapidly developed and the infection could be more serious than the comparatively harmless cold. Some forms of influenza would have swept through factory and home with the speed and intensity of a prairie fire, causing numbers of deaths among the aged and the very young from resultant pneumonia.

Influenza is a mysterious disease, not yet fully understood and with a controversial history. It is really not a single entity but a collection of diseases, caused by a mixture of quickly mutating viruses or even by cross-breeding between an existing human form of the influenza virus with some related virus of an avian or animal origin. This instability has so far defeated efforts to produce a truly comprehensive vaccine and is the reason why new types of the disease may well be a global danger. Most known types are characterized by a very short incubation period, a short but acute illness, and an almost complete lack of increased resistance or conferred immunity to a future attack. Three strains of virus, labelled A, B and C, are recognized and a bacillus, named after the German discoverer R.F.J. Pfeiffer, was once believed to be one of the causative organisms. It has been said of this bacillus that 'it inveigled many scientists into wasting a lot of time discovering its insignificance'. Certainly when Alexander Fleming first prepared crude penicillin in 1928, he used it as a 'laboratory antiseptic' to obtain uncontaminated cultures of Pfeiffer's bacillus, then often named *Bacillus influenzae,* and for over ten years totally neglected the potential of penicillin as an antibiotic for human medication.

Influenza may or may not be a comparatively modern infection. The name is Italian, dating from the eighteenth century or earlier, and implies that it was caused by the influence of heavenly bodies. One of the peculiarities of this common infection is that it disappears for quite long periods and then reappears as wide-spread epidemics of varying severity. Typically, though not invariably, an illness of the winter months, it may take the form of 'two-day flu', little more than a raised temperature, sore throat and headache, in one epidemic, to reappear a year later as a much more lethal sickness, carrying risk of pneumonia, and leaving the patient suffering from severe depression for many weeks.

So variable is influenza in its behaviour that no certain diagnosis can be made on the evidence of ancient records. In fact it is doubtful whether the disease existed as an infection of the human before the fifteenth century. A much disputed theory identifies influenza with the first appearance of the sweating sickness or 'English sweat' in the year 1485 when Henry Tudor defeated King Richard III at the battle of Bosworth Field on 22 August. It is said that a hitherto unknown illness struck the victorious army and that they carried the infection to London. Henry was proclaimed king on the battlefield and it was very necessary that he should establish his Divine Right by being crowned as soon as possible. The illness carried by his troops caused so many deaths and such disorganization that the ceremony had to be postponed until 30 October. This is the first recorded appearance of the *Sudor Anglicus.*

An attack was of short duration, the victim either dying in a matter of hours or remaining severely ill for several days before recovery. Symptoms were high fever, burning thirst, headache and painful joints, sometimes abdominal pain and vomiting, and always the profuse, stinking sweat which gave the infection its name. In those unwashed times any profuse sweat would probably have smelt badly, but the fact that sweating is described as the most noticeable symptom indicates that the disease caused a high temperature. Accounts suggest that the wealthier class suffered heavily and that many deaths occurred among young adults. This first epidemic seems to have lasted only a few weeks and then to have disappeared as mysteriously as it came.

Epidemics of a similar kind recurred for a century. Four have been identified, in 1507, 1528, 1551 and 1578. That of 1528 also spread to Germany where the infection was named 'the English Pestilence'. Meanwhile another form had appeared in Europe, bearing more resemblance to the modern 'ordinary flu'. That of 1516 which affected all Europe is often regarded as the first definite appearance of influenza. There were further European pandemics in 1557 and 1580. Then, for just over a century, there seem to have been small regional epidemics but nothing in the nature of a European pandemic until 1729. Major outbreaks followed in 1732, 1781 and 1788. That of 1781–2 not only became widespread but was very infectious. About three-quarters of the British population are said to have fallen ill and it reached as far as the Americas. The disease again receded, no epidemic being recorded until 1830. This was followed by a second in 1833 and a third in 1847. Then influenza seems to have disappeared almost entirely until 1889.

The pandemic of 1889–92 was much more serious than most of the previous outbreaks and is better documented. It is also the first type of influenza to be named after its supposed place of origin. 'Russian flu' appeared in the St Petersburg district during December 1889, and by March 1890 had spread over most of the world. This is also the first certainly known epidemic of influenza to occur in 'waves' of varying severity, acute in the winter of 1889, still worse in spring 1891, mild in autumn and winter 1891–2. It killed at least 250,000 Europeans and the total global death toll may have been as high as a million or more. This 'Russian flu' seems to have persisted for a number of years, gradually becoming less prevalent and less severe.

In 1918 the world had been ripened for a pestilence. Four years of trench warfare, fought under conditions of privation previously unknown to those engaged, had produced a breeding ground for infection. Starvation or near-starvation affected most of the peoples of Europe as well as the less privileged countries of the world. One would have expected a disease far worse than 'mere flu' to have ravaged Europe and been carried by the swiftly moving steamship to all other parts of the globe. In fact when the pandemic arrived, it took the form of a uniquely virulent strain of influenza.

One of the peculiarities of flu is that it seems to attack a number of widely scattered areas at the same time. For this reason it is difficult, if not impossible, to decide where the 1918 pandemic originated. The contemporaneous name 'Spanish flu' is certainly misleading and for an interesting reason. Belligerent governments, fearful that reported loss of manpower would encourage the enemy, imposed censorship upon reports of serious epidemic illness. Spain, not being a belligerent, permitted publication of the fact that the country was suffering from an unusually severe type of influenza.

The first wave occurred in the early summer of 1918, starting either in the USA or in American army camps in France, and attracted little attention because it was a mild illness. The second wave was quite different and appeared in several localities during August. Freetown, the capital of Sierra Leone, Brest, the French port of disembarkation for American troops, and Boston, Massachusetts, appear to have been all infected at the same date. The illness was not only unusually infectious but also exceptionally lethal. The symptoms were those of a typical severe influenza – high temperature, sore throat, headache, generalized pains in the limbs and prostration – but abdominal pain was frequent and pneumonia much more prevalent. Although the elderly and the very young suffered badly, there was an unusually high proportion of deaths from pneumonia in the 20–30 age group. At a military camp in Massachusetts the first case of influenza was diagnosed on 12 September. Less than a fortnight later 12,604 soldiers had been taken ill. Boston itself was severely affected, about 10 per cent of the total population suffering, of whom nearly two-thirds died. The San Francisco Hospital admitted 3,509 patients suffering from pneumonia, of whom a quarter perished. It is reckoned that 20 per cent of the United States Army fell ill between August and October. In all, about 24,000 American service personnel died from influenza and resultant pneumonia, compared with a total of 34,000 battle casualties.

These figures indicate the kind of morbidity and mortality experienced in the second wave. The third came in the spring of 1919 and was almost as severe but less wide-spread. During the whole pandemic only St Helena, New Guinea and a few Pacific islands are certainly known to have escaped infection, although there must have been unknown areas in Central Africa, Asia and South America which were not attacked. The death toll was appalling – over 150,000 in Britain alone – while between twenty-one and twenty-five million of the world population died. (Even that huge number may be an underestimate. A more modern accounting doubles the world-wide toll and adds 50,000 to the British figure.) The pandemic of 1918–19 undoubtedly produced the largest loss of lives by a single invasion of disease since the Black Death, though on a percentage of the population basis, the mortality rate was probably much smaller than in 1347–50.

Hunger, bad living conditions, stress and war-weariness lowered resistance on a massive scale and contributed to the incidence and death-toll. Travel was perhaps quicker than in 1889 and the war entailed large troop movements between nations. But, even making allowance for these abnormal factors, the pandemic of 1918–19 remains unique. The great killer was not influenza itself but the superimposed viral pneumonia. Never before nor since has a respiratory infection produced such a death-toll as this. At the time, and at intervals in the following years, blame was laid upon an animal infection, perhaps the organism of swine-fever, which transferred to the human. Pigs have been farmed as human food for centuries with the result that pig and human have lived in close contact. If pigs suffer from epidemics of a fever, then the infection could have been transferred to the pig-keeper without interposition of any vector such as a louse or flea.

For this reason and because of the similarity between the symptoms, there are those who believe that the pandemic of 1918 was a recurrence of the 'English Sweat'. But such a belief does not imply that the 1918 visitation was not influenza. Rather it suggests that the Sweat may have been the first recorded influenza epidemic, originating in and at first confined to England. The theory that it was a disease of pigs, or any other domestic animal, that transferred to the human might also account for the comparatively late appearance of influenza in the European disease pool. If this is correct, then influenza is one of the less acceptable gifts that Britain has made to the world.

It was said above that never before nor since has a respiratory infection imposed so great a mortality as that in 1918–19. But the statement is not true if we think in terms of a prolonged time-scale and include the insidious effect of pulmonary tuberculosis upon the world. Here we have a disease that is more ancient than Man, caused by an organism possibly descended from the oldest living thing on earth. Many scientists believe that the tubercle bacillus derives from a saprophyte, feeding on dead tissue, which transferred to living cold-blooded creatures, then to warm-blooded animals and so to the human. Part of this theory is borne out by the great prevalence of tuberculosis in the animal kingdom and the number of recognizably different strains of the causative bacillus.

We are concerned here with only two, the bovine and human strains, both of which can cause the disease in humans and cattle. The bovine type, usually acquired by drinking milk from tuberculous cows, tended to be a disease of childhood. The human type, usually acquired by direct spread from one person to another, tended until quite recently to be a disease of the young adult. Tuberculosis can affect every body structure, forming 'tubercles', from which the name derives, which are tiny nodes of inflamed tissue. These are formed by reaction to the bacilli which they contain and are sometimes microscopic, sometimes just visible to the naked eye. The bovine type more commonly affected glands or lymph nodes, which hardened in texture and became enlarged, or joints which developed the classical 'white swelling'. For a similar reason bones softened and lost their shape. This kind of lesion was known as scrofula or the King's Evil. The human type more often attacked the lungs, being known as phthisis or consumption. The invading organism caused increasing destruction of lung tissue, starting as 'the patch', typically in the apex of the lung, and extending throughout the whole organ, often causing collapse of the tissues and a massive exudate, heavily tinged with blood, purulent or serous. Symptoms were a cough, a high temperature with night sweats, rapid wasting and expectoration of blood.

One attack of the bovine type protects the patient against infection by the human type. Being almost confined to children, the bovine infection was an actual safeguard against a more lethal illness in later life. Although bovine infection could result in death or crippling deformity, many children suffered nothing more than an enlarged gland or a slight and temporary rise in temperature. They had been infected by the bovine bacillus but their natural resistance had been sufficient to overcome the small invasion. This 'attack' was sufficient to protect against further infection by the bovine type *and also to protect against the human type*. The importance of this fact must be emphasized. In closely packed communities, such as the industrial town, human invasion was likely to be far more massive and more difficult to resist, so that the immunity conferred by the bovine type was positively advantageous. In the years of high incidence many doctors, especially in industrialized Britain, believed treatment of milk to render it free of tubercle bacilli carried a danger because, although such treatment might save some children from death or deformity, it would place many more at risk through later and almost inevitable contact with a human source.

Evidence of tuberculous infection has been found in Eurasian and African remains at least from the Neolithic period onward and in Amerindian skeletons from about 800 BC. One of the more interesting medical-archaeological discoveries is the mummified body of an Ammonite priest named Nesperehan who died about 1,000 BC. He shows not only the typical hunch-back (kyphosis) of advanced spinal tuberculosis but also a cavity formed in the lower part of the abdomen above the hip-joint which would now be known as a psoas abscess. Hippocratic texts record recognizable symptoms and appearances. Aretaeus of Alexandria, writing in the second century AD, described the *habitus phthisicus*, accepted by nineteenth-century physicians as 'the tubercular diathesis', the appearance of a person in positive danger of pulmonary tuberculosis: 'the slender, with prominent throats, whose shoulder blades protrude like wings, who are pale and have narrow chests'. All civilizations and all nations have been subject to tuberculosis. Physicians have attempted cures in all ages. The Hindus advised out-door living, exercises and sleeping in goat-stables. Galen taught that the disease is contagious and warned against contact with infected persons. He sent his patients to Stabia, a resort on the coast of Italy opposite the Isle of Capri, just as an early twentieth-century physician might have advised his wealthy 'lungers' to live on the French Riviera. Rhazes and Avicenna of the medieval Arabian school recommended draughts of asses' milk and powdered crab shells. The latter, a long-lasting popular remedy, provided additional calcium, a treatment revived in the late nineteenth century.

Magic or miraculous cure played its part and took a strange form. The King's Evil or scrofula, commonly affecting the glands of the neck, was supposed to respond to the royal touch. Touching is an ancient custom, which may have been introduced by Clovis the Frank about AD 496 and is said to have been first used in England by Edward the Confessor, although there is no certain record until the twelfth century. Charles II of

England touched in exile and dealt with 6,275 sufferers in 1660, the year of his restoration. By the time of his death in 1683 he had touched no fewer than 92,107 people. History does not relate how many he cured, but the figure suggests a high incidence of glandular tuberculosis in the seventeenth century. William III continued the ceremony but had little faith in its value for he accompanied each touching with the words 'God grant you better health and more sense.' Queen Anne touched no less a person than the two-year-old Samuel Johnson in 1711/12. Johnson must have been among the last English subjects of this curious rite, for George I abolished it when he came to the throne in 1714. French kings regularly touched until 1775 and the custom was briefly resurrected by Charles X, an ardent believer in the Divine Right, when he ascended the throne in 1824. The last recorded ceremony took place in 1825.

The early history of the pulmonary form of tuberculosis is not altogether clear, partly because of confusing nomenclature. In England the word 'tissic' may have been attached to the disease. If so, the Tudor dynasty of kings suffered badly for both Henry VII and his elder son Arthur died of this mysterious ailment. So did the Duke of Richmond, illegitimate son of Henry VIII, and it has already been mentioned that Henry's only legitimate son, Edward VI, appears to have died of a combination of syphilis and tuberculosis which was a quite common end for town children in the nineteenth century. Some historians maintain that consumption was a disease of the well-nourished upper class rather than of the underprivileged until the eighteenth century. Deaths of notabilities attract attention, whereas deaths of lesser persons do not, so it is equally logical to infer from the large number of known royal and upper-class victims that pulmonary tuberculosis was wide-spread, attacking all classes including the highly privileged.

From the second half of the eighteenth century until the Second World War, roughly two hundred years, pulmonary tuberculosis was far more common among the under-privileged than among the privileged, though the latter suffered badly by modern standards. Tuberculosis became equated with poverty. The term 'consumption' was taboo among the more wealthy class who preferred to be afflicted with a 'decline'. The present view is that, while poverty was a major factor, poor living and working conditions combined with an inadequate and unhealthy diet do not wholly account for the very high incidence among the labouring population. The rise in the incidence of tuberculosis during all major wars may be mainly due to these causes but suggests that physical and psychological strain also play a part. This concept of 'strain' or 'stress' is supported by a markedly increased prevalence among pregnant women who are employed in industry. The industrial town was not solely to blame although it lacked those amenities supposed to lessen risk of infection: fresh air, sunlight, adequate leisure and proper facilities for personal hygiene. The sum of these inadequacies cannot wholly account for the high urban incidence in the nineteenth century, because all had existed in earlier if smaller towns. The new factors were exacerbation of previous evils, gross overcrowding in home and factory, acute strain consequent on overwork and stress caused by the nagging fear of losing the means of livelihood. The last is a particular phenomenon of tuberculosis because the illness is prolonged and the sufferer too weak to carry out heavy work.

The scientist Thomas Young stated in 1815 that phthisis caused the 'premature death' of one person in every four. At about the same time in Paris, autopsy showed that 40 per cent of all deaths were due to consumption. John Brownlee, a statistician and co-founder of the science of epidemiology, believed that the highest mortality in London occurred about 1800 and that provincial industrial towns reached their zenith a few years later. From 1838 to 1843 the pulmonary form, consumption, caused an average of over sixty thousand deaths a year in Britain. The death rate then started to fall, although pathologists stated that autopsy revealed that almost all individuals examined had suffered from some form of tuberculosis during their lifetime. The Registrar-General's figures show that in the decade 1881–90, 664,963 persons died from all forms of tuberculosis (that is about sixty-six thousand a year as compared with sixty thousand from consumption alone in 1838–43). In the following decade, 1901–10, deaths from all forms amounted to 566,162, an average improvement of ten thousand a year.

There is no simple explanation for this decline in mortality. The legislation briefly described in the last chapter was beginning to take effect at the end of the nineteenth century with the result described by William D. Johnston: 'The early stages of an industrial economy are generally those in which crowded and impoverished living conditions prevail for numerous people and lead to increased tuberculous mortality. Eventually, however, industrialization's material benefits improve housing and nutrition, and reduce risks for infection and reinfection, thereby lowering both morbidity and mortality rates.' This combination of social legislation, improved amenities and increased personal prosperity in the end made the industrial town more healthy than the agricultural countryside. But, as regards the single problem of tuberculosis, the continuing reductions in mortality are not attributable to any specific treatment until the 1940s.

The belief that tuberculosis is contagious dates from very early times but was not proven until 1865 when Jean Antoine Villemin, a young surgeon in the French army, showed that the infection could be transmitted to animals by inoculation. Even then, the cause of tuberculosis remained unknown until Robert Koch of Wollstein in Germany isolated the causative bacillus, now known as *Mycobacterium tuberculosis*, in 1882. Despite Koch's discovery, almost the most important in the whole history of medicine and certainly in the history of bacteriology, no direct attack upon the bacillus could yet be made. Attempts to destroy the organism by inhalations of 'antiseptics' such as carbolic acid ended in disaster. Until the Second World War treatment of tuberculosis depended on good food, sunlight, fresh air and rest. In the early years fresh air encountered much opposition because so many doctors believed 'miasma' carried by the air to be the cause of disease. A Birmingham doctor, George Boddington, appears to have been the first to establish a fresh-air sanatorium for consumptives at Sutton Coldfield in 1843, but he was forced to abandon his project. Herman Brehmer opened a sanatorium at Göbersdorf, Silesia, in 1859 and one of his patients, Peter Dettweiller, built a similar institution at Falkenstein in 1876. By now the germ theory was replacing the theory of miasma, which accounts for the success of Edward Livingstone Trudeau at Saranac Lake in the healthy Adirondack Mountains of America. Trudeau, himself a sufferer, planned a number of small separate cottages surrounding a central laboratory in 1884. His sanatorium formed the prototype of many others in many countries. Thomas Mann's famous novel of 1924, based on his own experience of Davos, relentlessly details the therapy available to those dwelling on the slopes of 'The Magic Mountain'.

The concept of pulmonary tuberculosis as a familial disaster rather than an illness of the individual was first understood by Thomas Beddoes who founded his Preventive Medical Institution at Little Tower Court, a Bristol slum area, in 1803. He purposed to examine not only the sick patient but the seemingly healthy members of the family with the object of detecting disease at the earliest possible moment. In 1799 Beddoes had noted that brassworkers and stonecutters were unusually prone to consumption and so confirmed the finding by Paracelsus in 1567 that there is a relation between pulmonary disease and mining. Gradually it became recognized that dusty trades, particularly when the dust is from silica, placed workers at special risk and legislation was introduced to protect them. One of the more beneficial advances in this field accidentally occurred during an attempt to make synthetic diamonds, resulting in the discovery of the harmless and efficient abrasive, carborundum, by Edward G. Acheson of Pennsylvania in 1891.

Beddoes's 'social approach' was not pursued until 1887 when Robert Philip, an Edinburgh physician, founded the Victoria Dispensary for Consumption. Philip taught the need to consider the whole family as the unit for investigation. Thus he started the tracing of tuberculous contacts. He also campaigned for notification, isolation, sanitorium care and formation of colonies to provide light work. Two years later three physicians, H.M. Biggs, T.M. Prudden and H.P. Loomis, developed a similar dispensary and investigation system in New York.

Attempts to prevent or to cure by vaccines prepared from tubercle bacilli failed. Tuberculin or 'Koch's fluid', an extract of killed bacilli, proved not only useless but actively dangerous as a treatment. Through the work of an Austrian, Clemens von Pirquet, and a Frenchman, Charles Mantoux, a much purified Koch's fluid has, however, proved invaluable as a skin test to indicate whether a person has suffered infection or not. The search for a safe and efficient vaccine continued, resulting in some strange but ultimately valueless treatments. In 1902 Emil von Behring of Marburg prepared an attenuated strain of human bacilli with which he hoped to stamp out tuberculosis in cattle. In 1906 Albert Calmette of the Pasteur Institute in Paris and his colleague Camille Guérin started work on von Behring's idea of using an alien bacillus, seeking a cure for human tuberculosis by using a bovine strain. Calmette worked for over thirteen years before satisfying himself that he had an attenuated and stable vaccine. He had moved to Lille just before the First World War. The Germans occupied the town from 1914 to 1918 and requisitioned all cattle so Calmette transferred his experiments to an avian strain of tubercle bacillus, using pigeons as his subjects. The number of pigeons aroused German suspicion and Calmette narrowly escaped being shot as a spy.

Bacille-Calmette-Guérin, the famous BCG, was first used for protection of very young children and calves in 1921. Calmette distributed a free supply for human use throughout France in 1924, warning that it must be given only to infants. By the end of 1925 1,317 babies had been treated, of whom 586 were known to have been in contact with a tuberculous relation. Six children died from tuberculosis within six months of inoculation, which aroused mistrust of the method. Then, in 1930, there occurred a frightful disaster at Lübeck in Germany which has never been satisfactorily explained. A total of 230 infants were inoculated from a single batch of BCG, of whom 173 developed pulmonary tuberculosis and 68 died, all within a few months. As a result BCG did not come into use again until after the Second World War when better laboratory control and standardization made such accidents virtually impossible. By 1963 a hundred and fifty million BCG vaccinations had been performed with only four known deaths.

Meanwhile Wilhelm Konrad Röntgen of Würzburg in Germany had discovered X-rays in 1895 and so revolutionized diagnosis, permitting foreign bodies to be located and broken bones examined much more exactly. The first satisfactory X-ray photographs of lungs in 1922 were greatly improved by introduction of a radio-opaque contrast fluid, lipiodol, in 1924. As methods improved and experience grew, tuberculous lesions could be detected at an earlier and earlier stage and, eventually, before any symptoms or clinical signs of disease appeared. Simplification made possible the use of mobile units for mass radiography which revealed an unexpectedly large number of sufferers not detected clinically. In the late 1940s screening revealed that the global incidence of tuberculosis had hitherto been underestimated by at least one-third.

There had been much controversy about the bovine type of tuberculosis. Was it or was it not a safety factor? Theodore Smith of Harvard University isolated the responsible bacillus in 1898 and showed that it would cause tuberculosis in the human as well as in cattle. In 1907 a British Royal Commission on tuberculosis reported that milk from infected cows is a potent cause and stressed the urgent need to prevent sale of infected milk. Louis Pasteur had already proved that heated milk will not sour if sealed from the air. In 1880 the German firm of Ashborn made the first commercial apparatus for 'pasteurization' of milk, the purpose being simply to delay souring. In 1907 Dr Charles North of New York introduced a pasteurizing plant that not only killed all disease-producing organisms but also delayed souring and was therefore commercially desirable. Meanwhile Smith's work had suggested an attempt to eliminate tuberculosis from dairy herds. This is comparatively easy, for cows can be tuberculin tested as can humans. But it is also expensive because the only practicable solution is to kill the infected cow.

In 1917 about 16 per cent of dairy cattle in USA and 25 per cent in Britain were tuberculous. A programme of eradication started that year in the United States which reduced the incidence of tuberculosis among American children to about half that obtaining in Britain at the equivalent date. Britain did not take strenuous action until 1922. From then onwards, the incidence of the bovine type affecting glands, bones and joints was very greatly reduced.

Direct attack upon the tubercle bacillus did not become possible until after the Second World War. Penicillin proved to be useless for the purpose. In 1944 Selman Waksman of New Jersey, USA, investigated a mould found growing in the throats of chickens reared in a heavily manured field. The mould proved to be one of a group, the *Actinomyces*, from which he prepared an antibiotic, actinomycin, lethal to a range of bacteria but too toxic for human medication. This led him to the discovery of a related mould to which the name *Streptomyces griseus* was given and from which he isolated the antibiotic streptomycin. In 1948 Professor W.H. Feldman of the Mayo Clinic tried it on a large scale for the treatment of tuberculosis. Unfortunately, streptomycin was too often followed by emergence of resistant strains of the tubercle bacillus. The potential was so good, however, that Professor Feldman determined to find some means of preventing bacillary resistance. After much experimental work, he found that a course of streptomycin combined with two drugs, para-aminosalicylic acid and isonicotinic acid hydrazide (PAS and isoniazid), could be used with excellent effect and with less danger of producing resistant strains.

A modernized tuberculin test, mass radiography, BCG vaccine prepared under strict control, and chemotherapy based on streptomycin are the weapons which have tamed tuberculosis. But it is too early to claim a total victory. In Britain 27,754 people died of tuberculosis in 1937 and in 1949 the figure fell below 20,000 for the first recorded time. Thereafter the number fell steeply, through 10,583 in 1952 to 2,282 in 1965. Britain is a wealthy and privileged country but even here there is still tuberculosis though it tends now to be a chronic illness of the elderly rather than of the young. Nor has the fall in morbidity been maintained. In Europe the incidence of tuberculosis increased by nearly 30 per cent between 1985 and 1991, and by 12 per cent in the United States. A great increase in tuberculosis appears to be associated with the drying-up of the Aral Sea in Uzbekistan. Today approximately ten million people suffer from tuberculosis, with about three million deaths a year; 95 per cent of these deaths are in the Third World. Thus, in the less privileged parts of the world tuberculosis still persists as a health problem despite all attempts at mass prevention. The reason is largely overcrowding of the home and undernourishment. Until those social evils can be rectified, there will be no total defeat of the scourge.

Even the partial defeat of an illness such as this must have affected world history. Though a cynic would probably remark that tuberculosis has killed as many budding Hitlers as potential Elizabeth Frys, the premature deaths of so many young people must have robbed us of potentially brilliant scientists, artists, and similar creative workers. Let us take as a single example one young Englishman whose story not only stresses the characteristically familial nature of the infection but is all the more apposite precisely because it encouraged the nineteenth-century habit of dignifying 'the decline' as essentially a romantic affliction. If ever there was a 'fashion' in disease, we have ample evidence of it here (though it seems often to have been confused with the less fatal but equally romantic 'vogue' malady known as chlorosis, where a similarly wan appearance resulted from iron-deficiency anaemia). In the novel and in the opera, in painting and in poetry, we repeatedly encounter pallid heroes and still paler heroines, all of whom project an increasingly ethereal radiance. However, such ivory beauty serves to reveal their consumption not only by the fires of love but also by the relentless advance of a paradoxically purifying corporeal decay. If such romanticism inspires us to shed a tear over the fictional fate of Verdi's Violetta or Puccini's Mimi, then we should be all the more affected by the reality of the final illness suffered by John Keats.

Born in London, John was the eldest child of Thomas Keats, manager of a livery stable owned by his father-in-law, Mr Jennings, on 29 October 1795. John was the eldest of four children; he had two brothers, George and Tom, and a sister named Fanny. They were well off, a happy and united family. The boys were sent for their education to a good school in Enfield under the headmastership of the Revd John Clarke. John Keats developed as a typical schoolboy, good at athletics, not so good at lessons, and in his early years rather too pugnacious for the comfort of others.

Then came tragedy. His father was killed after falling from his horse on 16 April 1804, a few months before John's ninth birthday. The widow married again within two months but the couple soon separated and she went to live with her mother at Edmonton which became the family home for the next five years. Edmonton being not far from Enfield, the boys stayed at school. When in his fourteenth year and entering puberty, John changed in character, becoming less pugnacious and more sensitive, a kindly and popular boy who spent less time on games and read widely in addition to his ordinary schoolwork.

At this point his mother fell ill of consumption. John, passionately fond of her, helped to nurse the patient devotedly but she died in February 1810. Not only was her death a terrible loss, but it left him the eldest of four orphans with little money. Their grandmother Jennings entrusted them to two guardians, one of whom, Richard Abbey, removed John Keats from school at the end of 1810 and apprenticed him to an Edmonton surgeon named Thomas Hammond. John had become a close friend of his late headmaster's son, Cowden Clarke, and often walked over from Edmonton to the school at Enfield. On one of these visits the master lent John a copy of Edmund Spenser's great verse-epic *The Faerie Queene*. This is the work that inspired Keats to write his poetry.

He had been apprenticed to Hammond for a term of five years, which meant that he could set up for himself as a surgeon at the end of 1815 when twenty years old. But something happened in the autumn of 1814. It is commonly said that he quarrelled with Hammond but the more likely explanation is that Hammond was an unqualified surgeon and Keats cherished the ambition to become fully qualified. The Apothecaries' Act, which empowered the Society of Apothecaries to regulate medical practice, was then under discussion and would become law in 1815. In October 1814 Keats moved to London to register for classes and walk the wards of one of the largest teaching hospitals, the United Hospital of St Thomas's and Guy's, then in the Borough on the south side of London Bridge. At first he lodged with some fellow-students in St Thomas's Street, but when his two brothers came to London to work in Abbey's office they lived together in Cheapside.

Keats studied hard and seems to have shown himself to be a promising student although one of his contemporaries, Henry Stephens, recorded his surprise when Keats passed the examination for the Licence of the Society of Apothecaries at his first attempt on 25 July 1816. His certificate is numbered 189 and he was elected to the coveted post of surgeon's dresser (now known as house surgeon) at Guy's Hospital. But his experiences in the wards and particularly in the theatre, where he himself operated, sickened him. We must remember that operations were performed without anaesthesia in those days and surgeons were becoming more ambitious, so that, despite the patient's agony, their procedures took longer than the one-minute lithotomy or the two-minute amputation. In the winter of 1816/17, Keats decided that he could not face a medical career.

Earlier in 1816 his old headmaster John Clarke had introduced Keats to James Leigh Hunt, the critic, poet and editor. Keats now became member of a circle of artists and writers, most of them of the second class but including Shelley and also an elderly merchant named Charles Brown who enjoyed helping young people of this kind. After spending some months on the Isle of Wight and the Kent coast, John joined with his younger brother Tom to share a house in Hampstead with Charles Brown. By now he had firmly decided to make his living by writing poetry.

Leigh Hunt had already published some of Keats's poems in his newspaper *The Examiner*. The circle of friends, Shelley in particular, urged publication of a book of verse which came out in March 1817, but it was not well received. Keats now started on the very long poem *Endymion* which he published in May 1818. In the summer of 1818 he went on a walking tour in the Lake District and Scotland with Charles Brown. The occasion was not a happy one, for his brother Tom was showing signs of consumption and had been sent to Teignmouth in Devon, while the other brother George had married and part of John's reason for going north was to see the couple off at Liverpool on the start of their voyage to a new life in America. John returned to Hampstead in September to find Tom very much worse. As he had done for his mother, he helped to nurse his brother devotedly but Tom died in the first week of December 1818.

In the autumn of 1818 John Keats met Fanny Brawne, the daughter of a man who had rented Charles Brown's house while they were in the north and had now become a neighbour. The two fell passionately in love and were engaged at Christmas. But now Keats himself began to show the first signs of the disease that had killed his mother and his younger brother. In April 1819 he met Samuel Taylor Coleridge who recorded his premonition of Keats's approaching death. This is of pathetic interest because Coleridge had been one of the circle surrounding Thomas Beddoes and his assistant, the young Humphry Davy, at Bristol where they experimented with inhalation of various gases in attempts to cure or relieve consumption.

There followed eighteen months of feverish composition in which Keats produced a new poem nearly every day. Almost the last of his poems, *La Belle Dame sans Merci*, contains a verse which in effect describes his own appearance in the terminal phase of consumption:

> I see a lily on thy brow
> With anguish moist and fever dew,
> And on thy cheeks a fading rose
> Fast withereth too.

It was during this period that he wrote the odes, *To a Nightingale*, *On a Grecian Urn* and *To Autumn*, among others, which many critics not only regard as his best work but declare to be some of the finest English poetry ever written.

Keats had been staying alone in London when, on a night in early January 1820, he turned up at the Hampstead house in a state resembling advanced intoxication. Charles Brown realized that the trouble was not drink but illness. Keats explained that he had come on an outside seat of the coach and, it being a bitter night, had caught a chill, adding 'I do not feel it now, but I am a little feverish.' Brown hastened to put him to bed and, as he climbed in, Keats gave a cough, put a handkerchief to his mouth and brought it away stained with bright blood. 'Bring me a candle. I must see that blood.' He looked steadily into his friend's face and calmly said 'I know that colour – it is arterial blood. I must die.'

He was better in the spring and experienced the *spes phthisica*, the false hope and sensation of well-being that is a quite common symptom of advanced pulmonary tuberculosis. He wrote hardly at all now and had spent his share of the small capital which came to him after his mother's death. Brown lent him sufficient for his needs and Fanny Brawne looked after him. His doctor ordered him to winter in a warmer climate and he received an invitation to join Shelley in Pisa, but Keats had never liked Shelley. The young artist Joseph Severn had won a Royal Academy scholarship to study in Rome for three years. He offered to take Keats with him and place him under medical care when they arrived. Keats accepted the offer and they sailed on 18 September. Owing to stormy weather in the Channel, the ship put in at Lulworth where Keats landed and wrote the last of his poems *Bright star! Would I were faithful as thou art.* When they arrived at Naples, Severn took him to Rome and put him under the care of Dr Clark, later Sir James Clark, the trusted physician and adviser of Queen Victoria.

Clark and Severn looked after their patient well and he seemed to improve but had a severe haemorrhage on 10 December from which he never really recovered. During the final month of his life he woke every morning disappointed that he had not died during the night. On the last morning he whispered to Severn that he wanted to be lifted up: 'I shall die easy – don't be frightened – be firm, and thank God that it has come.' John Keats died from consumption on that day, 23 February 1821, aged twenty-five.

Here, then, is one telling example of the loss that tuberculosis has inflicted on the world.

CHAPTER EIGHT

Mosquitoes, Flies, Travel and Exploration

Men and women have encountered and overcome terrible dangers as they have forced their way into every corner of the earth. A long sea voyage in tiny ships led the Spanish Conquistadores to a hostile terrain in Central and South America. The vast featureless plains and high mountain ranges of North America, inhabited by hostile indigenous tribes, failed to deter the pioneers in their covered wagons as they journeyed from the Atlantic to the Pacific. Geographical barriers can be overcome and even the fiercest of human opponents or the most aggressive of predatory creatures were powerless before a well-aimed musket.

It was not the larger animals that presented the greatest danger for, until almost the end of the nineteenth century, minute forms of life were the unbeatable enemy – the mosquitoes breeding in steamy swamps, the tsetse flies of the African savannahs and forests. While these were not dangerous in themselves, the saliva of their bites carried even smaller organisms: the tiny parasites that cause malaria, the virus of yellow fever, the trypanosomes that produce sleeping sickness. Tropical heat, damp and dirt also provide ideal conditions for the bacteria of disease.

We briefly noted in the first chapter that malaria contributed to the end of the Roman Empire. Greece had contact with Egypt, while Rome conquered and settled the Mediterranean coast of Africa, and it is probably by this means that malaria reached Europe, for there is little doubt that it is of African origin. Malaria is in fact the most dangerous and widespread of the African diseases. It is caused by a minute protozoon, known as a plasmodium, of which there are several strains. *Plasmodium malariae* or *P. vivax* is more common in Europe and America while *P. falciparum* is the prevalent African parasite. A European who has developed a resistance to the type of malaria caused by *P. vivax* will still be susceptible to the type caused by *P. falciparum*.

The parasites have a complicated life history, multiplying asexually in the human bloodstream and completing their sexual life-cycle in the body of the mosquito. To put it very briefly, the parasites are injected into the human by the bite of a female *Anopheles* mosquito, go through various phases, take up their lodging in the red blood cells, feed on the haemoglobin and burst the cell envelope, so releasing toxic products formed by the digestion of haemoglobin.

These toxins cause the typical malarial attack: a cold stage, a hot stage and a stage of sweating. The first signs of malaria appear about a fortnight after being bitten by a mosquito, the onset varying slightly according to the number of parasites injected by the bite. This 'incubation period' is the time taken for the rapidly dividing parasites to form a sufficient number – several hundred in every cubic millimetre of blood – to affect the victim's health. It takes between forty-eight and seventy-two hours to invade a red blood cell, grow to fill it, divide into six or twelve new individuals and burst the cell wall to release the toxins.

As all the parasites injected by one mosquito bite are in the same stage of development and as they keep to a fairly rigid developmental timetable, attacks of malaria occur at regular intervals. For this reason one kind of malaria was given the name 'tertian ague', describing an attack occurring every forty-eight hours, that is on the first, third, fifth day and so on. 'Quartan ague', with an attack every seventy-two hours (first, fourth, seventh day), is caused by a different but similar plasmodium which has a longer developmental cycle. The predominant African type, caused by *P. falciparum*, known as 'sub-tertian' or 'quotidian (daily)' malaria in which attacks are almost continuous, is a far more dangerous disease. It often causes quick death but, if death does not occur in the first attack and the subject is regularly reinfected by the parasite, the resultant attacks may be little more than chills and slight fever.

Untreated tertian or quartan malaria rarely kills of itself but is a chronic illness, which progressively weakens those who suffer from it, rendering them less resistant to other diseases. The chief reason for chronic ill-health is anaemia resulting from the parasites' destruction of the haemoglobin in the red blood cells, the iron-containing pigment essential for carrying oxygen to all parts of the body. Therefore if malaria attacks a community on a large scale, the vigour of the people will decline. This is why nineteenth-century travellers to malaria-infested regions such as the Pontine Marshes remarked on the feebleness of the population and their squalid life.

Malaria seems to have attained its widest distribution in Europe during the seventeenth century when very few countries, if any at all, escaped infection. Oliver Cromwell, born in the English Fenland, suffered from malaria all his life and died on 3 September 1658 'of a tertian ague'. A post-mortem examination revealed his spleen to be 'a mass of disease and filled with matter like the lees of oil'. This is a fairly common termination of malaria. The spleen is enlarged and may either be ruptured by a quite minor accident or suffer a spontaneous haemorrhage into its substance. The blood clot then becomes infected and forms an abscess which will cause death from toxaemia. Malaria was relatively common in England until 1840, after which incidence rapidly declined until by 1860 it had become a rarity except in the Isle of Sheppey off the Kentish coast. One of the present writers, while going through old case-notes in his hospital, found details of a patient who had never travelled abroad yet acquired malaria in 1874. He lived on the Plumstead Marshes, a waterlogged area bordering the River Thames and only separated from the London Docks by the river. This should remind us that the *Anopheles* mosquito is still found in malaria-free countries and people can be infected by a casually introduced malarial parasite.

Until the seventeenth century doctors treated malaria in the same manner as any other fever. Many physicians recognized only two kinds of fever, 'intermittent' and 'continuous', a classification which sometimes led to disaster. Purging, starvation diet and bleeding were the accepted remedies and must have hastened the end of many unfortunates who suffered from the anaemia of malaria. In 1632 the Spaniards sent from Peru a bark which was found to be an effective medicine. 'The Bark' as it was generally called has a curious story.

For many years it was taught that the bark known as cinchona took its name from the Countess of Chinchon, wife of the Governor of Peru, who had been cured of an obstinate fever by taking an infusion of this native remedy. As a thank-offering she distributed free supplies to the citizens of Lima and it was she who brought the original import on her return to Spain. The true story is less romantic. The Peruvian Indians applied the name quina-quina, meaning bark of bark, to a tree, myroxylon, which yielded a gum known as Balsam of Peru. This became such a popular remedy in Europe that apothecaries could not meet the demand and adulterated the extract with gums from other barks including that of the cinchona tree. The latter mixture proved particularly effective and so was the one most often prescribed. Physicians gradually realized that it was not the much-vaunted Balsam of Peru but the adulterating cinchona which helped to cure fevers. In 1820 two French chemists, Pierre Pelletier and Joseph Caventou, extracted the active alkaloid from cinchona bark but mistakenly gave it the name Quinine from the Amerindian quina-quina, the bark which produced Balsam of Peru.

Quinine is lethal to the malarial parasite and so can be used in the cure of the active disease. Quinine is also fairly effective in preventing malaria if taken regularly so as to maintain the blood-level necessary to kill the parasite. The drug is perhaps the classical example of effective empirical treatment. No one knew the cause of the illness or why the cure worked, but it did work. Quinine is not a pleasant medicine for, if taken in sufficiently large doses to kill the parasite, it has side-effects such as vomiting, headache, rashes, disturbance of vision and hearing. Many regular takers of quinine suffered from such severe tinnitus or 'singing in the ears' that they were almost stone-deaf. A better and more modern drug is a derivative of the alkaloid, chloroquine. Shortly before the Second World War an entirely new drug, mepacrine hydrochloride or atebrin, was found to be effective as a prophylactic and a suppressant (that is, it did not cure the developed disease but suppressed the worst symptoms). Mepacrine proved very successful during the campaigns in Burma and New Guinea and practically stamped out the most lethal form of malaria known as blackwater fever. This drug, too, had unpleasant side-effects. Not only did it stain the whole skin yellow but it caused vomiting and, sometimes, cerebral excitement. More recently two drugs, pyrimethamine and sulphormetoxine, used in single doses, have protected against the parasite. After the war in Vietnam a number of cases of malaria occurred in the United States and these were traced to returning soldiers who neglected prophylactic treatment. Sporadic cases still occur in plasmodium-free countries because travellers to malarial areas have thought it unnecessary to take precautions when going for a stay of only a few days. Parasites, like humans, can develop resistance and a strain of malarial parasite resistant to prophylactic drugs has appeared. Although much has been done to destroy mosquitoes by spraying breeding places with paraffin or insecticides, *Anopheles* still persists and can harbour the parasite.

Malaria, especially the malignant African type, was for many years confused with Yellow Fever, often known as Yellow Jack because it was a common cause for the quarantining of ships, which would then have to fly a yellow flag. Yellow fever is caused by a virus harboured by another type of mosquito, *Stegomyia* or *Aëdes*, injected into the human when the insect sucks blood. The distressing and dangerous symptoms include high fever, jaundice, vomiting, intractable diarrhoea, suppression of urine and profound exhaustion. One attack protects the patient for life. Thus, in areas where the disease is endemic, a considerable mass immunity develops and, as in measles, some maternal resistance is conferred upon uninfected children. Yellow fever is therefore at its most dangerous when introduced to communities which have never experienced it. Yellow Jack became particularly feared by seamen who plied between Africa and America in the eighteenth and nineteenth centuries. A single case occurring on board a ship that had never been infected could wipe out the whole crew.

The original habitat of yellow fever is not certain. There is a legend, which may well be true, that the *Aëdes* mosquito had a preference for breeding in ships' water butts. This would certainly account for the wide distribution and the mosquito may well have been carried by ship from Africa to the West Indies. Some epidemiologists believe the reverse: that the disease originated in the West Indies and was transported to the West Coast of Africa. They base their theory on the fact that the first well-documented epidemic occurred in Barbados, Guadeloupe and Yucatan in 1647. For a long time it was believed that the first known African outbreak was that described by J.P. Schotte at St Louis de Senegal in 1778. More recently it has been found that John Williams, a surgeon of Kingston, Jamaica, described a West Indian epidemic and continued: 'I do not apprehend this fever is what we call a local disorder, for I have seen it on the coast of Africa and am well informed that in the River Benin they have a bilious or yellow fever acuter than what is here, at the time of the expedition to Carthagena. The person seized with this fever dying there in less than twenty-four hours.' John Williams had been surgeon on a Guineaman, a slaving ship plying between Guinea and the West Indies. The date of his own African experience is not clear but the Carthagena expedition took place in 1740–1, nearly forty years earlier than the supposed first African epidemic.

Williams tried to differentiate between yellow fever and malaria. He was probably the first practitioner to understand the difference and the reason must be his experience in both Africa and the West Indies. The very prevalent and severe type of malaria endemic in West Africa, often associated with the lethal blackwater fever, may have obscured the presence of true yellow fever on the African coast. Williams's theory aroused much opposition in Jamaica. So angry were the arguments that his chief critic, Dr Parker Bennet, challenged Williams to a duel in which both men were killed.

Whether yellow fever originated in Africa or America, it became a common disease in many parts of the world during the seventeenth, eighteenth and nineteenth centuries. Particularly severe epidemics developed on the eastern seaboard of America, extending as far north as Halifax, Nova Scotia, which experienced a severe outbreak in 1861. New York suffered at the end of the seventeenth century and a hundred years later in 1793 Philadelphia was ravaged by an epidemic that must have equalled in its horrors a visitation by the Black Death. At least one-tenth of the population died between April and September. Morale fell to a low level. In his *Devils, Drugs and Doctors* Howard W. Haggard quotes the following comment from a witness of the epidemic:

> While affairs were in this deplorable stage and the people at the lowest ebb of despair, we cannot be astonished at the frightful scenes that were enacted, which seemed to indicate a total dissolution of the bonds of society in the nearest and dearest connections. Who, without horror, can reflect on a husband deserting his wife, united to him perhaps for twenty years, in the last agony, a wife unfeelingly abandoning her husband on his deathbed, parents forsaking their only child without remorse, children ungratefully flying from the parents and resigning them to chance without an enquiry after their health or safety?

A shining light in this dark tale is provided by the behaviour of Philip Syng Physick, sometimes called the Father of American Surgery. Physick left America for London to study under the great John Hunter who pressed him to remain as his assistant but he preferred to return. Only twenty-five years old, he had just settled in practice in Philadelphia when the epidemic started. Physick attended his patients devotedly until he was himself attacked. He recovered but never regained his previous strength. Later he was appointed surgeon to the Pennsylvania Hospital and Professor at the University.

The battle against malaria and yellow fever is of great importance in the history of travel, as are any of the attempts to combat major transmissible diseases, so the story will be very briefly told here. In 1857 Louis Pasteur,

Professor of Chemistry in the University of Lille, studied the problem of fermentation and concluded that the cause was not miasma, or bad air, as previously thought, but microscopical particles carried in the air. He thought that these particles were endowed with life and could multiply, as did other living creatures. He gave the particles their name on 7 April 1864 when telling his audience at the Sorbonne of a flask of milk which he had sterilized and kept airtight for some months:

> And I wait, I watch, I question it, begging it to recommence for me the beautiful spectacle of the first creation. But it is dumb, dumb since these experiments were begun several years ago. It is dumb because I have kept from it the only thing Man cannot produce, from the germs which float in the air, from Life, for Life is a Germ and a Germ is Life.

So was born the germ theory, not yet applied to the cause of infection and wrongly applied to the genesis of life. Joseph Lister, taught the use of the microscope by his father, a wine merchant, could appreciate the existence of micro-organisms as the agents of fermentation. He applied Pasteur's theory to the prevention of surgical sepsis by trying crude carbolic acid, then used to deodorize sewage, as a wound dressing for the first time on 12 August 1865. There were many who believed that germs were not the cause but the product of disease. The large bacillus causing anthrax had been seen under the microscope by Franz Pollender as early as 1849 but Pollender did not understand what he had discovered. In 1876 Robert Koch succeeded in isolating the bacillus and growing it in a culture medium.

Louis Pasteur, unaware of Koch's work, started to investigate anthrax, then a plague among French cattle, early in 1877. He found by experiment that the bacilli would multiply rapidly in urine. He took one drop of blood from an infected animal and added it to 50 cubic centimetres of sterilized urine in a flask. He allowed the culture to grow, then seeded a second 50 cc of sterilized urine with one drop of the first. Proceeding in the same manner, he produced a dilution of the original drop approximating to 1 in 1,000 million. The blood was now imperceptible but the urine teemed with anthrax bacilli. Pasteur found that one drop of his end product when injected into a warm-blooded animal caused death from anthrax just as certainly as did one drop of blood from an anthrax-infected animal.

Robert Koch widened the scope of his own investigations. In 1878 he identified six different types of bacteria which caused surgical infections and proved that each of the six bred true through several generations. His preparations had been more or less contaminated by alien micro-organisms but in 1881 he succeeded in producing pure cultures by transplanting selected colonies from generations grown on glass plates covered with a medium of gelatine and meat extract, protected from the air. In 1882 he made perhaps his most important discovery, the bacillus which causes tuberculosis, and in the same paper laid down the rules governing the relationship between bacteria and disease:

- The organism must be found constantly in every case of the disease.
- It must be possible to cultivate the organism outside the body of the host in pure cultures for several generations.
- The organism, isolated and cultured through several generations, must be capable of reproducing the original disease in susceptible animals.

These are known as Koch's Postulates and, when they are applicable, prove conclusively that a specific disease is caused by a specific organism.

The work of Pasteur, Koch and others made it possible to uncover the microscopical cause of infections but the method of transmission had yet to be demonstrated. In 1877 (Sir) Patrick Manson, then of Hong Kong, showed that embryos of a minute worm called *Filaria*, one of the causes of elephantiasis, were ingested at night from human blood by the *Culex* mosquito, that they developed in the insect's body, and were transmitted when the mosquito bit another individual. Manson's theory was not believed but in 1881 Carlos Finlay of Cuba made a similar suggestion that yellow fever was spread by mosquito bites, although he could produce no evidence in support. Meanwhile in 1880 a French army surgeon stationed in Algeria, Alphonse Laveran, had observed malarial parasites in the red blood corpuscles of infected patients when examined under a microscope. The parasites were also observed by an Italian, Camillo Golgi, who noted a difference between the parasites of tertian and quartan malaria.

In 1894 Manson, now working in London, met Ronald Ross, a young surgeon on leave from the Indian Army, and showed him Laveran's parasites in a blood film. Manson told Ross that he believed the parasites developed in 'some suctorial insect', just as the eggs of *Filaria* were incubated in the body of the *Culex* mosquito. Back in India Ross undertook a long investigation and eventually, on 20 August 1897 (a date which he thereafter always called 'Mosquito Day'), discovered malarial parasites in the stomach of the *Anopheles* mosquito. His finding was confirmed in the following year by Giovanni Grassi of Rome, who also showed that the female *Anopheles* is the only type of mosquito capable of transmitting malaria. The parasite's life cycle was gradually worked out. In 1900 infected mosquitoes, sent from Italy to London, were allowed to bite Ross's son who developed malaria. A control experiment was equally successful when three of Ross's assistants lived for some months in specially mosquito-proofed huts in the heavily infested Roman Campagna and failed to develop malaria.

These findings renewed interest in Carlos Finlay's unproven theory that yellow fever is spread by mosquito bites. Walter Reed was an army surgeon who had studied under the eminent pathologist William Welch of Baltimore. In 1900 Reed joined Carlos Finlay in Havana with two assistants from Baltimore, James Carroll and Jesse Lazear, to form a Yellow Fever Commission. Lazear and Carroll allowed themselves to be bitten by the *Stegomyia* mosquito. Both developed yellow fever. Lazear died within a few days but Carroll recovered after a severe illness. Walter Reed carried on with the work and, having proved the association between mosquitoes and yellow fever, suggested methods of control which virtually freed Havana from infection within three months, although the causative virus was not isolated until 1928. Reed died in 1902 and was succeeded at Havana by William Crawford Gorgas who had himself suffered from yellow fever earlier in his career as an army surgeon in Texas. Colonel Gorgas took command of the dramatic campaign which now opened against malaria and yellow fever during the construction of the Panama Canal.

If ever disease has hindered the travels of Man and the defeat of disease has demonstrably removed the hindrance, it is in the first failure and later success of driving the Canal through an infected terrain. The Pacific Ocean could only be reached from Europe by the long and notoriously dangerous voyage round Cape Horn at the extreme tip of South America. In 1879 Ferdinand de Lesseps, engineer of the Suez Canal, started to investigate the possibility of digging a canal across the narrow Isthmus of Panama, following the line of a railway which had already been constructed. It is said that a labourer died for every sleeper laid upon that railway track. De Lesseps estimated that completion of the canal would take about eight years. He encountered immense problems, and some financial difficulties, but the terrible sickness rate among his workmen was the primary cause of failure. Mosquitoes abounded in the undrained lakes and swamps through which the canal must pass. The death rate from all causes among the workers amounted to 176 per 1,000. Lesseps abandoned his project in May 1889. No more work was attempted for eighteen years and at one time the idea of the Panama route was entirely given up and a much longer canal through Nicaragua proposed.

In 1904 the United States became actively interested in reopening the Panama route and put William Gorgas in charge of health. One of the preventive measures introduced by Walter Reed in Havana had been isolation of all yellow fever patients in mosquito-proof rooms. This, combined with an active campaign against mosquitoes, had been the reason for success. Gorgas now proposed a similar campaign but encountered stubborn opposition from the authorities who failed to appreciate that mosquitoes and not dirt caused malaria and yellow fever.

After a hard battle, lasting nearly a year, he at last persuaded the American Government-run Canal Commission to take action on the Havana lines. He organized sanitary brigades on a large scale and conducted intensive warfare against the mosquito. Special buildings were prepared for workers and officials, all of them protected by fine copper-gauze netting. Stagnant pools were drained and filled in wherever possible. Very good results followed spraying of choked drainage channels with weedkiller, which not only allowed a freer flow but destroyed the resting places of adult mosquitoes. When drainage proved impossible, water surfaces were regularly sprayed with kerosene to destroy the larvae. The work of digging started again in 1907 and by then yellow fever had been beaten, the last case occurring in 1906, and the incidence of malaria had fallen very considerably. On 17 November 1913 the first ship passed through the Panama Canal which opened fully for traffic in August 1914. The 'official' opening arranged for 1 January 1915 had to be delayed because of an earth-slide in the previous October and, owing to the First World War, did not take place until 1920. By 1913 mortality from all causes among workers on the project had fallen to only six per thousand. This compared with an overall death rate of fourteen per thousand throughout the United States and fifteen per thousand in London. Colonel Gorgas, whose efforts had achieved this magnificent triumph, organized the medical services of the United States Army in the First World War.

Exploration of Africa was delayed by fly-borne, mosquito-borne and water-borne diseases which so weakened expeditions that the interior long remained impenetrable. The white man clung precariously to the coastal areas. James Lind, a naval surgeon well remembered for his introduction of lemon juice to prevent scurvy aboard ship, believed that the upland interior must provide better living conditions for the European. The practical difficulties of reaching the central plateau were unknown and unsuspected. The rivers teemed with mosquitoes; dysentery and other enteric fevers waited all along the route; wounds caused by thorns or other means festered and refused to heal. The terrible trypanosomiasis affected humans in the form of sleeping sickness and horses with the fatal infection called nagana. Borne by the tsetse fly, this last was perhaps the decisive factor. Because of it the horse – which in the different circumstances of Central America had flourished even in the same tropical latitudes – could not be used for transport in equatorial Africa. There all cross-country journeys had to be made on foot, goods being carried on the heads of natives.

Hardy men attempted the hopeless journey for four hundred years. In 1569 a party of Portugese settlers started from the coastal plain on horseback, explored part of the lower and middle Zambezi River, then struck inland searching for gold. Much later news came back that all the horses had died and the men had succumbed to disease and attack by hostile tribes. In the late 1770s a Scottish surgeon named Mungo Park endeavoured to find the source of the Niger River. Having failed once he tried again, setting out on 28 April 1805 with a party of forty-four Europeans, including scientists, soldiers, four carpenters and two seamen. He reached the Niger on 19 August after travelling over five hundred miles through disease-infested country. By now all the party were suffering from dysentery and fevers and by 11 October all except four were dead. Park, probably with the only remaining white man Lieutenant Martin, contrived a canoe with which they tried to reach safety by river. He appears to have been drowned or killed by hostile natives while negotiating rapids with the remnant of his party. One native servant escaped to recount this tale about five years later. A few belongings were recovered but Mungo Park's journal has never been found.

In 1816 Captain James Tuckey RN tried to explore up the River Congo. He took his ship as far as the rapids where he landed with a shore party containing one or two scientific assistants. They found the climate 'pleasant, the thermometer seldom exceeding 76°F or being lower than 60°F, with scarcely any rain and the atmosphere dry'. Despite these favourable conditions the whole expedition was attacked by an intense 'remittent fever' with black vomit, almost certainly the African type of malignant malaria. Fourteen men died on land and four more after boarding the ship. The total European mortality can be expressed as 37 per cent. The dead included Captain Tuckey and the scientists.

In 1832 Major M'Gregor Laird headed an expedition carried by two ships, *Quorra* and *Albrukah*, intending to explore the Niger delta and push on up the river. They entered a tributary, the Benue, on 18 October. By 12 November nearly all the crew were sick with fever and two days later only one European was fit for duty. The *Quorra* reached the sea in August 1833, only five of the Europeans having survived. *Albrukah* returned in November having lost fifteen out of nineteen Europeans.

Travel by steamship proved no more successful. A much larger expedition led by Captain H.D. Trotter in 1841 consisted of 145 white Europeans, 25 non-Europeans recruited in Britain and 133 Africans recruited in Sierra Leone travelling in three iron-built steamboats, *Albert*, *Wilberforce* and *London*. The steamers reached a point on the Niger about a hundred miles from the sea on 26 August. Fever broke out at the beginning of September and 'paralysed the whole expedition'. They pushed further on but sickness became so prevalent that *Wilberforce* and *London* were sent back to the coast on 19 September laden with their own sick and those from *Albert*. *Albert* steamed on further but was forced to return on 4 October, reaching the coast ten days later, having been on the river for nine weeks. Of the 145 Europeans, 130 fell sick of fever and 50 died. Eleven of the non-Europeans from Britain fell ill but all recovered. None of the 133 Africans recruited in Sierra Leone developed fever. The fate of these expeditions – and there were many more, equally disastrous – clearly shows why the interior of Africa remained unknown territory for so long a time.

We now know that many Africans in malarial areas suffer from a genetic disorder known as sickle-cell anaemia. The malarial parasite cannot develop in the thin crescent shaped red blood corpuscles and so the subject is immune, although anaemic. The susceptibility of Europeans to 'fever' compared to the exemption of Africans puzzled medical men who put forward many theories to account for the immunity of the natives. Perhaps God had purposely arranged matters thus so that the Africans might live in peace. Or perhaps they did not develop fevers because they had not experienced the European's more luxurious style of life. A favourite theory maintained that Africans had a greater capacity for perspiration and so were better able to throw off the 'foul and nasty vapours' which poisoned the European body in hot climates.

Most medical authorities held that Africans must be differently constituted. They invented a pseudo-scientific or at least a pseudo-medical basis for racism. The African could perform manual labour in a tropical climate without falling sick while the white man inevitably succumbed. Therefore the function of the latter was to direct and govern leaving the native population to carry out the heavy work. These vacillating and erroneous ideas resulted in gross injustice and the abandonment of hopeful policies. They also explain why, in its early stages, so much of tropical medicine had to be concentrated on avoiding 'white men's graves' rather than on the afflictions of the natives themselves.

For four centuries the European exploited the tropical coast of Africa. Unable to penetrate further inland, he made treaties with native chiefs and Arab traders who searched out unknown inland communities, overwhelmed them, and herded the survivors to the coast. The white man eagerly bought their captives for a handful of shoddy goods, packed them head to foot in his insanitary sailing ship and sold those who survived the sea passage to Bristol or across the Atlantic for a hundred times the price he had paid in Africa. Some of these slaves, particularly boys in the eighteenth century, were bought as servants for fashionable houses and probably enjoyed a much better life than in their native land. Many more laboured in the sugar plantations of the West Indies and in the cotton fields of the Southern States of North America under masters of varying degrees of kindness and brutality who paid them with scanty food and primitive lodging. Often regarded and treated as animals, the bitter resentment of these slaves outlasted manumission and even today helps to shape the folk-memory of their descendants.

Experience of the African terrain, greater knowledge of disease and massive dosage with quinine enabled white explorers to penetrate more deeply in the second half of the nineteenth century. There remained the deadly infection known as sleeping sickness which attacked native Africans and, to a lesser degree, immigrant Europeans too. Sleeping sickness is caused by a minute parasite belonging to the genus *Trypanosoma* carried by the tsetse fly, a species of *Glossina*, a genus of which many varieties infest different areas in Africa. There is also a form of trypanosomiasis called Chagas's Disease, carried by a louse, which is only found in Brazil and Venezuela.

African trypanosomiasis occurs widely in the area lying roughly between the Gambia River on the north-west coast and the Limpopo River on the south-east, thus embracing the whole of the Great Central Plateau and all equatorial Africa. Two types of sleeping sickness affect the human: the *gambiense*, distributed in west and central Africa, and the *rhodesiense* occurring in east and central areas. The two types are carried by different varieties of tsetse which also differ in habitat. Those which carry *gambiense* thrive in shade and high humidity, while the vectors of *rhodesiense* live in open, scrub-covered country. This differing habitat implies that few parts of central Africa are free from one or other form of the disease, the first belonging to the humid forest regions, the second to the dry savannahs.

The bite of the tsetse is described as like a red-hot needle, commonly in the soft skin behind the ear or on the neck. The spot bitten swells up and then subsides, much like the bite of a common horse-fly. If the tsetse is infected, the bitten place again becomes swollen and painful about ten days later. This swelling is sometimes called the chancre, on the analogy of the chancre produced by syphilis. The trypanosomes invade the subject's bloodstream within two or three weeks and the generalized disease process then begins. The clinical picture varies with the type.

Gambiense is the more chronic. There are irregular bouts of mild fever and the glands, particularly at the back of the neck, become enlarged with a distinctive rubbery feeling when palpated. The bouts of fever now last longer, often for as much as a week. The liver and spleen enlarge. After some months the central nervous system is affected. Those afflicted complain of severe headache and their behaviour is not entirely rational, unusual lethargy alternating with outbursts of senseless anger accompanied by physical violence. Typically, there is reversal of the normal sleep rhythm, insomnia at night and somnolence by day. They develop tremors and paralyses of the limbs, lose their appetite, and start to waste away until reduced to little more than skin-covered skeletons. Gradually the sufferer sinks into coma which deepens until death.

Rhodesiense is a much more acute illness. Fever is higher and constant rather than intermittent, the patient is seriously ill within only a few weeks of being bitten and death often occurs quickly from the direct effect of high fever on the heart. If this does not happen, the final stages will resemble *gambiense*, with tremors of the limbs, increasing drowsiness and coma.

Sleeping sickness is undoubtedly of ancient African origin but the first and classic description comes from Cuba. In 1803 Doctor T.M. Winterbottom, an Englishman working in the West Indies, observed this strange illness in slaves imported from the west coast of Africa, who must have shown the first symptoms on the long Atlantic crossing. He is still remembered by 'Winterbottom's sign' – the prolonged swelling and peculiar rubbery texture of glands at the back of the neck. David Livingstone, the great missionary-explorer, described the tsetse fly in 1857 and stated that horses and cattle died from its bite. Livingstone treated horses suffering from 'nagana' or stallion sickness with arsenic. His treatment must have been empirical because the cause was not yet known, but arsenical preparations were the first hopeful medicines even after the trypanosome had been identified.

Tsetse flies tend to colonize belts of countryside rather than spreading haphazardly. This fact was recognized by the African native but not by the European. Epidemics of sleeping sickness among the indigenous populations became more frequent in the last years of the nineteenth century because white men opened new trade routes and there was increased movement and ecological disruption in the hitherto almost static equatorial area. At the same time there was a corresponding increase in the nagana of horses and cattle. Prevalence of nagana limited mobility. In 1894 (Sir) David Bruce, an army medical officer, arrived in Natal to investigate the problem, accompanied by his wife who actively assisted him in the work. They examined the blood of all infected horses and cattle brought to them and discovered the parasite which became known as *Trypanosoma brucei*. Bruce showed that the parasite was conveyed to animals by the bite of tsetse flies, thus confirming and expanding Livingstone's observation of 1857.

In 1901 Joseph Everitt Dutton, a doctor working in Gambia, found trypanosomes in the blood of human patients suffering from sleeping sickness, hence the name *T. gambiense*. Dutton's investigation ended prematurely in the following year when he died while researching another insect-borne disease, relapsing fever, on the Congo River. In 1903 a large epidemic of sleeping sickness caused many deaths in Uganda. David Bruce and his wife went to investigate with a team including the famous Italian expert on tropical diseases, Aldo Castellani. Castellani was particularly interested in the nervous symptoms, the tremors and paralyses, the alternating violence and drowsiness. He examined the cerebro-spinal fluid, which is contained between the two membranes enclosing the brain and spinal cord, and found a minute parasite. Bruce, informed of this finding, turned his attention to the blood of patients suffering from sleeping sickness and discovered similar parasites, identical to the trypanosomes he had discovered in the blood of cattle suffering from nagana. All the pieces of the puzzle fell into place. Bruce showed beyond question that both nagana of animals and sleeping sickness of humans are due to a trypanosome carried by tsetse flies. He advocated control of spread by restricting movement of infected humans and cattle, and by destruction of the flies.

Unfortunately it was not so easy as that. Control of the *gambiense* type is comparatively simple, for the vector fly is not common and will only thrive in humid shade. Stripping the hot, damp river banks of their vegetation destroyed the breeding grounds and soon diminished the fly population. But *rhodesiense* is carried by the fly of the arid scrubland savannahs. The parasite infests domestic cattle causing a high mortality which limits production of meat and milk. This is the chief reason for prevalence of the disease known by the Ghanaian name Kwashiorkor which affects fast-growing children and is due to a deficiency of high-grade protein foods. Control of the fly depends on clearing wide areas of scrub and restricting movement of cattle. The latter derives from the ancient observation of African herdsmen, for the fly is only active by day and the herdsmen found that they could safely drive cattle from one grazing ground across scrub country (the fly belt) to another ground at night. Farming of herded wild game in large reserves has been suggested as an alternative means of providing protein. Wild animals have developed sufficient resistance not to be affected but they may act as a reservoir of parasites and so spread the disease to domestic animals and humans unless kept under conditions of strict control.

Treatment of both types of sleeping sickness was practically useless until the early 1920s. A drug, atoxyl, and very large doses of tartar emetic, given intravenously, were often prescribed. European travellers to fly-infested districts were advised to wear gauze veils over the face and neck, gloves, and long trousers tucked into boots, an uncomfortable kind of attire in a hot and humid climate, but the reason why the European was much less commonly infected than the naked or semi-naked African. In 1922 the German firm Bayer introduced a useful drug, the arsenical compound tryparsamide, and this has been followed by increasingly effective compounds both in treatment of the developed disease and as prophylactics. Combined with intensive warfare against tsetse flies, using persistent insecticides, these measures brought sleeping sickness and nagana under some measure of control by the 1960s. However, since then political instability in many areas has resulted in displacement of populations with consequent disruption of public health services on a scale that has brought these diseases again into prominence.

The long battle of almost four centuries against the African pool of disease has presented the native peoples with an extraordinary problem. The northern areas – Morocco, Algeria, Tunisia and Libya – have evolved more or less in parallel with their European neighbours. The ancient civilization of Egypt succumbed to barbarian attack but has also developed on lines similar to Europe. The pleasant climate and rich farmland of South Africa, curiously neglected by the early Portuguese settlers, has attracted first Dutch and then British emigrants since the early seventeenth century. With the discovery of diamonds and gold in the 1870s and 1880s a migratory flood from all parts of the world brought both the benefits and the ills of the European type of civilization into South Africa.

None of this penetrated to the African interior. When the conscience of the white man awoke to the fact that traffic in humans is offensive and the slave trade ended in the 1830s, communication between the coast and the Central Plateau practically ceased. Then interest in the mysterious interior was aroused. Missionaries and doctors, battling against immense difficulties, forced their way inland. As knowledge of disease increased and as quinine became more readily available, they met with greater success. Most notable of these devoted men is David Livingstone who, from 1841 until his death on 1 May 1873, founded mission stations, preached to the natives, treated their illnesses and explored large areas of equatorial Africa. His exploratory work was continued by another remarkable man, the Welsh orphan John Rowland, who ran away from the workhouse at the age of fifteen and sailed to America as a cabin boy, to be adopted by a New Orleans merchant, Henry Morton Stanley, whose name he assumed. Dispatched by the *New York Herald* to search for Livingstone after his reported death in 1869, Stanley found him alive but reduced almost to a skeleton on 28 October 1871. Disease had most certainly not yet been conquered. Both Stanley and Livingstone almost succumbed to attacks of malaria and dysentery on many occasions, and not one of the mission stations founded by Livingstone survived for more than a few months.

The true importance of Livingstone and Stanley lies not in what they directly accomplished but in the enthusiasm which their example inspired. They were the first in a long line of later nineteenth-century pioneers who stimulated international interest in the potential opportunities of unexplored Africa. They found communities, often uncivilized by European standards, sometimes entirely unclothed, living the kind of existence described in the introduction to this book. Their reports suggested that here were whole nations, not only to be saved by Christianity and educated to be citizens of the modern world, but also to be commercially exploited.

Until 1877, in which year Stanley completed his journey down the Congo River, the only foreign powers established in Africa were Great Britain, Portugal and France. The Portuguese claimed sovereignty over 700,000 square miles but effectively controlled less than 40,000. The French, almost confined to the Mediterranean sea-board, held 170,000 square miles, and the British with the Dutch Boers held 250,000, largely in the south. The total area 'ruled' by the European amounted to 1,271,000 square miles, about one-tenth of the continent. Apart from the large deserts of Sahara and Libya, roughly half the total area of Africa was wholly inhabited and ruled by native tribes. Much the larger part lay in the unexplored tropical zone.

The Franco-Prussian War of 1870–1 greatly affected the future. Victorious and united, Germany became eager for overseas dominions. Defeated France saw her own hope of renaissance in an enlarged colonial empire. The struggle for African colonies was precipitated by an initially benevolent movement on the part of King Leopold II of Belgium. In September 1876 Leopold summoned representatives of all the powers to a conference in Brussels, the object being to suppress the slave trade and discuss the future exploration and civilization of Central Africa. Delegates to this conference did not represent their governments, who gave no official support. The conference agreed to set up an International African Association with its headquarters in Brussels. As the result of international jealousy and lack of cooperation, the Association failed and the venture became purely Belgian. The Congo Free State came under the personal sovereignty, rapidly approaching the personal ownership, of Leopold II.

Leopold's rule very soon aroused hostility and other countries were not slow to see the material advantages of opposition to his unenlightened management. The Congo River, which Stanley had shown to be a navigable waterway from its deep estuary on the coast for nearly a thousand miles inland, was an attractive feature. In January 1879 Stanley received an appointment as an accredited agent of Leopold II in the Congo Free State. He established trading stations and entered into treaties with native chiefs along the south bank of the Congo. Portugal made renewed claims, traditional rather than justified. The French became suspicious of Belgian penetration. In 1880 Savorgnan de Brazza, acting for France, made treaties and founded stations along the north bank of the Congo, in an endeavour to link the coast with Timbuktu, the theoretical southern extremity of the French colonial empire. In 1884 Germany announced the annexation of a long stretch of the west coast together with the hinterlands of Togo and Cameroon. The British, who had lagged behind except in South Africa, now formally declared their sovereignty over the Niger Delta, Lagos and Sierra Leone.

The great land-grabbing operation had clearly got out of hand and would inevitably lead to large-scale warfare unless the countries could reach some kind of agreement. The Berlin conference of powers, opened on 15 November 1884, decided that possession by a European country of any part of Africa must be actual and effective to be valid and that all signatory powers must be notified of intention to annex any part of the continent. The ominous phrase 'spheres of influence' appeared for the first time in this treaty. The 'scramble for Africa' occupied slightly less than a quarter of a century. By 1914 nearly eleven million square miles had passed into European possession, leaving only 613,000 independent. The consolidation of effective control over the partitioned regions owed as much to quinine as it did to the rifle.

Only three independent states remained at the beginning of the Second World War in 1939, the Union of South Africa, Egypt and the Republic of Liberia which had originally been founded by American abolitionists as a home for freed slaves. Just over twenty years later, in 1962, twenty-eight independent African states had become voting members of United Nations. Within twenty-three years the whole population of Central Africa acquired the rights of self-government and self-determination. There is no doubt that the change had been too rapid. In 1962 there were many equatorial Africans who had hurtled from a Stone Age civilization into the Atomic Age within their own lifetimes.

We can gain some idea of the headlong speed of this change by estimating the length of railroad in the Africa of 1934, at a time when steam transport was giving way to the internal combustion engine in Europe and America. In the whole of equatorial Africa there existed only 318 miles of track and the total mileage for the huge continent, including that of 'white' South Africa, was 42,750, just double that of the relatively tiny Britain at the same date. The equivalent figure for Europe and Russia is 235,719. Africa, hardly touched by the horse or steam power, passed directly from pedestrian transport to the internal combustion engine.

The continent of Africa is in fact the seat of a vast technological and social experiment. By the end of the twentieth century the experiment was by no means complete, for poverty, famine, sickness, primitive housing, tribal hostility and race-hatred still remained. No one can usefully prophesy what the future holds or what the result of the experiment will be. The difficulties are derived not least from the sheer speed of change. This is the sense in which the danger of African diseases still existing in the last quarter of the nineteenth century, and the rapid but incomplete social and medical advances directed against them in the ensuing hundred years, may well have posed one of the greatest world problems of the future.

CHAPTER NINE

Queen Victoria and the Fall of the Russian Monarchy

At first thought, Queen Victoria would be a most unlikely candidate for the dubious honour of bringing Lenin and his Bolsheviks to power. But strange things happen in history and, in fact, the 'Great Queen' was one of the primary causes of the troubles which overwhelmed tsardom during its last years, even if her contribution was made only indirectly and unwittingly. The royal families of Europe may have begun to doubt that they ruled by Divine Right but still clung to the absurd principle that only they were fit to wear a crown. No commoner might be allowed to debase the royal blood. Marriage was limited to the royal circle and, since that circle was a comparatively small one, a wife would often be quite closely related to her husband.

Until the late nineteenth century no one seems to have fully understood just how dangerous intermarriage of closely related spouses can be. The Christian Church forbade union between the closest degrees of affinity but even first cousins, that is the children of brothers or sisters, were permitted to intermarry. It could be, and was, argued that if two brothers showed exceptional intelligence then the grandchildren, issue of a son and daughter of the brothers, would be likely to possess an even higher degree of intelligence. There was a tendency to forget that intelligence is not the only attribute which may be transmitted by both mother and father.

To understand Victoria's role in the collapse of tsardom, we need to turn back to the middle of the nineteenth century when a quite unknown Roman Catholic monk named Gregor Mendel became interested in the growth of peas. He worked in the garden of his abbey at Brunn in Austria and was puzzled by the fact that if he sowed seed from tall peas the plants produced were not always tall. He tried crossing a short breed of pea with a tall breed, sowed the seed, and to his surprise found that the plants produced were nearly all tall, not half tall and half short or all medium as he had expected. He worked on until he had one strain that produced all tall peas and another that produced all short. Then he crossed a tall with a short and sowed the seed. Three quarters of the resultant plants were tall and only a quarter short.

Mendel decided that there must be a 'hereditary factor' that determined tallness and shortness but that the factor must be double, as it appeared that the factor for tallness would override the factor for shortness. If the factor was double and a true tall pea (T) was crossed with a true short pea (t) then the two factors could form four possible combinations: TT, Tt, tT and tt. But what really interested Mendel was that tallness must be dominant because three-quarters of the progeny proved to be tall (TT, Tt, tT) and only the remaining quarter were short (tt). But of the tall peas only one-third (TT) would breed true when crossed with another TT to produce uniformly tall progeny and two-thirds (Tt and tT) contained a factor for shortness and even if crossed with a TT would produce a proportion of short plants.

After over ten years of research Mendel described his theory of 'hereditary factors' in 1866. Unfortunately he buried his findings in the pages of an obscure journal and they attracted no attention at the time. The history of Europe might conceivably have been a little different had their implications been understood more swiftly. In fact thirty-five years elapsed before three botanists in three different countries had the same idea. During the course of their researches they came across Mendel's paper and, having proved his theory correct, assured him posthumous fame. In 1905 William Bateson, working on the hybridization of sweet peas at Cambridge, gave to Mendel's hereditary factors or elements the name 'genes'.

These genes, derived from each parent, decide the physical appearance of the child and the basic manner in which he or she will react to environmental influences. The human is derived from a single female cell, the ovum, and a single male cell, the sperm. Both cells contain a nucleus and each nucleus contains a material called chromatin, visible under the microscope as fine tangled threads, largely composed of nucleic acid – the very important constituent now usually termed DNA. When the ovum is fertilized by the sperm, the two nuclei fuse and form a single cell. The billions of cells that compose the adult body are all ultimately derived from this single cell. When the single cell first divides into two, the new cells contain equal male and female elements and this process continues throughout growth of the embryo and of the developing body. Before the fertilized cell first divides, the tangled threads of chromatin coalesce to form a number of roughly X-shaped bodies called chromosomes. It is these chromosomes that carry the genes of inheritance.

Mendel's original theory was based on naked-eye observation. He could not see what was happening when he crossed his peas. Modern microscopical studies have confirmed his postulate that his hereditary factor or element (TT or Tt for instance) is always doubled in the individual and that only half of this element is transmitted by each parent to the offspring. In the human, the female ovum and the male sperm cells each contain twenty-three chromosomes so the fertilized cell will contain forty-six, although very occasionally an extra chromosome is transmitted with unfortunate results. The number of chromosomes remains constant with each cell division in all members of the human race, but the size and shape of the chromosomes differ, and this difference affects the nature of inheritance.

As chromosomes bear differing genes and as only half the maternal and paternal chromosomes are transmitted to the offspring, it is extremely unlikely that a child, deriving twenty-three gene-bearing chromosomes from one parent and twenty-three from the other, will exactly resemble either of the parents. It is also extremely unlikely that there will be no resemblance. It is also unlikely that one child in a family will exactly resemble any other, except in the case of identical twins who are formed from the splitting of a single fertilized cell and are therefore genetically the same.

Quite often a familial resemblance can be traced back for centuries by examining portraits, such as those of the Habsburgs with their drooping lips and narrow chins. However, if we could find a full-length picture of a Habsburg who existed as far back as one million years BC, we should not expect any resemblance to the descendant who ruled Austria at the beginning of the twentieth century. The differences would be even greater than any that could be explained by the constant infusion of fresh genes by marriage. Face and body would in fact bear little resemblance to any human who lives today.

This is because the genes themselves change and it is the mutation of genes which has, in the course of many centuries, produced the human from his more ape-like ancestor and, going back to an unknown period in time, from creatures that preceded the hominids. Such genetic changes are essential to the orderly process of evolution because they enable a creature to adapt itself to a gradually changing environment and to a more complex life. In our present state of scientific knowledge and technical ability there is a temptation to encourage the mutation artificially. One of the chief reasons why we must recognize that 'genetic engineering' is risky derives from our knowledge of the accidents which have already occurred during the natural process.

For things sometimes do go wrong. The mutant gene produces an undesirable trait which was not present in the genetic pattern before. The change may take the form of a disease. True genetic disease is by no means common because, if the disease limits viability of the individual, the family is likely to die out completely within only a few generations. An exception, and one of the first genetic disorders to be recognized, is Huntington's Chorea which causes progressive mental deterioration accompanied by continuous involuntary twitching movements. It was first fully described in 1872 by an American physician George Huntington, who attended several patients in Long Island suffering from these symptoms. Some of the patients belonged to families treated by Huntington's father and grandfather, who had started practising there in 1797. The Huntington grandson was thus able to trace the families back. He showed that the disease – that is the mutant gene – existed in a family from Bures, a small village in Suffolk, who landed at Boston in 1630. The violent twitching and mental symptoms aroused suspicion and caused some of those affected to be accused in the notorious Salem witch trials of 1692. Huntington's Chorea is a rare example of persistent genetic disorder because, although incurable, it most commonly appears in middle age. Thus there is time for children to be born before onset and about half of these will be affected. In one case, the unbroken line could be traced back through an immigrant for twelve generations.

Among other genetic diseases, porphyria is of particular interest because it stimulated one of the most brilliant pieces of medical detective work, and may also have had some effect on the course of history. The name 'porphyria' means 'purple urine' and refers to the most common sign, occasional passing of urine which turns a purplish-brown colour on standing. The disorder usually becomes apparent in the second or third decade of life, taking the form of a sudden attack associated with abdominal pain and constipation, local nervous symptoms such as a hypersensitive skin, rheumatic pains and mental disturbance. Through the meticulous investigation of the late Doctors Ida Macalpine and Richard Hunter, King George III of Great Britain and Hanover has become the most widely known sufferer from this ailment. Cruelly treated in his lifetime as 'mad' or, in more modern terminology, as suffering from a manic-depressive psychosis, George is now considered by many physicians to have been a victim of porphyria. Macalpine and Hunter traced the disease back through six generations to Mary Queen of Scots. Among those in whom they found evidence of the disease were Queen Anne, Mary's great-granddaughter, and King Frederick I of Prussia. Four of the sons of George III showed symptoms as did two tactfully unnamed royal personages still living in the 1960s, one descended from Frederick I and the other from a sister of George III.

King George III, born in 1738 and dying in 1820, had eight attacks of illness, all of a similar character, between 1762 when he was twenty-four years old and 1804. In October 1810 he again fell ill and, after two years of exacerbations and remissions, lapsed into hopeless insanity. He died, mad, blind and stone deaf at the age of eighty-one. His final illness, which started when he was seventy-two, was probably not related to porphyria, bearing more resemblance to advancing senility of the Alzheimer type.

Many attempts have been made to link his 'madness' with the most notable event of his reign, the loss of Britain's colonies in America and the birth of the independent United States. Undoubtedly George was a stubborn, not very intelligent, unimaginative man and he backed his Prime Minister, Lord North, in the foolish provocation that precipitated the War of Independence in 1775. But he showed no sign of mental aberration between attacks. He was garrulous, prone to ask strange questions such as 'How does the apple get into the dumpling?', often seemed more interested in turnips than statecraft, but he ruled adequately and with some firmness. He had no attack between 1762 and January 1766, when he suffered a mild one lasting for a month. He was then free of symptoms until July 1788. Since there is no evidence of 'madness' between 1766 and 1788, we can hardly blame porphyria for the loss of the American colonies in the war of 1775–81. The king's bad judgement may have helped to precipitate the crisis and his obstinacy may have prevented an amicable settlement, but his faults were shared by his ministers, the majority of the House of Commons and a large proportion of the British public.

It was on Irish rather than American issues that George's malady had the greater impact. During the eighteenth century Protestant settler and Catholic native lived fairly amicably together in Ireland, although

Catholics were not allowed to sit in the Dublin Parliament. In the last years of the century Republican France offered to liberate Ireland from the yoke of England, an offer which provoked the rebellion of 1798 when Catholics attempted to set up a Celtic Republic dominated by priests. After the revolt had been cruelly suppressed by a combination of English troops and Irish Protestants, the Prime Minister, William Pitt, decided that union of the two islands in one Parliament at Westminster offered the best hope of restoring order and justice. He induced the Irish Parliament to abolish itself and to declare for union with Britain in 1800, on the understanding that Catholics would be eligible to sit in the new United Parliament. In other words Pitt committed himself to Catholic emancipation.

But Pitt omitted to inform King George III of his intention. George regarded himself as the Defender of the true Protestant Faith. When the Lord Chancellor drew the king's attention to Pitt's proposal, he at once objected and Pitt resigned. Ten days later, in February 1801, George suffered another attack of porphyria with severe mental derangement. He recovered in March and Pitt made the solemn promise that he would never again mention Catholic emancipation in the king's lifetime. 'Now my mind will be at ease,' George answered. So, to set the royal mind at rest, the subject of Catholic emancipation was shelved for twenty-eight years. Lacking this essential ingredient, Pitt's scheme for the pacification of Ireland was doomed to failure. Union with Britain denoted to the Irish Catholic nothing more than domination by the alien and oppressive Protestant. Perhaps porphyria is partly to blame for the Irish troubles of the nineteenth and twentieth centuries.

Queen Victoria's most fateful role in history was to transmit the rare genetic disorder known as Haemophilia A to a number of her descendants. An almost invariable characteristic of this condition is that, while females are the means of passing on the disease, it is their male progeny who suffer the ill-effects. Even an afflicted father cannot transmit haemophilia directly to his sons, as distinct from siring daughters who may act as carriers to their own male offspring. A female can suffer from haemophilia only if the mother is a carrier and the father is a haemophiliac. The disease itself involves the failure of blood to clot within the normal time. This abnormality has been noticed for centuries, particularly among people, such as the Jews, who practise circumcision. The first clear description was given by a physician, John C. Otto of

Philadelphia, in 1803: 'an haemorrhagic disposition existing in certain families. It is a surprising circumstance that the males only are subject to this strange affection. Although the females are exempt, they are still capable of transmitting it to their male children.' The defect is lack of a protein in the serum, the liquid part of the blood, which is essential for clotting. Whereas normal blood takes from five to fifteen minutes to clot, the haemophiliac's blood will take at least half an hour and generally several hours or even days. Thus the haemophiliac lives in extreme danger. A small wound, trivial in the normal individual, will place him at risk. A bruise, caused by a subcutaneous wound to a blood vessel, will be exceptionally painful as the extravasated blood forces its way into the tissues. Such internal bleeding is particularly dangerous because the surgeon can deal with it only by making an open wound.

The defect or mutant gene seems to have originated with Queen Victoria or perhaps her mother the Duchess of Kent. Victoria was an only child, so there can be no certainty. There is no known history of haemophilia in either the British royal family or that of Saxe-Coburg-Saalfeld, the mother's family. One of Victoria's four sons, Prince Leopold, died from haemophilia. Of her five daughters, two transmitted haemophilia to their sons or grandsons. The worst history is that of the youngest, Princess Beatrice, who married Prince Henry of Battenberg. Two sons of the marriage died of the defect. A daughter, Ena, married King Alfonso XIII of Spain. Two haemophiliac sons of this marriage died aged twenty and thirty-one. This is a family history typical of the disorder and, since no sufferers can be traced on either the maternal or the paternal side of Victoria's acknowledged ancestry, questions have inevitably been raised about illegitimacy. Was she really the Duke of Kent's daughter, or rather the child of some man unknown? Despite her facial resemblance to the Duke and to his father George III, and the possibility that a genetic mutation might have spontaneously occurred for the first time (as happens in about a quarter of recorded cases of haemophilia) in Victoria or in either of her ducal parents, a trace of doubt about her paternity remains.

Victoria's third child and second daughter, Alice, was born in 1843 and married Louis IV, Grand Duke of Hesse-Darmstadt. There were two sons of the marriage, of whom one died of haemophilia aged three. Of their five daughters, the youngest survivor, always known as Alix, married Nicholas II, Autocrat, Tsar and Emperor of All the Russias, thus bringing Queen Victoria's haemophiliac gene into the Romanov family.

Alix or, to give her full name, Alice Victoria Helena Louise Beatrice, Princess of Hesse-Darmstadt, was born at Darmstadt on 6 June 1872. At the age of six she lost her mother and her younger sister during an epidemic of diphtheria. The family had regularly visited 'Granny Victoria' once a year. After her daughter's death, the Queen tended to regard the widower as her own son and the visits to the British court became more frequent.

Alix grew up to be beautiful, a tall slender woman with red-gold hair, blue eyes, a pink and white complexion, her classical features marred only by a withdrawn, cold expression. If not outstandingly clever as an adolescent, she was by no means unintelligent for she was well grounded in history, geography, literature and music by the age of fifteen. She also developed an interest in medicine. The great ideals of the Victorian Age, hard work, discipline and service, remained with her throughout her life. She became a prude, the typical Victorian 'lady' who was secretly obsessed by sex but regarded any overt discussion of the subject as disgusting. Pathologically shy, she lacked charm, that essential quality of royalty. Not many people knew her well but, to those who did, she was 'Sunny', a name given as tribute to her bright hair and sparkling eyes.

In 1884 this quite unimportant twelve-year-old princess of a minor royal family travelled for the first time to the court of the mightiest land empire in Europe, the occasion being the marriage of her elder sister to Grand Duke Serge, brother of Tsar Alexander III. Here she met Alexander's sixteen-year-old son, the Tsarevitch Nicholas, born on 18 May 1868. It was a case of love at first sight.

If Alix had genetic problems, so did Nicholas. The root of his trouble lay in the first 'hereditary factor' observed by Mendel, the vagaries of tallness. Alexander III was gigantic, six foot six inches in height, and broad in proportion. He could bend a silver coin in his fingers and once held up the roof of a wrecked railway carriage on his shoulders while his family escaped. When the Austrian ambassador tactlessly remarked at the dinner table that it might be necessary to mobilize an army division or two on the frontier, Alexander picked up a heavy silver fork, casually tied it in a knot, and threw it at him with the words 'That is what I will do with your divisions.' This great strong bull of a man, practically solid wood from the neck up but downright in word and action, married a tiny woman of more complex character. Nicholas inherited much more from his mother, Maria Dagmar, than he did from his awe-inspiring father. Charming, brave, athletic, shy and hesitant, intelligent but fatally at the mercy of stronger personalities, Nicholas grew into a small, slight man, only just over five feet six inches in height, surrounded by a mob of gigantic Romanov relations.

Queen Victoria warmly supported the couple, because their marriage seemed a brilliant opportunity for one of her favourite granddaughters. But a shadow overlaid it from the start. Neither Alexander nor his wife approved, for both of them disliked Germans. Also, the future Tsaritsa of Russia must be a member of the Orthodox Church and Alix was a fervent Lutheran. The dutiful son Nicholas told his diary: 'For a long time I resisted my feeling, trying to deceive myself by the impossibility that my dearest dream will come true.' His dream did come true two years after he wrote those words. In April 1894 the Tsar fell seriously ill with a kidney disease and his son's marriage quite suddenly became a matter of state importance. Nicholas would hear of no one else but Alix, and there was nothing his parents could do but give in.

Alexander went downhill rapidly. In October he was obviously close to death. Alix, hastily summoned, reached Livadia in the Crimea on 23 October and the formal ceremony of betrothal took place in the Tsar's bedroom. Typically the dying man insisted on dressing in full uniform for the occasion. On 28 October Alix wrote in Nicholas's diary an interpolation prophetic of the future: 'Sweet child, your Sunny is praying for you and the beloved patient. Be firm and make the doctors come alone to you every day – so that you are first always to know – don't let others be put first and you left out – show your own mind and don't let others forget who you are.' On 1 November 1894 the mighty Alexander died aged forty-nine and at the age of twenty-six Nicholas II assumed the title of Autocrat, Tsar and Emperor of All the Russias.

Alix's reception into the Orthodox Church under the name of Alexandra Feodorovna and the marriage, on 26 November, took place in an atmosphere of deep mourning. Nicholas, flung into the business of state, could afford no time for a honeymoon. But the prime purpose of a royal marriage, whether a love match or one of policy, had to be fulfilled and Alexandra did not show herself laggard in her duty. The first child was born in October 1895 and three more followed in the next six years. Each birth proved an increasing disappointment, for all four of these children were girls. At last, on 12 August 1904, in the middle of the disastrous Russo-Japanese War, the cannon of St Petersburg thundered news of the event which, more than any other, was to change the course of Russian history. That day was born the unfortunate boy Alexis, the longed-for son to whom Alexandra transmitted Victoria's mutant gene for haemophilia.

The first sign showed itself by bleeding from the umbilicus when Alexis was six weeks old. Very soon the appearance of bruises, resulting from quite minor knocks while crawling or toddling, confirmed the diagnosis beyond doubt. Alexandra, a devotedly possessive mother to all her children, was forced to recognize that she had transmitted the terrible disease to her innocent son. The revelation came as a shock from which she never recovered. No one who has not experienced the bearing of a haemophiliac boy can fully enter into the mother's agony. She enters a dark, sunless world of loneliness. If the boy is heir to a throne, the distress must be all the greater, for no one can be told and life becomes a lie.

Such is the reason for the withdrawal of Nicholas and Alexandra into seclusion at Tsarskoie Selo, for their bourgeois family life amid a dull and restricted court circle. In many ways Alexandra resembled her grandmother Victoria. She hid her despair at Tsarskoie just as did Victoria in the suburban castle of Windsor when robbed of her beloved Albert. They were both dominant personalities, but both demanded to be dominated and both chose their masters from the lower ranks of society. Victoria had her John Brown and her Munshi, Alexandra had her drunken peasant. Existence such as this inevitably bred rumour. At one time popular gossip told that the hidden Victoria had followed her grandfather into insanity. Petersburg society whispered that the Tsarevitch could not be allowed in public because he suffered from epilepsy or congenital idiocy. And, as the haemophiliac boy was the only direct heir to the throne of Russia, the truth could not be told.

Nicholas could do nothing, nor could the doctors or courtiers. The prayers of royal chaplains were equally unavailing and supplications to orthodox saints went unanswered. But God could not entirely desert one who, like Alexandra, believed in His goodness so fervently, who worshipped Him so wholeheartedly. Somewhere there must exist a human of sufficient spiritual purity and strength to wring from God the miraculous intervention which alone could save the child Alexis. Because such a being was so ardently desired, his appearance was inevitable. It just happened that he took the form of Rasputin, a *staretz* or wandering holyman.

In July 1907 Alexis lay for three days at the point of death. Rasputin was summoned to Tsarskoie Selo by the Empress, on the advice of either a grand duchess or her dowdy but intimate friend Anna Vyroubova. The holy man sat quietly beside the boy's bed, held his hand, and whispered to him fairy stories and Siberian folk tales. Next day Alexis was free of pain and able to sit up. A temporary 'cure' by this kind of treatment is quite possible, for keeping the patient quietly at rest is half the battle.

The next incident falls into a quite different category. In September 1912, when Alexis was eight years old, the imperial family paid a visit to Bialowieza in East Poland. The boy fell when jumping out of a boat and sustained a large bruise on the upper part of his left thigh. He complained of severe pain so the family physician, Dr Eugene Botkin, confined him to bed for a few days. Two weeks later, when he seemed to have recovered, the family moved to Spala, a cramped and dark hunting box in dense forest. Alexis made no progress in these gloomy surroundings, seemed in discomfort, pale and unhappy. Alexandra decided that a long drive in an open carriage would do him good, but the roads were uneven and the carriage jolted unmercifully. After a few miles, Alexis began to suffer agonizing pain in his upper thigh and lower abdomen. His terrified mother ordered an immediate return. The homeward journey became a nightmare. It was obvious that Alexis must be put to bed under medical care as soon as possible, but any attempt to speed the horses resulted in increased jolting which caused the boy to scream in pain. By the time they reached Spala he was only semi-conscious.

When jumping out of the boat two weeks earlier, Alexis had fallen heavily on the butt end of an oar. The superficial bruising misled the doctors. He had ruptured a small blood vessel, deeply situated in either the upper part of the thigh or the internal abdominal wall. The bleeding was minimal so long as he remained quiet. The jolting of the carriage not only caused fresh bleeding but probably widened the wound in the small blood vessel which had already been injured.

Nothing would stop the haemorrhage. For eleven days Alexis hovered between life and death, exsanguinated, with a high temperature, tortured by pain. For eleven days Alexandra sat beside his bed, hardly sleeping, snatching brief moments of rest on a sofa in his room. At last the surgeon Feodorov warned the Tsar that his people must be prepared for the heir's death. National prayers were ordered, bulletins issued, but the nature of the illness was not mentioned. On 10 October priests administered the Last Sacrament and that day the bulletin was worded in such a manner that the next could announce the death of the Tsarevitch.

That night Alexandra decided to call in Rasputin. He had gone home to Siberia and could only be reached by telegraph. He did not immediately board a train and rush to Spala. Instead he telegraphed back: 'God has seen your tears and heard your prayers. Do not grieve. The Little One will not die. Do not permit the doctors to bother him too much.'

Twenty-four hours later the bleeding stopped.

There is no doubt that this story is substantially true. Unless the doctors were parties to some mysterious plot, it is also inexplicable. But that does not affect the outcome. Can we wonder that Rasputin now became essential to the mother of Alexis? Is it probable that any report of bad behaviour would turn her against him? Here is the one man for whom she had been praying, a man who possessed the miraculous power to intercede directly and successfully with God. Since God listened to him, Rasputin must be a good man. Since he was a good man, anyone who opposed his will or spoke evil of him must be bad. It was as simple as that.

Many books and learned articles have been written about the man Grigori Efimovich, known as Rasputin, but he remains a mystery. Here we are concerned only with his strange relationship with the Tsaritsa and her son, and the effect his domination of her exerted upon the future of Russia. Rasputin, born in the Siberian village of Pokrovskoie about 1860 or 1865, first appeared on the St Petersburg scene in 1903. On 1 November 1905 the Tsar entered in his diary: 'We have today met a man of God, Gregory, from the province of Tobolsk.' 'Holy fools', soothsayers and monstrosities had always formed part of the Russian court retinue. Rasputin was not the first wonder-worker to gain access to the closed circle of the imperial family. Alexandra, desperate for a male child, had at one time been so influenced by a charlatan named Philippe Nizier-Vachot that she had developed a pseudocyesis or false pregnancy. Rasputin rarely visited the royal family, probably not more than half a dozen times in any one year, but his association with Tsarskoie Selo, his intimacy with some of the grand duchesses, wealthy industrialists and wives of the nobility, his public drunkenness and open lechery, were reported in the press (uncensored after 1905) and alarmed many responsible Russian leaders.

As one of the few outsiders to gain admission to the closed circle of Tsarskoie Selo, Rasputin was obviously of use to anyone who desired to influence governmental policy. He could hardly be expected to choose his clientele wisely, and this is the worst, most disastrous aspect of his hold on the imperial family. But, even in the days when he was unknowingly destroying all confidence in the regime, Rasputin's advice was by no means always bad. He possessed plenty of common sense and he knew his fellow peasants. During the 1914 war he continually urged more equitable division of food supplies and he prophesied serious trouble unless something was done to speed up distribution and so prevent long queues waiting for hours in the bitter cold. His prophecy proved correct, for the revolution of March 1917 would start in the food queues of Petrograd. Had the Empress been less dependent on him, his presence at court could have been a stabilizing influence, for the majority of peasants were less impressed by stories of his orgies than by the fact that one of their own number had broken through the barrier of the nobles to reach their Little Father the Tsar.

And what of his ability to arrest the internal bleeding which caused Alexis agonizing pain and jeopardized his life? Was he in league with the royal physicians who told him the exact moment at which to exercise his alleged power? Did he have access to 'mysterious Tibetan remedies' supplied by the quack doctor Peter Badmaiev? Was it done by hypnosis? Had he stumbled on the possibility that all disease, even uncontrollable haemorrhage, may be psychosomatic and that cure can be aided by psychiatric treatment? Or was it just luck? We shall never know the answer to these questions, but the essential fact is that Alexandra firmly believed in Rasputin's power.

There is evidence that the Tsar did not altogether share his wife's obsession. Nowhere in his diary nor in his letters to his mother and to Alexandra, does he so much as mention the miraculous power of Rasputin. He attributed the recovery at Spala to administration of the Last Sacrament. Nicholas regarded Rasputin as an ordinary Russian peasant: 'He is just a good, religious, simple-minded Russian,' he wrote. 'When in trouble or assailed by doubts, I like to have a talk with him, and invariably feel at peace afterwards.' The Tsar, who received the police reports, must have known much better than Alexandra of Rasputin's scandalous life, and he was no doubt at times disturbed by her dependence upon one who, however good and simple, behaved in so dissolute a fashion. There is a story that one of his favourite courtiers, Admiral Nilov, dared to ask the Tsar why he continued to put up with Rasputin's insolent behaviour. 'Better Rasputin than hysterics,' answered Nicholas shortly.

In July 1914, when war with Germany became imminent, Rasputin was at home in Siberia, convalescing from a stab wound. On hearing of the order for mobilization, he telegraphed to Tsarskoie Selo: 'Let Papa not plan war for with war will come the end of Russia and yourselves and you will lose to the last man.' The Tsar angrily tore the telegram to pieces. He wished to take immediate command of his beloved army and was only with great difficulty persuaded to appoint as commander-in-chief Grand Duke Nicholas Nicholaievitch, the most experienced soldier in the imperial family. The war went badly for unprepared Russia. The Battle of Tannenberg on 26–30 August saved France by diverting German troops from the western front but almost destroyed the regular army. Lack of munitions continually hampered recovery. Although Russia achieved some startling successes against Austria, she could make no headway against Germany. By August 1915 most of Russian Poland had been lost, and nearly four million men killed, wounded or captured. The Tsar now decided to take supreme command. He did so against the advice of all his ministers, but with the enthusiastic support of Alexandra.

Her eagerness for this absurd if understandable move on the Tsar's part was dictated by her determination that her husband must never be second to anyone in the empire. The royal couple usually corresponded with each other in English whether by letter or telegraph. On 24 June 1915 Alexandra had written to Nicholas, then touring the front line, 'Sweetheart needs pushing always and to be reminded that he is the Emperor and can do whatsoever pleases him – you never profit of this – you must show you have a way and will of yr. own, and are not led by N [Grand Duke Nicholas] and his staff, who direct yr. movements and whose permission you have to ask before going anywhere. No, go alone, without N by yr. very own self, bring the blessing of yr. presence to them.'

From 5 September 1915, when Nicholas left Tsarskoie Selo to take over command of his armies, until 20 March 1917, the day before his arrest at Moghilev, we can follow the tragic and almost incredible events of these last months of tsardom through the letters which passed between Nicholas and his wife. This series of letters forms one of the most astonishing and important of historical archives. But we cannot possibly understand them unless we recognize and sympathize with the terrible dependence of these unfortunate parents upon the only person who could restore their beloved son to health.

On 4 September 1915 Alexandra wrote her husband a letter to await his arrival at headquarters: 'Do not fear for what remains behind . . .

Lovy, I am here, don't laugh at silly old wifey, but she has trousers on unseen.' Nicholas was overjoyed: 'Think, my wifey, will you not come to the assistance of your hubby now that he is absent? What a pity that you have not been fulfilling this duty for a long time or at least during the war!' On 10 September Alexandra accepted her commission: 'Oh Sweetheart I am so touched you want my help, I am always ready to do anything for you, only never liked mixing up without being asked.' So, by these few absurdly childish words, was the supreme government of Russia handed over to the Empress. Loving power, she gladly accepted. But she still demanded to be dominated. There was only one man upon whom she could lean and that man was Rasputin.

The scandal of Rasputin did not become an urgent problem until the Empress Alexandra began tampering with governmental affairs at the end of 1915. The Tsar started his reign determined to uphold the principle of autocracy but, in the near revolution of 1905, he accepted a compromise, a form of parliamentary government known as the Imperial Duma. Alexandra detested the Duma for two reasons. First, this body instigated a public enquiry into the scandalous behaviour of Rasputin in 1911. Secondly, the very existence of an elected Duma implied a check on the absolute authority of her husband and, worse still, upon the future autocracy of her son. Her sick fear for the child's life was translated into a determination that he must reign as the all-powerful monarch. To this end, Nicholas must himself be Ivan the Terrible, Peter the Great, a harsh tyrant who could transmit unchallenged power to his son. She returns to the theme again and again: 'For Baby's sake we must be firm as otherwise his inheritance will be awful, as with his character he won't bow down to others but be his own master.' 'We must give a strong country to Baby, and dare not be weak – for his sake, else he will have a yet harder reign, setting our faults to right and drawing the reins in tightly which you have let loose.' 'He has a strong will and mind of his own, don't let things slip through your fingers and make him have to build up all again.' Such was the driving force which steered Nicholas into the fatal and avoidable errors of his last eighteen months in power.

At the outbreak of war the Premier had been a wily old bureaucrat named Goremykin, who held that ministers were no better than butlers to the Tsar. Even he protested against the Tsar's decision to take command and was unexpectedly dismissed on 2 February 1916, to be replaced by B.V. Stürmer, a Master of Ceremonies at the Palace. There is little doubt that Alexandra had suggested his name. At first he showed himself a firm friend of Rasputin and received Alexandra's support, being granted the additional and key appointment of Minister of the Interior. He knew nothing of his duties and made less attempt to carry them out. Even had he been capable, Stürmer's Teutonic name would have rendered him suspect. As it was, many influential people, among them the allied ambassadors, thought he would urge the Tsar to conclude a separate peace with Germany. The Duma launched an angry attack on him at the beginning of November. Having already described him as 'such a devoted, honest, sure man', on 7 November 1916 Alexandra wrote to Nicholas: 'for the quiet of the Duma, Stürmer ought to say he is ill and go and rest for three weeks – being the red flag for that madhouse, it's better he should disappear for a bit and then in December when they will have cleared out – return again.'

Nicholas agreed with his wife's description: 'He, as you say rightly, acts as a red flag not only to the Duma, but to the whole country, alas! I hear this from all sides, nobody believes in him. Alas! I am afraid he will have to go altogether.' On 22 November he dismissed Stürmer from both offices and appointed the senior member of the Cabinet, the Minister of Transport A.F. Trepov, to be temporary Premier. Alexandra was not in the least pleased: 'Trepov, I personally do not like and can never have the same feeling for him as to old Goremykin and Stürmer . . . if he does not trust me or our Friend, things will be difficult. I told Stürmer to tell him how to behave about Gregory and to safeguard him always.'

Trepov lasted until January 1917, to be replaced by the final Tsarist prime minister, Prince Nicholas Golytzin, whom Bernard Pares described as 'an honest old gentleman in weak health, who was known to the empress as her deputy-chairman of a charitable committee'. Golytzin, horror-struck at the proposal, pleaded his infirmities and inexperience but could not disobey the direct imperial command. He certainly need not have worried for neither he nor Trepov counted for anything in these last days of tsardom. The Empress and Rasputin had found the ideal partner to complete a triumvirate in the person of A.D. Protopopov, first an acting minister, then the last tsarist Minister of the Interior.

At first sight Protopopov seems a very sensible choice, for he was a Vice-President of the Duma. In fact he was hopelessly unsuited even for his first post, to which he was appointed on 23 September 1916, after repeated appeals from Alexandra to the Tsar. Some years before, he had suffered from syphilis and been treated with 'mysterious Tibetan remedies' by the charlatan Badmaiev, who was a possible source of

Rasputin's success with the Tsarevitch and one of the more unsavoury members of 'the Rasputin gang'. There is little doubt that Protopopov now suffered from the cerebral form of late syphilis known as GPI. Many Russians who had contact with him as minister regarded him as insane. He knew nothing of his work and spent most of his time when Minister of the Interior in drawing up fantastic plans, illustrated by complicated graphs and charts, for sweeping reforms of the army, the government and the whole empire. He rarely troubled to attend meetings of the Cabinet and wisely kept away from the Duma.

Nicholas doubted the wisdom of retaining a lunatic as minister in charge of internal affairs. On 10 November 1916 he wrote to his wife: 'I am sorry for Prot – he is a good, honest man, but he jumps from one idea to another and cannot make up his mind on anything. I noticed that from the beginning. They say that a few years ago he was not quite normal after a certain illness (when he sought the advice of Badmaiev). It is risky to leave the Ministry of Internal Affairs in the hands of such a man in these times. . . . Only, I beg of you, do not drag our Friend into this. The responsibility is with me, and therefore I wish to be free in my choice.' But the Tsar was not 'free in his choice', for 'our Friend' Rasputin had decided that Protopopov must remain. Alexandra delivered one of her heaviest broadsides on her husband: 'I entreat you don't go and change Protopopov now – he is honestly for us. Oh Lovy, you can trust me. I may not be clever enough – but I have a strong feeling and that helps more than the brain often. Don't change anybody until we meet, I entreat you, let's talk it over quietly together. Protopopov venerates our Friend and will be blessed. He is not mad, the wife sees Badmaiev for her nerves only. Quieten me, promise, forgive, but it's for you and Baby that I fight.'

Alexandra had already arranged a visit to her husband at Moghilev. On 12 November, two days after writing this letter, she set out for headquarters and stayed for three weeks. It was not an easy visit, for Nicholas proved uncharacteristically obdurate. He argued that there was antipathy to Protopopov on every side. She pleaded with him to be 'firm', to be 'sharp and bitter', to show that he was the master who took no account of popular clamour. Above all, he must trust in Rasputin. A little while before the present crisis she had written: 'Ah, Lovy, I pray so hard to God to make you feel and realize that He is our caring, were He not here I don't know what might have happened. He saves us by His prayers and wise counsels and is our rock of faith and help.' It should be noticed that Rasputin is now not only 'our Friend' but merits the divine capital when referred to by a pronoun. On 4 December, the day that Alexandra left him, Nicholas wrote apologizing for having been so 'moody and unrestrained' during her visit. But she had got her way. Protopopov was confirmed in his office.

The Tsar, his wife and Rasputin were now, in the autumn of 1916, intensely unpopular among all classes in Russia. This hatred had developed in little less than eighteen months. Many well-meaning attempts were made to open the Tsar's eyes to the true position. His mother, several Grand Dukes, the British and French ambassadors, the President of the Duma, besought him to get rid of Rasputin and 'throw in his lot with the people'. Grand Duke Paul, Alexandra's favourite uncle by marriage, and her own elder sister Grand Duchess Elizabeth, pleaded with her to rid herself of Rasputin's evil influence. They tried to make her understand that his interference in military matters gave the impression that she was treacherously helping the German High Command. They all failed, for she would hear nothing against Rasputin. As a result, certain members of the imperial family decided upon direct action.

Unfortunately they could not agree on the best way to set about it. Most were of the opinion that Alexandra could now be considered insane, but they saw no method of removing her unless the Tsar abdicated. This extreme course was considered but rejected as too dangerous. At last they decided on the murder of Rasputin, arguing that his loss would force Alexandra into a state requiring asylum treatment and the pliable Tsar could then be persuaded to stop acting the commander-in-chief and rule in cooperation with the Duma. The murder was planned by Prince Felix Yusupov, nephew of the Tsar by marriage. He was assisted by Grand Duke Dmitri who was the Tsar's favourite cousin and son of Grand Duke Paul, and by V.M. Purishkevitch, an ardent monarchist and extreme right-wing member of the Duma.

The story of the sordid and ill-planned killing of Rasputin, on 30 December 1916, has been recounted so many times and with so many variations that it need not be discussed in detail here. There must be considerable doubt about the quantity of cyanide (if any at all) in the wine that he drank and the cakes that he ate, but he was certainly shot once with a revolver at point-blank range and a second time from a little further off. He was then thrust under the ice covering the River Neva, and subsequently found to have died only after inhaling water. All of this suggests that, if the other Romanovs were so inefficient as murderers, they would not have made better Tsars than Nicholas. The effect of Rasputin's death on Alexandra seems to have been the reverse of that expected. So far from relapsing into hopeless mania, she quickly recovered after the initial shock. One of the most remarkable chapters in the whole story is the amazing fortitude of this sick woman who supported the family throughout the miseries and indignities of the next eighteen months.

The Tsar was the one who collapsed. On his wife's urgent demand, he hurried back from headquarters to Tsarskoie Selo where he stayed for just over two months. All who met him during this time were startled by his changed appearance and manner. The old charm had gone, his face became lined and apathetic, the whites of his eyes yellowed and the pupils lacked lustre. He was moody, hesitant, sometimes seeming not to know the day of the week nor to be aware of his surroundings. Some thought that he drank heavily or took drugs ('supplied by Badmaiev'). There is no evidence in support of either allegation but we can postulate both a psychological and a physical reason for his collapse. During the past eighteen months the Tsar had not only lived under intense strain but had become almost completely isolated, for all his advisers and his old devoted friends had either resigned or been removed by order of Alexandra. He must have known that his isolation resulted from loyalty to his wife and her concept of Rasputin. The latter had become essential to her and therefore must be retained at all costs. Now Rasputin had gone and Alexandra seemed virtually unmoved. All these sacrifices and errors had been unnecessary.

The physical reason is to be found in two of the Tsar's letters. Back in June 1915 he had replied to Alexandra's enquiry: 'Yes, my darling, I am beginning to feel my old heart. The first time it was in August of last year, after the Samsonov catastrophe, and again now – it feels so heavy in the left side when I breathe.' On 11 March 1917, when he had returned to headquarters, there is a much more ominous paragraph: 'This morning during the service, I felt an excruciating pain in the chest, which lasted for a quarter of an hour. I could hardly stand the service out, and my forehead was covered with drops of perspiration. I cannot understand what it could have been, because I had no palpitation of the heart, but later it disappeared, vanishing suddenly when I knelt before the image of the Holy Virgin. If this occurs again I shall tell Feodorov.' The Tsar appears to have suffered a small coronary infarct or perhaps an attack of angina.

Three days earlier Nicholas had left Tsarskoie Selo for headquarters, having been urgently summoned by General Alexeiv, probably because the discipline of some units gave cause for alarm. On the same day disorders broke out in Petrograd. The weather had been unusually severe, even for a Russian winter. The railways were brought almost to a standstill by the number of engines with boilers cracked by frost, and little coal or food could reach the city. There is said to have been plenty of flour but too little fuel to bake bread. The Duma furiously attacked the government's food policy, while large crowds wandered aimlessly about the streets demanding bread, but doing little damage and quietly dispersing when ordered by the police. Next day the crowds increased and some food shops were looted. Cossacks helped the police to restore order, but neither demonstrators nor law enforcers seemed willing to attack one another.

Not until Saturday 10 March did any political flavour appear in the demonstrations. A few of the crowd carried red flags and there were some shouts of 'Down with the German woman.' In other respects the disorders were little more than a rather widespread food-riot. On Sunday the mood became more ugly and the police summoned troops who fired on the crowd. The Pavlovsky Regiment mutinied and refused to fire but were disarmed by the famous Preobrazhensky Guards. Order had been restored by nightfall but during the day the Volynsky Regiment had proved unreliable and returned to barracks. That night they mutinied and killed at least one officer. On Monday morning, 12 March, they joined the crowd on the streets. This was the action which changed an aimless bread-riot into a revolution.

In fact Russia had had no effective government since the preceding Friday. That day Alexis and his sister Olga went down with measles, to be followed shortly by the three other girls and Anna Vyroubova. Alexandra nursed them all devotedly and had no time left to spend on business. Protopopov ruled almost alone with such help as he could receive from the shade of Rasputin conjured up in a series of spiritualistic seances.

Later on Monday 12 March Alexander Kerensky, a left-wing Duma deputy, advised the Volynsky to go to the Tauride Palace where the Duma met. The Volynsky sent deputations to all regiments in the garrison inviting them to leave their barracks and join them 'in defence of the Duma'. By evening the whole of the Petrograd garrison had mutinied except for three companies of the Ismailovsky Guards and three companies of Chasseurs. Urgent messages were sent from the Duma to the Tsar at headquarters.

The Duma had now become the centre of a kind of mob rule, feebly trying to restore order with the alternate help and opposition of the Council (Soviet) of Workers and Soldiers, hastily elected by show of hands on the basis of one representative per thousand. During the night of 14/15 March, after much angry discussion, Duma and Soviet agreed that Nicholas must abdicate but the Tsardom should continue with Alexis as constitutional monarch under the regency of his uncle Grand Duke Michael. Nicholas had attempted to reach Tsarskoie Selo but had been turned back and was now at Pskov in contact with Army command. Two members of the Duma, Alexander Guchkov and Basil Shulgin, drew up a deed of abdication and left for Pskov at dawn on 15 March.

Meanwhile the generals had been conferring and had also decided that Nicholas must abdicate. He consented after some hesitation and in the afternoon of 15 March composed his own deed, naming Alexis as his successor and his brother Michael as regent. Then he consulted the surgeon Feodorov and changed his mind. When Guchkov and Shulgin arrived at ten o'clock that night he told them he could not be parted from his haemophiliac son. He would abdicate, but only in favour of Grand Duke Michael.

The Duma representatives, both monarchists, were horrified, for Nicholas had wrecked the whole plan. A boy of twelve under the tutelage of the Duma might have been acceptable. Michael would be just another Romanov autocrat. And so it turned out, for when the deputies proclaimed Tsar Michael at the Petrograd station, they were howled down by the crowd and had difficulty in escaping from an angry mob. Twenty-four hours later Michael, too, abdicated the crown of Russia. Haemophilia had destroyed the last chance of saving the Romanov dynasty.

There followed a summer of anarchy, disillusion and defeat under the ineffectual rule of a Provisional Government awaiting confirmation by a Constituent Assembly to be elected in December. But the only call which would rally the despairing people of Russia in the autumn of 1917 was that of bread and land and peace. These the minority Bolshevik party promised them and so came to power. In the civil war which followed, the imperial family were taken to the Bolshevik-held mining town of Ekaterinberg on the eastern side of the Ural Mountains. There, on the night of 16 July 1918, they were all shot by order of the Ekaterinberg Soviet. They died as they had always lived, a united family.

Eighty years later, to the very day, the remains of most of the Romanov victims killed in Ekaterinberg were given a ceremonial reburial in the former capital of the tsarist empire. By 1998, after the ending of Soviet rule some seven years earlier, their bones were returned to a city no longer called Leningrad, but to one with the restored name of St Petersburg. There the coffins containing the remains of Nicholas and Alexandra, with those of their daughters Olga, Tatiana and Anastasia, and of four faithful servants, were entombed together in a chapel of the Romanov mausoleum within the fortress cathedral of St Peter and St Paul. As yet, the relics of the third-born daughter Marie remain undiscovered. And so, too, do those of the boy who is surely the most tragic single figure in the tale which links Queen Victoria to the fate of the Russian imperial house – the haemophiliac Tsarevich Alexis himself.

One notable feature of the ceremonies in St Petersburg was the attendance of about fifty Romanov relations of varying degrees of kinship to Nicholas II. Some of these visitors took the opportunity of inspecting, at her moorings on the River Neva, the cruiser *Aurora* of the former Imperial Navy, the guns of which had threatened the ministers of the Provisional Government in the Winter Palace at the start of the Bolshevik coup and thus inaugurated the seven decades of communist dictatorship. No doubt these members of the imperial family derived some satisfaction from the recent collapse of the Soviets, but they were clearly less pleased to discover that the funeral service of the last of the Romanov rulers had been denied the personal presence and spiritual approval of the Patriarch of St Petersburg. He had dismissed the obsequies as meaningless, giving as the reason his dogmatic belief that forensic DNA-testing was utterly incapable of authenticating the imperial remains. Sadly, such conduct merely served to demonstrate – nearly fifty years after Watson and Crick established the structure of the DNA molecule and no less than a century after the rediscovery of Mendel's hereditary elements – that no understanding of genetics had yet penetrated the minds of those who simply found it convenient to ignore or deride much of modern science and of biology in particular. As the twentieth century drew to a close, Russians were experiencing grave difficulty in elaborating stable governmental and economic structures for their post-Soviet era of development. It was therefore all the more regrettable that, in July 1998, at the solemn moment of political reconciliation symbolized by the reburial of the Tsar, they should find ecclesiastical obscurantism, one of the major defects of the tsarist regime, again added to the many problems facing Russia. Recalling the agonies of the Revolution and civil war, followed by the terrors of Stalin's Gulag system, one is moved to wonder whether the change from an inefficient tsarist dictatorship to an even more oppressive communist regime had been of any benefit to the world in general and to the Russian people in particular. A great opportunity wasted may have been the true legacy of Victoria's haemophiliac gene.

CHAPTER TEN

Mob Hysteria and Mass Suggestion

Broadly speaking there are two main types of disease, somatic and psychiatric. Somatic, sometimes called organic disease, is demonstrable by lesions which doctors can identify by the patient's description of the symptoms and the physical signs which they can elucidate, using the ancient methods of palpation and auscultation or more modern aids such as X-rays and blood tests. In psychiatric or emotional disease there is no demonstrable physical lesion but the patient suffers from very real symptoms. Cancer is a somatic disease recognizable by definite signs and symptoms. Cancerophobia is a fairly common psychiatric disorder in which the patient may be able to present symptoms suggestive of cancer but no signs demonstrable on physical examination. The above is an over-simplification because disease is seldom purely somatic or purely psychiatric. The very fact that the patient is ill may give rise to symptoms which cannot be related to a physical cause. Troubles such as financial difficulties, frustration, sleeplessness and loss of appetite may result in psychiatric symptoms that are not part of the somatic disease from which the patient is suffering. Conversely, a psychiatric illness will often produce physical signs such as tics, paralyses or disorders of appetite which are not symptoms of the disease itself.

For these reasons we may state that all disease is to a greater or lesser degree psychosomatic. Consider two examples, discussed in previous chapters. Henry VIII almost certainly suffered from the somatic infection syphilis. If so, the effects were exaggerated by his powerful position, by his arrogance and intolerance. The two latter are psychiatric defects. His main trouble was undoubtedly a somatic disease (or diseases, if preferred) and the psychiatric element was secondary. Napoleon, in contrast, suffered from a number of minor somatic ills throughout his life but his real illness was psychiatric. He conceived himself to be master of the world and thus a greater man than he really was.

We find an instructive example of this psychosomatic combination in the puzzling case of Joan of Arc. Born of a prosperous peasant family at Domremy in Lorraine, Joan began to hear mysterious voices at the age of thirteen, about the year 1425. She later claimed that her voices came from St Michael, St Margaret and St Catherine. The voices told her that she had been chosen by God to deliver France from the English invader. They commanded her to go to the Dauphin and persuade him to be crowned king. His mission must be to drive the English and Burgundians from France and to dedicate his cleansed kingdom to the service of God. In this, Joan was undoubtedly abnormal, for normal people do not hear supernatural voices nor do they see visions of saints. But Joan was certainly not insane, any more than Florence Nightingale can be regarded as insane because she heard God speaking to her in her seventeenth year. Joan showed herself to be thoroughly practical, as did Miss Nightingale, and elaborated a policy which was ultimately successful. It is therefore unwise to dismiss her voices and her visions as the hallucinations of a diseased mind. While admitting that she was a 'strange girl', that is she did not behave as would an ordinary girl, we ought to look for a somatic cause of these aberrations of sight and hearing.

The only real evidence is to be found in the statements which she made at her trial before the Bishop of Beauvais in February–March 1431. At first Joan showed great unwillingness to speak of her heavenly visitors. Her judges were anxious to show that the Black Arts had inspired her and, at one point, suggested drug addiction. They asked what she had done with her mandragora. Joan replied: 'I have no mandragora and never had any. I have heard it said that near to my town there is one. I have heard it said that it is a thing evil and dangerous. I know not what use it is.'

She defended herself bravely and firmly throughout the trial. Asked about the voices, she told the Court that she first heard them at age thirteen and that they frightened her. She could not understand what they tried to tell her until the third time they spoke to her. They spoke again and again but she could never understand their meaning unless her surroundings were perfectly quiet. The figures of the saints, who seemed to be speaking, did not appear until later. She refused to give any details of their physical appearance but said she embraced them and they had a pleasant odour. On further questioning, she twice declared that the apparitions frightened her so much that she fell on her knees. Then comes, from a medical point of view, her most significant statement: 'I heard the voice on the right hand side . . . and rarely do I hear it without a brightness. The brightness comes from the same side as the voice is heard. It is usually a great light.' On one occasion she was asleep and the Voice woke her, not by touch but by sound alone. The Voice did not seem to be in the cell where Joan slept but she was sure it was somewhere in the castle building. She thanked the Voice by getting up, sitting down on the bed and clasping her hands.

A little more evidence is to be found in the Trial of Rehabilitation held in 1456, twenty-five years after Joan died at the stake. Two priests testified that they visited her in her cell on the morning of her burning. She told them that her saints, or spirits, appeared to her in the form of minute specks, in great numbers and of the smallest size. The only other suggestive evidence is the rather mysterious illness which attacked her during her trial, causing it to be adjourned for three days. Her gaolers attributed this to eating shad, a great Loire delicacy, while Joan herself blamed a carp sent to her by the Bishop of Beauvais. John Tiphaine, the surgeon who attended her, made enquiry and found that she had been unwell, with vomiting, on several occasions and that the present attack only differed from the others in being rather more prolonged.

There is not enough here to attempt a definite and exact diagnosis but sufficient to hazard a guess. Joan's disability started at the age of puberty. She suffered from intermittent attacks of tinnitus, the singing or ringing in the ears, which some people translate into speech. (A patient of one of the present writers complained of the hymn *Onward Christian Soldiers* repeated over and over again in her ears). Joan's tinnitus was unilateral, on the right side only, again a quite common manifestation. She also suffered from visual disturbance which took the form of bright or flashing light mingled with dancing black specks. The specks are a common symptom of nausea, in Joan's case sometimes so severe that she actually vomited. At the same time she experienced giddiness, which forced her to sit down or fall on her knees. Joan probably suffered from the syndrome first described by Prosper Menière as aural vertigo in 1861, now usually known as Menière's Disease.

But Joan's somatic disorder, whatever it may have been, is obviously only of secondary importance in the story. She had convinced herself that her Voices required her to liberate France. So convinced was she of her mission that she convinced many others and thus sparked off a great mass movement. France was in a dreadful state, her people hopeless after seventy years of unsuccessful warfare and foreign occupation. Joan infused her countrymen with a new hope by her own example. In her case we can identify with certainty the one person who triggered off a great mass-change in behaviour. There are many examples in history of these mass changes. Sometimes we can select the individual or the incident which has started a chain reaction but in other cases we can detect no individual stimulus, for there seems to have been a general perception that something which has been accepted without question is no longer desirable. A simple example is the attitude of the British to the hunting of foxes and deer. At the beginning of the twentieth century hunting was generally regarded as a desirable and colourful 'sport', the meet being an occasion when all classes mingled together and those who could not afford horses followed on foot. Less than a hundred years later the 'sport' had aroused massive opposition as being cruel to animals and there was wide demand for its abolition. In this case no one could possibly identify an individual who started a considerable mass movement, a change in the way of thinking and pattern of behaviour.

Foxes have been hunted as vermin and deer as human food for many centuries and it is only in very recent years that the feelings of the animal have aroused concern. Consideration for the animal may be regarded as an advance in human civilization, the imposition of another in a series of covering skins. Underneath the skins there still lie hidden the primitive instincts of animal Man. Fear, hate, anger, greed, self-preservation and preservation of the human race are ever-present. There comes a time in the life of any individual when the skins break and a primitive instinct emerges. Then the control imposed by civilization is lost and we may rightly speak of the individual's bestial rage or animal fear.

But Man is a gregarious animal and such creatures do not like to be different from their fellows, for fear that they may be cast out of the pack. This is why we tend to copy one another and, given the right conditions, why unreasoning and causeless fear or anger can pass from the individual into a crowd. Men and women who are apparently sensible in their face-to-face dealings with each other as individuals may, as part of the mass, suffer a persistent delusion that whole categories of their fellow-beings are inimical. There are all too many instances in world history when one crowd has regarded another, very similar crowd, as monstrous, as tools of the devil, as non-men, as instruments of destruction. This is one of the phenomena to which the name mob hysteria has often been attached.

Mob hysteria in its simplest form can be exemplified by the not infrequent occurrence of mass fainting. One worker faints on the factory floor, another follows, and a dozen are 'out' within a few minutes. Sometimes an organic cause – perhaps an overheated workshop or noxious fumes – is apparent. Quite often there is no obvious cause. In fact the first girl fainted because she was suffering excessive blood-loss from her period, or the man had come to work without breakfast. The remainder were cases of 'sympathetic fainting'. The fainting is hysterical or emotional in that it has no physical cause.

Fear can also be contagious and hysterical, sometimes with tragic results. A well-known example occurred on 30 May 1883, soon after the new Brooklyn to Manhattan bridge was first opened. Somehow an unreasoning fear that the structure was on the point of collapse swept through the crowd. In the rush to get off the bridge, which was perfectly safe, twelve people were trampled to death and twenty-six injured. The precipitating cause of panic has never been identified. A similar baseless panic fear caused many deaths on the stairway leading to a deep air-raid shelter during a flying-bomb attack on London in 1944.

Sympathetic fainting and panic fear depend upon mass suggestion, the fainting or panic of one individual suggesting to others that they should do the same. This is how the crowd can be manipulated. A good example is the hysteria which followed the tragic death of Princess Diana on 31 August 1997. Death of a passenger, sometimes attractive or well-known, when the car driver is under the influence of alcohol, is unfortunately too common an event to arouse much public attention. The princess was certainly attractive, her marital difficulties aroused sympathy, and a relatively small circle of people knew of and admired her love of children and her humane efforts to outlaw land-mines. Had an enquirer gone from house to house anywhere in Britain a few days before the accident and asked the simple question 'What do you know of Princess Diana?', many of the answers would have run along the lines of 'Not very much at all.' Yet, less than a week later, thousands of these people, united by a mass process of imitative behaviour, would be depositing bunches of flowers at the Kensington Palace gates as though mourning a close relation or an intimate friend.

Such is the power of the media today and such has been the power of demagogues in the past, whether ranting from their cathedral pulpits or on a street corner soapbox. The wise ruler knows only too well that the crowd which cheered him vociferously last week may be crying for his blood tomorrow. Patriotic loyalty to the crown can be aroused by appeal to the mob, but so too can the more primitive urges of fear, hate and anger. These suggest to the individual that he or she should take immediate and preferably violent action, but there may be nothing to hit or the object of our protest may be too strong for us. When this demand for immediate action transfers itself from the individual to the crowd a mass movement will result. This may take a bizarre form because the participants cannot translate their protest effectively.

The dancing mania of medieval Germany is an example of the latter. We can probably uncover an initiating cause, ergot of rye. Rye, a common bread-corn in northern Europe, sometimes becomes infected with *Claviceps* fungus in wet seasons. The resultant product, ergot, is chemically complex. One of the compounds present is D-lysergic acid diethylamide, commonly known as LSD, the initials of its Swiss name. This was one of the drugs which used to be taken at pop-music sessions in the 1960s because it increases the response to rhythm. Other effects include hallucinations, agitation and intensely coloured vision.

Small outbreaks of dancing mania occurred in Germany from early in the Middle Ages until late in the sixteenth century. The phenomenon was not confined to Germany but has been reported from many countries. The last known 'dancing epidemic' affecting a number of people was observed in 1911 close to the Mediterranean outlet of the Dardanelles. The most serious incident started at Aix-la-Chapelle in July 1374. Sufferers danced uncontrollably in the streets, screaming and foaming at the mouth. Many suffered hallucinations, some declaring they were immersed in a sea of blood, others claiming to have seen the heavens open to reveal Christ enthroned with the Virgin Mary.

At first these dancers had no definite aim but they rapidly gained adherents who imitated their unrestrained movements. Thousands became affected and, as the craze grew, it crystallized into anti-clerical protest largely directed against the hated Prince-Bishops. Streams of dancers invaded the Low Countries and moved along the Rhine, gathering new adherents throughout Germany. Mobs stormed monastic houses, chased out abbots and priors, shouted filthy abuse at priests. It is interesting that no ruling Prince-Bishop was killed or even dislodged. In the later stages, the dancers often appeared insensitive to quite severe pain or other external stimuli, a symptom of hysteria rather than LSD intoxication. The mania bears a marked resemblance to the flagellant movement which we noticed in Chapter Two. It will be remembered that this started as an intercession against plague and developed into a protest against riches, the Church and established government.

Both flagellant movement and dancing mania produced increased sexual activity. Violent action and violent emotion both stimulate the most primitive instinct, the sexual urge or instinct of race preservation. This is why the dance is part of the ritual of witchcraft. The witch craze is mysterious in more than one respect. It has been convincingly argued that it is essentially a devil doctrine purposively established by the Church during the early Middle Ages, which might account for the marked similarity in witch practices in widely separated countries. There is little evidence that apostles of the diabolical religion travelled extensively in search of converts, but there is much to suggest a wide distribution of knowledge through the written denunciations made by churchmen.

The mob hysteria of the cult and the hysteria of those who would suppress the cult are of equal interest. We cannot divorce the craft from the hunt. If witch-hunting took the form of a mass movement at times, then so did witchcraft itself. The cult became widespread at the same periods as did suppression. Thus, when we speak of the witch craze, we should apply the term both to the witch and to the hunter. The three main periods of witch hysteria roughly coincide with the Renaissance, the Protestant Reformation and the Catholic Counter-Reformation. Within each of these we observe a loosening of the hold of conformity which in turn stimulated aberrations and repression. Witchcraft was only one of these aberrations and witch-hunting was only part of a general repression of non-conformity, practised by Catholic and Protestant alike.

The practice of witchcraft bears the stigmata of hysteria. The myth of the witch flying long distances on her broomstick to the sabbat is levitation, the sensation of being airborne, a symptom of hysteria. The sabbat itself with its wild exhausting dance, weird music and sexual orgy is mass hysteria. The feast of nauseous delicacies lacks any taste, the kiss or copulation with a diabolical leader holds no warmth. The witch often complains of formication, the sensation of ants crawling over her skin. The witch-finder searched with his bodkin for areas of anaesthesia on the suspect's body. All these are well-known symptoms of hysteria.

A witch, endowed with supposed diabolical power to bring disease and ill-fortune, must be an object of terror to the uninitiated. But we may be able to uncover an even more primitive urge for the witch-hunt. The witch is commonly, although by no means invariably, a woman who possesses the supernatural power. She is the embodiment of *feminine* evil. To the celibate priest, to the grim Protestant who believed in the subjection of women, she was a special object of hatred and fear. Such men saw in witchcraft not only an obscene parody of religion but a threat to male supremacy. The witch became a symbol of the primitive love-hate relationship, the age-old struggle for domination between the sexes.

The real increase in witch practices that occurred in times of unbridled repression bred panic exaggeration. Fear bred fear, hatred bred hatred, witches were seen everywhere. The gentle, scholarly Nicolas Remy of Lorraine sent between two thousand and three thousand victims to the stake in the years 1595 to 1616. The pious Archbishop of Trier burned 368 witches from twenty-two villages between 1587 and 1593, leaving only one woman alive in each of two villages in 1595. From 1623 until 1631 the Prince-Bishop of Würzburg burned over nine hundred people for witchcraft, including his own nephew, a number of children and nineteen priests. France, Germany, Switzerland, Spain, Sweden and Scotland all joined in this form of mass murder. Germany was the country worst affected, a fact that will have some significance later in the story. At the height of the terror, belief in witchcraft became an article of faith and to deny the existence of witches could lead to condemnation.

The worst excesses in England and the American colonies were associated with extreme puritanism. Though repression never equalled that on the European continent, two outbreaks are notorious. The first affected the eastern counties of England in 1644–7 when the puritanical parliamentary army was in the ascendant. The hysterical denunciations and accusations were instigated by Matthew Hopkins who, in 1645, procured a commission as Witch-finder General. An Ipswich lawyer, he journeyed about the countryside in search of witches, supported by a barrister named John Godbolt who had been appointed a judge for this special purpose by vote of parliament. Within just over a year the two villains hanged over sixty women in Essex alone, besides many others in Norfolk and Huntingdonshire. Hopkins published a treatise, *The Discovery of Witches*, in 1647, and in the same year was denounced as an imposter. He failed to pass the trial of swimming; that is, he floated when thrown into water with his hands and feet tied. He was condemned to be hanged as a sorcerer.

The American episode occurred at Salem, then a village about fifteen miles north-east of Boston, Massachusetts. The witch-craze began in 1692 with an accusation made by ten young girls that they had been bewitched by two old women and a West Indian slave named Tituba, property of the Revd Samuel Parris. The latter seems to have been largely responsible for fanning the hysteria which spread rapidly. Within four months hundreds of women had been arrested and tried. The judges condemned nineteen women to be hanged, one to be pressed to death for refusing to plead, and many to imprisonment.The hysteria passed almost as quickly as it had arisen and a swift reaction against the witch-hunters followed. In May 1693 Governor Phelps ordered the release of all prisoners held on a charge of witchcraft.

Cotton Mather, the Boston Congregational minister who was to become a Fellow of the Royal Society in 1713, played a curious part in this episode. He is sometimes named as the instigator of the hunt and there is no doubt that he firmly believed in witchcraft and wrote several papers on the subject before 1700. On the other hand he warned the judges of their unfair methods and that they had unjustly sentenced some of their victims. Whatever the truth may be, it is certainly of interest that a serious scientist, as was Mather, could have believed in the existence of witches.

Over two hundred years later the rise of Adolf Hitler and the Nazi party was to show what terrors can be inflicted when a diseased individual, a capacity for mass suggestion, a persecutory craze and a state of mob hysteria are brought together to infect a whole nation. Hitler himself unwittingly exemplifies how history may be affected not only by disease itself, but by the individual's ideas about disease. His concept of a diseased nation was based upon two assumptions. The first was that society is not merely comparable to a biological organism but that actually and for all purposes it is such an organism. Society is often compared to an organism in phrases such as 'the body politic'. But Hitler, like many before him, mistook the metaphor for reality. In *Mein Kampf* he declared: 'As Aryans, we can consider the state only as the living organism of a people.' His second assumption followed from the first and is the linchpin of his racist ideology: since human society is a biological organism, it can become diseased or degenerate in much the same way as the individual. Further, just as the union of two individuals may produce a physically or mentally inferior second generation, so the union of two societies or 'races' can result in the degeneration of the product.

In order to justify this hypothesis, Hitler had to postulate the existence of a 'pure stock'. So he intensified and developed the 'Aryan myth': the fallacy that Nordic Teutons are pure Aryans. Since he thought that the most immediate threat to Aryan rule and culture came from the supposed 'Jewish race', the Jew was represented as the leading degenerate element. Hitler's theory of heredity was based on the ancient idea of the literal blending of blood. Thus he was able to use such meaningless expressions as 'poisonous contamination of the race' and 'the pestilential adulteration of the blood'. Logic suggested a further extension of the disease metaphor. Since he regarded the 'Jewish race' as the major contaminant, he depicted the Jew as a bacillus or parasite sapping the vitality of the society in which he lived: 'On putting the probing knife carefully to that kind of abscess, one immediately discovered, like a maggot in a putrescent body, a little Jew who was often blinded by the sudden light.' This concept of disease lies at the heart of Hitler's vision of the universe and thus contributed to the most horrifying events in all recorded history. Yet, in one curious sense, Hitler was right. From 1918 until 1945 he did live in a diseased community. The disease was not physical but of the mind.

In the First World War Germany made greater sacrifices than any other belligerent. Victory seemed at last to be in sight in the spring of 1918. Russia had signed a humiliating peace treaty at Brest-Litovsk, Romania had surrendered, the German armies had broken the stalemate of trench warfare and were hurling the Allies back to Paris and the Channel ports. All this was announced to the German people in exultant communiques. But when the advance faltered, halted, turned to retreat, no inkling of the truth appeared in the press. Knowledge that the position was rapidly becoming hopeless remained almost confined to the High Command. The announcement at the beginning of October that the government was seeking peace terms stunned and bewildered the German nation. Up to that moment the home front stood unbroken and the news came as a shattering blow which produced near-panic. It is often forgotten that even on 11 November, when the world learnt of the Armistice, the German armies still held their lines on foreign soil and not a single Allied soldier had penetrated German territory.

The economic situation in Germany now moved from bad to worse. During the next months a demobilized army, flung on to a labour market already staggering under a burden of unemployment, added to the general discontent. Demand for reparation payments caused a fall in the mark, from 4 to the dollar in mid-1914 to 75 in July 1921 and to more than 17,000 in January 1923. In that month French troops occupied the industrial district of the Ruhr, cutting off 80 per cent of Germany's coal and steel production. By August 1923 the mark had fallen to four million to the dollar and to an unbelievable 4,200,000 million by 15 November. Total collapse of the currency resulted in loss of all savings, bankrupt businesses, mass unemployment and renewed food shortages. The foundations of German society were far more shaken by the collapse of the mark than by the war, the revolution of 1918 and the Treaty of Versailles combined.

Slowly Germany began to recover, only to be faced with the world depression which began in the USA in 1929 and intensified during the years 1930–1. German industry could not cope. In 1929 unemployment rose towards two million and by 1932 the figure was growing well beyond five millions. Germany was now a sick nation in that so many of her individual members were half-starved and idle, defeated and disillusioned, translating their sufferings into a fantasy of persecution.

This was the only Germany known to Hitler. He had no personal experience of the efficient, prosperous Germany of pre-1914, for he was not a German national. The son of a minor official in the Habsburg customs service, he was born on 20 April 1889 at Braunau on the border between Austria and Bavaria. His father Alois was an illegitimate child of Maria Anna Schicklgruber, the father not being certainly known but presumed to be Johann Georg Hiedler. Alois legally adopted the name 'Hitler' thirteen years before Adolf's birth. There is no evidence that J.G. Hiedler was a Jew, but Adolf may have believed this disputed grandfather to be partly Jewish. Here is one possible basis for Adolf Hitler's virulent anti-semitism, for there would have been no stigma of illegitimacy in the family tree had his grandmother not been seduced by a Jew. At the very least this seems a more likely explanation than the theory propounded by more than one writer that his obsession derived from some sexual experience with a Jewish prostitute.

Adolf Hitler spent his boyhood in a small village outside Linz in Upper Austria, where his father died in 1903, a few months before his son's fourteenth birthday. He made little progress in the local school except in such subjects as he himself desired to learn. Aged sixteen in 1905 he left school without acquiring the customary Leaving Certificate. He continued to live with his widowed mother whom he loved in his own strange way though he did nothing to support her financially. He became fired with the ambition to be a brilliant architect but made no attempt to undergo any regular training, preferring to fill notebooks with drawings and elaborate plans for rebuilding Linz. In 1907 he decided on an artist's career and applied to join the Academy of Fine Arts at Vienna. He failed the entrance examination and, when he applied again a year later, was not even permitted to retake it. His mother had died at the end of 1907. Early in 1908 Adolf, friendless, incompetent and work-shy, disappeared for five years into the Viennese world of cheap boarding-houses and odd jobs, shifting to Munich in 1913.

But Hitler was something more complex than a mere work-shy drop-out. It is now known that he invented some of the more squalid parts of his autobiographical account. In doing so, he was excusing himself, for Hitler is a good example of that most pathetic of beings, the would-be creative artist without talent or acquired ability. Of such are the dreamers who make dreams their master, in whose fantasies the great book is written, the picture painted, the symphony composed without any intermediate step from inception to completion. Their dreams never produce anything second-rate, for the figment of their minds is always a masterpiece. It naturally follows that they are themselves great and find themselves surrounded by a crowd of petty beings, who will not acknowledge their pre-eminence or allow them their dominating place, through jealousy, misunderstanding and ignorance. Thus the persistent illusion of grandeur is accompanied by hatred and contempt for their worthless fellows.

Adolf Hitler's early history clearly shows that he suffered from this type of paranoia, behaviour dependent on a fixed belief totally divorced from reality. He was of the schizophrenic type which believes itself to be the subject of persecution and whose actions are dictated by a revulsion against the supposed persecutors. Paranoia caused his indolence, his sudden bursts of feverish work when work was inescapable, his maniacal rages when affairs would not arrange themselves exactly as he wished, his alternating moods of sullen despair and irrational hope. But how on earth did such a man ever achieve supreme power?

He would never have done so had it not been for his service in the First World War. Had it not been for that service, his sordid career must have inevitably ended in gaol, by suicide or in an asylum. He was twenty-five years old in 1914 and war conditions gave him exactly what he urgently needed: inescapable reality, an outlet for violence, membership of a gang, the security of strict discipline. Hitler had managed to evade compulsory military duty before the war, but the moment it broke out he enlisted voluntarily. He did not join his own national Austrian army, but asked to be recruited into a Bavarian regiment forming part of the German forces. Hitler made a good soldier because he had voluntarily offered his services to a country which he admired and because he found in its army the stabilizing conformity he could no longer avoid. For this reason he ended the war more competent and more stable than he had been in 1914. But he had not been cured. He still suffered from paranoia, was still obsessed by the delusion that he towered far above his fellow-men.

Hitler seems to have always been mildly interested in politics, the type of political thought found in the beer-cellar and at the street corner. He is said to have expressed extreme opinions with intemperate violence, showing no control in face of reasoned opposition or restrained debate. Such a man, whether of the political right or left, has no use for the forms of democratic government. The Aryans must be the Master Race solely because he, as a Teuton, was a member of that elite. Therefore it was their mission, but only under his leadership, to restore broken Germany to her former greatness. This Hitler could do only by winning absolute power.

Hitler's following or gang was the party of discontent, of envy, of resentment. The ex-officers like Hermann Goering, disappointed intellectuals such as Alfred Rosenberg and Joseph Goebbels, out of work labourers, small shopkeepers ruined by inflation, all these found a place in it. Hitler refused to permit a class or age identification. He wrote of his mass following: 'These fine chaps, what sacrifices they were willing to make, all day at their jobs, and all night off on a mission for the Party. I specially looked for people of dishevelled appearance. A bourgeois in a stiff collar would have bitched up everything.' The Austrian bourgeoisie had failed to support the great Hitler, had forced him to scratch a living in the gutters of Vienna. As it turned out, he had to have middle-class support, for unlike Lenin he could not ride to power on the shoulders of the workers alone. Yet he often felt nothing but contempt for his white-collar supporters.

During the thirteen years of Hitler's struggle towards absolute power, his organization reached its tentacles into the heart of German youth, creating new and aggressive gangs. Hitler Youth, that frightful parody of scouting, was founded about 1926 and grew quickly in numbers until in 1931 over a hundred thousand members paraded before their leader in the torch-lit stadium at Potsdam. The Students' League and the Nazi Schoolchildren's League were other ways of indoctrinating youth. The active spearhead of Nazism, the SA, rose rapidly in numbers from 27,000 in 1925 to 178,000 in 1929. But Nazism itself, the party of militant discontent, could make little headway while Germany was struggling back to prosperity in the years 1923–9. The turning point came with the global economic depression. In 1928 the Nazi Party polled 810,000 votes in the Reichstag elections. In the first year of depression, 1930, they polled 6,409,600, nearly a fifth of the total cast, and in July 1932 they gained no fewer than 13,745,000. Hitler had now become a major political figure. More ominous was his turbulent SA which he himself found difficulty in controlling. A paramilitary force, largely drawn from the unemployed, they now numbered over four hundred thousand – four times the size of the regular army permitted to Germany by the Treaty of Versailles.

Adolf Hitler came to power as Chancellor on 30 January 1933. Having dropped two million votes in yet another Reichstag election as late as November 1932, he commanded only 33 per cent of the national vote, and he achieved his ambition, not by a great upsurge of patriotic heroism (as the carefully fostered legend declared) but by a shoddy deal with the parties of the Right, the 'Old Guard' whom he and his followers had been attacking for years past. The Right aimed to regain its old function as the ruling class, to destroy the Republic and restore the Hohenzollern monarchy, to repress the workers and their trades unions, to reverse the Treaty of Versailles and rebuild the military power of Germany. Led by the octogenarian Hindenburg, now in his dotage, and the aristocratic Franz von Papen, they made the fatal mistake of believing that in Adolf Hitler they had found the man who would help them attain those ends. So they did not doubt their own ability to control Hitler and trusted the promises that he made. They were not alone. Neville Chamberlain, Edouard Daladier and Joseph Stalin among others fell into a similar error with disastrous results. Psychiatry is not a compulsory subject in the training of politicians, so we cannot altogether blame them if they failed to understand that no one should rely upon the behaviour or promises of a paranoiac.

So Germany passed into the rule of the gang. The gang demanded conformity with its laws and usages. Any person who did not conform was an outcast, a non-man. Hitler and his associates, the narcissist Goering, the malignant Goebbels, the sadistic Himmler, preached the virtues of Nazism to the mass which responded with mobs shrieking hysterical admiration, just as mobs of mindless teenagers screamed hysterical worship of their adored pop stars forty years later. But the teenager, though silly, was harmless. The German mob was not. They attacked their supposed enemies, destroyed their property, condoned their murder.

Within months of taking over the chancellorship, the Führer had ensured that his was the only political party officially remaining in Germany. There followed a modern version of the witch-hunt, aimed at the extermination of every person who would not conform to the pattern of the gang. Since Hitler had labelled the Jews as the diabolical agents or instruments of organic decay, it logically followed that the 'Jewish race' suffered the greatest hardship. They were persecuted, just as witches had been persecuted in sixteenth- and seventeenth-century Germany, but to a greater extent and with all the refinements made possible by technological advance. Some five million Jews died in German-controlled concentration and extermination camps during the Third Reich. In places such as those, the rhetoric of bacillus and parasite was converted into a hideously literal reality. To the earnest Nazi, the Jew was not human. Those who shared Hitler's world-view had reverted to the thinking of their remote ancestors who described their tribe as 'the men', thus implying that other tribes, groups or villages had no part in human virtues or even in human nature.

The Nazis aimed to preserve their supposed race uncontaminated, fearing and hating anything that menaced their self-preservation. Thus the primitive instincts of fear and hate, self-preservation and race-preservation broke through the skins of civilization and came to the surface. The despairing Germans of the 1920s and 1930s sloughed off those thin skins or veneers under which Primitive Man still lies hidden. They found their immediate satisfaction in violence and in conformity with the Gang. The whole Hitler episode, with its hysterical Nuremburg rallies, indoctrinated youth, witch-hunts and insane racial theories, was in part spurred by the distinctive anxieties of the inter-war years. Yet it also embodied a return to the hates and lusts and fears of a primitive era. It is a terrible example of the dangers and delusions consequent upon mass suggestion and mob hysteria.

CONCLUSION

Current Problems of Survival

Earlier parts of this book have already made clear many of the remarkable achievements registered by the 'scientific' medicine of the West, particularly over the last century or so. Even allowing for the various insights afforded by different versions of 'traditional' medical practice rooted in other regions of the world, there is no alternative approach to the treatment and cure of major diseases which has proved more generally effective, nor any rival system which has attained comparable influence on a global scale. In this sense it is understandable that historians of modern Western medicine should have had such frequent resort to the rhetoric of 'progress'. Yet the present volume has also suggested that instances of complete conquest over particular diseases have remained rare, and that in many other respects as well the overall story is far too complex to be properly presented as a simple chronicle of unbroken advance.

We need to note, for example, that the development of scientific medicine has brought with it a formidable set of social, economic and ethical dilemmas. The earlier achievement of figures such as Chadwick and Simon in promoting the notion of health care as an on-going responsibility to be discharged by society as a whole was one of the foundations for the twentieth-century experience of an ever-closer linkage between, on one hand, the growing authority of medicine and, on the other, the enlargement of state power within liberal as well as more autocratic regimes. Almost regardless of their particular ideological stance, governments became leading agents of collective mobilization for the preventative and therapeutic battles against disease. This process was assisted by the tendency of doctors (who themselves were now increasingly likely to be public employees) to urge the greater medicalization of an expanding range of policy issues, such as those dealing with the quality of the environment, or of diet, or of housing and working conditions, or of other components of a 'welfare' society.

These developments meant that, by the end of the twentieth century, medicine within the advanced economies was also big business. Here, whatever the particular balance between public and private outlay in each instance, the expenditure on health care within the most prosperous societies of the West had risen generally to something approaching 10 per cent of Gross National Product. In the trend-setting case of the USA, however, the figure had already spiralled higher – to one of 15 per cent, which reflected a doubling since the early 1970s. Such statistics indicate that the processes by which these societies were now seeking to combat disease and produce a healthier and longer lifespan had turned medicine into a major service industry. It was one whose operation required huge investment in various forms of professional education, as well as in the construction and servicing of the complex hospital systems which now served as the principal sites of 'high-tech' innovation. It was also an enterprise offering the prospect of huge commercial gain to companies active in fields like health insurance or the production of pharmaceuticals. All too often patients were becoming mere units of accountancy, especially when viewed from the perspective either of those intent on maximizing private profit or of those seeking to limit public expenditure.

In the latter context nothing was more striking about the health economics of the late twentieth century than the inclination of Western societies to generate an almost infinite demand for improved medical care. Within the fields of heart surgery and organ transplantation, for example, the scientific and technical advances of the last thirty years have fuelled far more hopes than currently available resources can readily meet. There, and at many other points, rising expectations have constantly clashed with rising costs. As the new millennium dawned those who lived in the West were now generally healthier than any preceding generations. But at the same time they were, arguably, also more anxiously obsessed about their health than those who had lived in earlier ages. Among the more justifiable of their concerns was a fear that the 'rationing' of medical services, which had already become prominent as a topic for public debate, would prove to be an increasingly pressing problem as a longer-living, and thus longer-ageing, population made ever greater demands upon resource. However, when contrasted with the fate of those living on poorer continents, these anxieties appeared simply as side-effects arising from the difficult choices imposed upon the West even by its relative prosperity. At the close of the twentieth century there remained extensive regions of Africa, Asia and Latin America where chronic political instability and unsolved poverty precluded all such choice and imposed far more radical limitations on the diffusion of scientific medicine as a potentially vital means of combating disease. Even today, as Ralf Dahrendorf reminds us, 'the globalized world has an underside of destitution and death'.

Some of the dilemmas and anxieties current at the close of the twentieth century were linked to an understandable ambivalence about much of the impact of science. In the domain of medicine this was particularly clear from the attention devoted to 'iatrogenic' conditions – illnesses or disabilities attributable to the intervention of physicians themselves. Such problems demonstrated the complexity of modern treatment. A drug might be invaluable in the cure of a certain disease, yet have distinct and sometimes dangerous disadvantages too. Perhaps the most notorious example from the modern epoch was thalidomide, first introduced during the 1950s in West Germany and soon widely available without formal prescription. As a means of inducing sleep, it seemed safer than any of the barbiturates, being non-addictive and having a margin of safety wide enough to make lethal overdose virtually impossible. Around 1960, however, German paediatricians found themselves dealing with an unprecedentedly large number of babies suffering from phocomelia, or 'seal extremities', a hitherto rare congenital deficiency of the long bones which produces normal or rudimentary hands and feet springing directly from the trunk. These children also presented deformities of the eyes, ears and heart, as well as of the alimentary and urinary tracts. It became quite swiftly evident that there was a connection between these defects and a drug retailing as Contergan, which had been taken by the babies' mothers during early pregnancy (the second month being the crucial phase). Other thalidomide-based agents, such as that being sold as Distaval in Britain and that being trialled as Kevadon in the USA, were soon similarly implicated. It is reckoned that about 20 per cent of the women who had taken the drug at the relevant stage of their pregnancies produced deformed offspring. In West Germany the Ministry of Health estimated that about ten thousand abnormal babies had resulted, of whom only half survived. Britain experienced five hundred cases, with much the same rate of mortality.

Thalidomide was an outstanding example of something which appeared to meet a public need, to add an amenity to life, to replace a more perilous agent, yet which carried an unsuspected and even graver danger. In other instances doubts about the side-effects of drug usage, especially over the longer term, have been frequently but less conclusively expressed. Such unresolved worries have shadowed the history of 'the pill', as a means of female chemical contraception that has proved so convenient as to have played a major role in the rapid increase of sexual 'permissiveness' during the later twentieth century. A similar pattern of anxiety may yet develop with regard to Viagra, a 'cure' for male impotence which was launched with huge publicity in 1998 and which seemed destined quickly to become an object more of recreational than of strictly medical usage. Even more generally, there were serious dangers stemming from the habit of over-prescribing antibiotics. The fact that it was often the patients themselves who pressed most eagerly for this kind of chemical 'fix' did not in any way lessen the resultant risk. In essence, they became increasingly vulnerable to the kind of genetic mutation within bacteria which could serve only to heighten the resistance of the latter to the operation of previously effective antibiotic controls.

That particular issue also illustrates the point that, by the end of the twentieth century, the areas of interaction between physicians and geneticists were precisely those where prospects for further scientific breakthroughs looked not only brightest but, paradoxically, also most threatening. Nearly two generations after Crick and Watson's decoding of DNA, the principal focus of fundamental science in relation to the battle against disease was directed towards molecules rather than cells. This emphasis was reflected in the Human Genome Project, launched as a scheme of international collaboration in the 1980s and due to be completed during the opening years of the twenty-first century. Here scientists were aiming to map the position of every gene on every chromosome, and to plot the sequence of three thousand million molecular 'base pairs' running through the double helix of DNA. Having established such a matrix, investigators hoped to be able to identify the precise genetical origin of any disease or other defect attributable to inheritance. Thereafter the most pressing challenge would almost inevitably become that of manipulating the hereditary material so as to eliminate the disorders at issue. By the year 2000 genetic screening was already being increasingly applied during pregnancy to check the unborn for their vulnerability to such inherited disorders as cystic fibrosis or haemophilia, and techniques of adult testing were also being refined in ways that might permit predictions concerning the susceptibility of particular individuals to the eventual onset of afflictions like

Huntington's Chorea or Alzheimer's disease. Within such contexts the ethical dilemmas associated with the potentialities of modern science seemed constantly to deepen, especially where questions arose about the nature and limits of justifiable alterations to genetical processes. Under what circumstances did beneficial 'improvement' become potentially perilous 'tampering'? After cloned sheep, for example, the chilling prospect of a Huxleyesque 'brave new world' where human babies might be 'bioengineered' into supposed physical perfection moved significantly closer. Similarly, with respect to patterns of nutrition, there were growing fears that rapid advances in the genetic modification of food-crops were being most strongly driven by considerations of imminent commercial profit, and in a manner that paid inadequate heed to the dangers of triggering unanticipated, and even uncontrollable, risks to health over the longer term.

Towards the end of the 1970s, those inclined to interpret the modern history of mankind's battle against disease in broadly triumphalist terms seemed to have something very substantial to encourage them. Most specifically, as we saw in Chapter Four, this was the epoch that witnessed the final stage in the global eradication of the scourge of smallpox. On the basis of such an undoubted achievement, it was tempting to argue that scientific medicine would now swiftly continue to register major advances against epidemic infections in general. Yet one can see with hindsight that, in strictly relative terms, smallpox had actually been one of the easier targets. As Geoff Watts has noted: 'It had no animal reservoir; it was easily recognized and diagnosed; there was a very effective vaccine against it; and it was widely feared.' These considerations had far less bearing on a number of other familiar major diseases. Still more crucially, however, none of these factors (not even, at the very outset, that of fear as distinct from sheer ignorance) proved immediately applicable to the particular form of epidemic illness which began to be identified as a new and dramatic threat to global health very shortly after the campaign against smallpox had been won.

This was the infection soon labelled as AIDS (Acquired Immune Deficiency Syndrome). Allan M. Brandt has commented on the historical significance of the timing of its eruption as follows: 'The epidemic began at a moment of relative complacency, especially in the developed world, concerning epidemic infectious disease. Not since the influenza of 1918–20 had an epidemic with such devastating potential struck. The

Western, developed world had experienced a health transition from the predominance of infectious to chronic disease and had come to focus its resources and attention on systemic, non-infectious diseases. AIDS thus appeared at a historical moment in which there was little social or political experience in confronting a public-health crisis of this dimension.' Neither the nature nor the potential scale of the problem was fully appreciated during the initial phase of investigation, commencing in 1980. Although there had almost certainly been a few earlier but as yet undiagnosed cases, this was the point at which some puzzling immunological deficiences started to be observed among a small number of male homosexuals resident in Los Angeles, and then among similar communities in San Francisco and New York. Before long the same problem began to appear in major European cities too. At this early stage the names given to the illness included 'gay plague' and 'GRID' (gay-related immune deficiency). The sufferers showed severely weakened resistance to infection, especially in the forms of pneumonia and tuberculosis. By 1983 the causative agent had been identified as an RNA retrovirus, subsequently called HIV (Human Immunodeficiency Virus), and the means of infection had been established as the transmission of blood and other body fluids. It had also become worryingly plain that someone could carry the virus for a number of years before any signs of the infection (and thus of a previous capacity to pass it on unknowingly) became apparent, and that once the symptoms did reveal themselves then an AIDS-related death was eventually inevitable.

The disease appeared to be unprecedented, at least in the sense that it had not been previously the object of specific identification nor had it ever taken epidemic form. Yet virologists soon strongly suspected that HIV itself had been around for quite a long time. In 1985 the discovery within West Central Africa of a second strain (designated as HIV-2) suggested that these kinds of virus might well have been present for many years among isolated communities living in that region. By the late 1990s the work of an international team coordinated from the University of Alabama would indeed be demonstrating that the human infection almost certainly originated as a result of the 'bushmeat trade' common in countries such as Gabon and Cameroon. It is now known that chimpanzees of the sub-species *Pan troglodytes troglodytes*, with a very high degree (98 per cent) of genetic similarity to *Homo sapiens*, have long been carriers of a virus almost identical to HIV. Though seemingly harmless to the apes themselves, this was capable of bringing disease to humans once the species barrier had been crossed through the blood contamination that must have stemmed from the slaughtering and eating of these animals. Thus AIDS – even if undiagnosed as such while it remained masked by the many other infections ravaging West Central Africa – appears to have become endemic in a number of self-contained localities before breaking out of the region as an epidemic illness.

The nature and speed of this eventual eruption testify to an increased human mobility, as well as to other behavioural changes (including a more 'permissive' climate of sexuality) which help to characterize the life of our 'globalized' epoch. As William H. McNeill observes, 'The exact path whereby the HIV virus escaped the older limits on its habitat before being propagated along truck routes in Africa and then around the world by aeroplane is not known, but its global propagation in less than two decades is not in doubt.' Nor could there be any reason for doubting that other previously unrecorded viral diseases might also have the potential to reach epidemic level – a consideration sharpened by the discovery of the dangerous Marburg, Lassa, Rift Valley and Ebola fevers. Whereas those infections have so far been contained, the continuing history of the spread of HIV-AIDS looks very different. The fact that in the West the disease was first transmitted largely by sexual activity between men provoked a great deal of scapegoating (reminiscent, for example, of responses to leprosy in past ages) and of facile moralizing in a homophobic mode. Just as harmfully, it also lured many into supposing that there was nothing more to this affliction than the 'gay plague' of their initial imaginings. However, by the time that WHO established its global AIDS programme in 1986, there was urgent need to raise public consciousness about a far wider range of risk. It was now becoming more evident that modes of transmission included heterosexual contact (markedly so in the case of HIV-2), perinatal linkage between mothers and infants, blood transfusions, and shared use of needles on the part of those engaged in the intravenous consumption of illegal drugs. There was also increasing evidence that the viruses causing AIDS were capable of even more rapid mutation than those whose transformation into new strains had already frustrated any comprehensive control of influenza.

By the 1990s epidemiologists were tracing the pattern of HIV distribution in terms of three broad areas. In North America, Western Europe, Australasia and urban parts of Latin America most of the impetus for diffusion has come from homosexual activity, even though there has also been a rise in the rate of heterosexual transmission as a result of intravenous drug use and thus in the number of paediatric cases generated by perinatal infection too. A second pattern of spread, apparent in sub-Saharan African and in much of rural Latin America, has been far more heavily dependent on heterosexual infection and has taken as much toll upon women as upon men. The third region embraced North Africa, the Middle East, Eastern Europe, Asia and the Pacific, where HIV seems not to have been present at all until the mid-1980s and where the illness has developed principally through contacts with those infected in the other two areas mentioned. Towards the end of 1998 WHO reported that the tally of global mortality since the start of the epidemic was approaching twelve million, and that the figure for those currently living while infected with HIV had already risen beyond thirty million. Regarding this latter statistic, more than two-thirds is attributable to the plight of sub-Saharan Africa. In at least four countries – Zimbabwe, Botswana, Namibia, and Swaziland – the infection rate among adults now exceeds 20 per cent. Despite the importance of California and New York as the primary foci during the earlier 1980s for the rapid diffusion of AIDS as a fully epidemic force, it must be stressed that by the close of the 1990s the disease had become predominantly yet another affliction of the Third World. Most tragically, it had now 'returned' to Africa in an unprecedently virulent way. There its swift and seemingly relentless advance served only to enlarge the potential for further social and political destabilization across this troubled continent in the early years of the twenty-first century.

The international mobilization not simply of governments but also of medical science against this pandemic threat was in many respects impressive. As Mirko Grmek has commented, 'The grandeur of modern medicine – its highs – may be displayed in the rapidity with which some complex problems of AIDS are resolved: its semiotics and pathology, the nature of the causal agent, its routes of infection and epidemiologic surveillance.' However, as he readily concedes, in this context we have also to register that the miseries and lows of such medicine 'are no less evident at the moment when we pass from understanding to action, from knowledge to power'. The vital role that had been increasingly played by immunology in modern battles against disease was never more clearly evident than at the juncture when scientists were suddenly outflanked by an infection which radically subverted the workings of the immune system itself. Even with the new developments in molecular medicine that were occurring towards the end of the twentieth century, no vaccine nor cure for this particular disease had yet been devised. Expensive drug therapies based on 'protease inhibitors' had shown some success in enlarging the span between infection and the onset of full-blown AIDS. But even these carried the danger of encouraging reduced concern for the stricter precautions about sexual activity which, after massive publicly funded campaigns of health education, had served to slow the advance of the affliction in North America and Western Europe. As for the regions of the world that were now in the direst need of rescue from HIV-AIDS, poverty continued to limit their access to any prophylactic more sophisticated than condoms or to any significant pharmaceutical palliative. Here millions were fated to enter the new millennium under the shadow of a 'plague' as dark as any in recorded history.

Many of the broader expectations aroused by the specific achievement of eradicating smallpox have been disappointed not only because of the AIDS epidemic but also due to the intractability of other major diseases of a more familar kind. One of these was cancer. In the West 'the Big C' was the affliction that aroused the most generalized anxieties during the second half of the twentieth century, at least until the threat from HIV produced a surge of rival fears. In contrast to AIDS, here was a chronic degenerative illness of a non-infective kind which took its principal toll of those who had reached middle or old age. Thus cancer served paradoxically as witness to the generally improved longevity registered within Western societies. Though known since ancient times, it was something which most of those living in previous eras had simply not survived long enough to be likely to face. The affliction was, strictly, not a single disease at all. Rather, the term 'cancer' had come to cover a cluster of disorders, numbering more than a hundred according to the tally kept by WHO. Their linking feature was a loss of control over the normal processes of cellular division, which resulted most typically in a multiplication of cells that formed tumours tending to spread into secondary lesions. Areas most vulnerable to attack included the stomach, lungs, breast, cervix, colon, rectum, prostate, and liver.

Despite long years of major investment in research, no general explanation of the causes behind these cancerous processes – let alone any comprehensive approach to cure – has yet been achieved. It seemed probable, however, that genetic predisposition or mutation played an important part in shaping the incidence of at least some cancers, while other forms had dietary, environmental or other exogenous factors as their more likely triggers. As early as 1755 the London surgeon Percivall Pott had already described a cancer of the male genitals which seemed to be confined to chimney sweeps and other workers whose clothing was persistently contaminated with sooty tars. Since then the list of chemicals known to be carcinogenic has vastly grown. During the 1920s questions began to be raised in Germany about possible linkage between smoking and lung cancer especially. By the early 1960s both the Royal College of Surgeons in London and the Advisory Committee of the US Surgeon-General were expressing their unequivocal confirmation of such a connection. Thereafter the medical profession found itself engaged in a long (and still unfinished) struggle against a rich and powerful lobby of tobacco industrialists prone to self-delusive denial of increasingly damning evidence, as well as against the reluctance of governments to forgo the immense tax revenues generated by addictive smoking. As for nuclear technology, its development over the last fifty years or so has also prompted growing and justifiable fears about the carcinogenic effects of atomic radiation. Similar concerns have surrounded other environmental issues, such as the connection between a rising incidence of skin cancer and changes in the intensity of solar ultraviolet light. Towards the end of the 1990s it was being estimated that one-third of those then living within the advanced economies would suffer sooner or later from some kind of cancerous invasion. That prospect appeared all the more alarming in so far as the most commonly available surgical, chemotherapeutic and radiotherapeutic responses to the major cancers had not yet produced any really radical transformation in survival rates.

It may well be correct to claim that in the course of the twentieth century cancer replaced consumption as what David Cantor has called 'the dominant disease metaphor' of the age. However, as we observed towards the end of Chapter Seven, tuberculosis too has proved much more difficult to eradicate than medical scientists anticipated a couple of generations ago. Though not currently epidemic, it remains a far from defeated force, stubbornly persisting as a widespread problem that affects especially but not exclusively the populations of the developing world. Further examples of the continuing intractability of certain major diseases are the cholera whose latest manifestations we noted in Chapter Six, and also the malaria whose role in the nineteenth-century exploration of Africa we surveyed in Chapter Eight. By the 1950s and 1960s the latter affliction had become the object of an international eradication programme, comparable in aim to that which eventually conquered smallpox. Sadly the campaign against malaria met with only limited success. Although it has been largely eliminated from North America, Europe and most of the former USSR, there remains a large band of tropical and subtropical areas in Africa, Asia and Latin America where this illness persists as a major hazard. The increasing resistance shown by mosquitoes against insecticides has been matched by that of the malarial parasites themselves when exposed to drugs like chloroquine, and meanwhile the expansion of international air travel has also threatened to facilitate distribution of the infected insects. Estimates at the end of the 1990s suggested that the number of sufferers was already exceeding three hundred million – a figure far greater than that recorded a generation earlier, and one now accompanied by at least three million deaths per year.

Malaria is also significant for exemplifying the potential linkage between disease and the unprecedentedly rapid changes which have recently been affecting the world's ecosystem. As with the tsetse fly in relation to sleeping sickness, it would take only a couple of degrees of 'global warming' to produce a very dramatic enlargement of the areas which the anopheline mosquito might succeed in colonizing or recolonizing. Such unanticipated climatic shifts may well produce new patterns of drought and famine too. Prominent among other environmental concerns has been the fouling of air, soil and water, particularly by industrial chemicals. Toxic emissions have certainly contributed to that depletion of the ozone layer in the upper atmosphere which has led to less effective filtering of ultraviolet radiation and thus to greater risk of skin cancers. Perhaps most dramatically of all, in 1986 the 'meltdown' of the Chernobyl nuclear reactor in the Ukraine served to underline the globalized perils to health which have become inseparable from mankind's harnessing of atomic power, even in avowedly peaceful forms.

Current millennial debates on the 'poisoning' of our planet, and thus of ourselves, cannot be detached from the extra strain imposed upon the global environment by the forces of population growth. Here the very success of twentieth-century medicine – for example, in deploying antibiotic and immunological techniques against the scourge of infant and child mortality – eventually proved to be a source of problems as well. Between 1750 and 1900 global population grew, roughly, from 1 billion to 1.6 billion. By 1950 the figure had climbed to 2.6 billion, and thereafter the numbers rose at a pace unparalleled in any previous era.

The 6 billion mark was passed during 1999, at which stage estimates from the United Nations Organization predicted that the graph would ascend to 9 billion in the middle of the twenty-first century and not reach a 'plateau' until 11 billion was attained in around the year 2100. The history of the last hundred years or so suggests that humanity is already in the midst of a process of quantitative transformation huge enough to carry vast qualitative implications as well. These are perhaps most evident from the calculation that some 95 per cent of the current and foreseeable demographic increase is and will be concentrated in the poorer regions of the globe. But what might prove to be the significance of the fact that many of these areas were also the ones where, as the twentieth century closed, HIV had already taken strongest hold? Even now, the work of Malthus and Darwin still serves to remind us of the possibility that massive mortality – whether produced by AIDS, or indeed by some other epidemic force similarly arising unforeseen amid the environmental and social upheavals of the contemporary world – might slow the demographic surge altogether sooner than present projections suggest.

As a result of its continuing battle against disease, modern medicine – social, therapeutic, and preventative – has offered much of the human race a prospect of longer and healthier life. In promoting the expansion of global population, it has generated difficulties which *may* be insoluble. Similarly, advancing technology has spread to many societies the kind of comforts and amenities which were virtually unimaginable two centuries ago. In doing so, it too has brought some problems which *may* defy solution. With respect to material things, the combination of these two processes has caused mankind to run ahead of its own state of civilization. The primitive is not buried deeply enough for safety. This may be why humans still live all too often like animals: breeding unchecked, fouling their surroundings, exhausting their resources, taking no thought for the future. Governments tell us that 'we must come to terms with our environment', but this is begging the question. Rather, mankind must come to terms with itself. If we do not learn self-discipline and if we fail to tackle the difficulties which we ourselves have largely created, then our problems seem destined to be resolved, at least temporarily, in an altogether harsher way. The solution will then surely lie in the hands of one or all of humanity's age-old enemies, Famine, Pestilence, and War – those Riders of the Apocalypse who also bring with them Death upon his Pale Horse.

Further Reading

GENERAL

Ackernecht, E.H., *A Short History of Medicine* (Baltimore: Johns Hopkins University Press, 1968)
——, *History and Geography of the Most Important Diseases* (New York: Hafner, 1965)
Bett, W.R. (ed.), *The History and Conquest of Common Diseases* (Norman: University of Oklahoma Press, 1954)
Bynum, W.F. & Porter, R. (eds), *Companion Encyclopedia of the History of Medicine* (2 vols, London: Routledge, 1993)
Cartwright, F.F., *A Social History of Medicine* (London: Longman, 1977)
Gale, A.H., *Epidemic Diseases* (Harmondsworth: Penguin, 1959)
Henschen, F., *The History of Diseases* (London: Longman, 1966)
Hudson, R.P., *Disease and Its Control: The Shaping of Modern Thought* (Westport: Greenwood, 1983)
Kiple, K.F. (ed.), *The Cambridge World History of Human Diseases* (Cambridge: Cambridge University Press, 1993)
McGrew, R.E., *Encyclopedia of Medical History* (New York: McGraw-Hill, 1985)
McNeill, W.H., *Plagues and Peoples* (Harmondsworth: Penguin, 1979)
Morton, L.T., *A Medical Bibliography (Garrison and Morton): An Annotated Checklist of Texts Illustrating the History of Medicine* (4th edn, Aldershot: Gower, 1983)
Porter, R., *The Greatest Benefit to Mankind: A Medical History of Humanity from Antiquity to the Present* (London: HarperCollins, 1997)
—— (ed.), *The Cambridge Illustrated History of Medicine* (Cambridge: Cambridge University Press, 1996)
Ranger, T. & Slack, P. (eds), *Epidemics and Ideas: Essays on the Historical Perception of Pestilence* (Cambridge: Cambridge University Press, 1992)
Scott, H.H., *Some Notable Epidemics* (London: Arnold, 1934)
Scott Stevenson, R., *Famous Illnesses in History* (London: Eyre & Spottiswoode, 1962)
Shrewsbury, J.F.D., *The Plague of the Philistines, and other Medical-Historical Essays* (London: Gollancz, 1964)
Sigerist, H.E., *Civilization and Disease* (Ithaca: Cornell University Press, 1943)
Singer, C. & Underwood, E.A., *A Short History of Medicine* (2nd edn, Oxford: Oxford University Press, 1962)
Sournia, J.-C., *The Illustrated History of Medicine* (London: Starke, 1992)
Walton, J., Barondess, J.A., & Lock, S. (eds), *The Oxford Medical Companion* (Oxford: Oxford University Press, 1994)
Yearsley, M., *Le Roy est Mort* (London: Unicorn Press, 1935)

DISEASE IN THE ANCIENT WORLD

Allbutt, Sir T.C., *Greek Medicine in Rome* (London: Macmillan, 1921)
Chadwick, H., *The Early Church* (Harmondsworth: Penguin, 1967)

Grmek, M.D., *Diseases in the Ancient Greek World* (Baltimore: Johns Hopkins University Press, 1989)

Hornblower, S. & Spawforth, A. (eds), *The Oxford Classical Dictionary* (3rd edn, Oxford: Oxford University Press, 1996)

Jackson, J., *Doctors and Diseases in the Roman Empire* (London: British Museum, 1988)

Jones, A.H.M., *The Later Roman Empire* (3 vols, Oxford: Clarendon Press, 1964)

Lloyd, G.E.R. (ed.), *Hippocratic Writings* (Harmondsworth: Penguin, 1978)

Nutton, V. (ed.), *Galen: Problems and Prospects* (London: Wellcome Institute, 1981)

Phillips, E.D., *Greek Medicine* (London: Thames & Hudson, 1973)

Procopius, *The Persian War* (Loeb Classical Library, London: Heinemann, 1914)

Scarborough, J., *Roman Medicine* (Ithaca: Cornell University Press, 1969)

Schouten, J., *The Rod and Serpent of Asklepios* (Amsterdam: Elsevier, 1967)

Sherwin-White, S., *Ancient Cos* (Göttingen: Vandenhoeck & Ruprecht, 1978)

Smith, W.D., *The Hippocratic Tradition* (Ithaca: Cornell University Press, 1979)

Temkin, O., *Hippocrates in a World of Pagans and Christians* (Baltimore: Johns Hopkins University Press, 1991)

Thucydides, *History of the Peloponnesian War*, Book Two (Harmondsworth: Penguin, 1954)

THE BLACK DEATH

Bell, W.G., *The Great Plague in London in 1665* (London: John Lane, 1924)

Cohn, N., *The Pursuit of the Millennium* (London: Secker & Warburg, 1957)

Creighton, C., *A History of Epidemics in Britain* (2 vols, Cambridge: Cambridge University Press, 1891)

Dols, M.W., *The Black Death in the Middle East* (Princeton: Princeton University Press, 1977)

Goodridge, J.F., *Langland, Piers the Ploughman* (Harmondsworth: Penguin, 1959)

Gottfried, R.S., *The Black Death: Natural and Human Disaster in Medieval Europe* (New York: Free Press, 1983)

Hatcher, J., *Plague, Population, and the English Economy, 1348–1530* (London: Macmillan, 1977)

Hirst, L.F., *The Conquest of Plague* (Oxford: Clarendon Press,1953)

Ormrod, W.M. & Lindley, P. (eds), *The Black Death in England* (Stamford: Watkins, 1996)

Poliakov, L., *The History of Anti-Semitism* (Vol. 1, London: Elek, 1966)

Slack, P., *The Impact of Plague in Tudor and Stuart England* (London: Longman, 1988)

Southern, R.W., *The Mediaeval Church* (Harmondsworth: Penguin, 1970)

Ziegler, P., *The Black Death* (Harmondsworth: Penguin, 1970)

THE MYSTERY OF SYPHILIS

Chapman, H.W., *The Last Tudor King* (London: Cape, 1958)

Crosby, A.W., *The Columbian Exchange: Biological and Cultural Consequences of 1492* (Westport: Greenwood, 1972)

Elton, G.R., *England under the Tudors* (3rd edn, London: Routledge, 1991)

Goodman, H., *Contributors to the Knowledge of Syphilis* (New York: Froben, 1944)

Graham, S., *Ivan the Terrible* (London: Benn, 1932)

Guy, J., *Tudor England* (Oxford: Oxford University Press, 1988)

Holcombe, R.C., *Who Gave the World Syphilis?* (New York: Froben, 1937)

Hudson, E.H., *Non-Venereal Syphilis* (Edinburgh: Livingstone, 1958)

Maclaurin, C., *Post Mortem* (London: Cape, 1923)

Macnalty, Sir A., *Henry VIII: A Difficult Patient* (London: C. Johnson, 1952)

Quétel, C., *History of Syphilis* (Oxford: Polity, 1990)

Scarisbrick, J.J., *Henry VIII* (Harmondsworth: Penguin, 1971)
Uden, G., *They Looked Like This* (Oxford: Blackwell, 1965)
Yanov, A., *The Origins of Autocracy: Ivan the Terrible in Russian History* (Berkeley: University of California Press, 1981)

SMALLPOX, OR THE CONQUEROR CONQUERED

Elliott, J.H., *The Old World and the New, 1492–1650* (Cambridge: Cambridge University Press, 1970)
Fisher, R.B., *Edward Jenner, 1749–1823* (London: Deutsch, 1991)
Gruzinski, S., *The Conquest of Mexico* (Cambridge: Polity, 1993)
Hassig, R., *Mexico and the Spanish Conquest* (London: Longman, 1994)
Hemming, J., *The Conquest of the Incas* (London: Macmillan, 1970)
Hopkins, D.R., *Princes and Peasants: Smallpox in History* (Chicago: University of Chicago Press, 1983)
Parry, J.H., *The Spanish Seaborne Empire* (London: Hutchinson, 1970)
Prescott, W.H. (intro. by Fernández-Armesto, F.), *History of the Conquest of Mexico* (London: Folio Society, 1994)
Rolleston, J.D., *The History of the Acute Exanthemata* (London: Heinemann, 1937)
World Health Organization, *The Global Eradication of Smallpox* (Geneva: WHO, 1980)

GENERAL NAPOLEON AND GENERAL TYPHUS

Ellis, G.J., *The Napoleonic Empire* (London: Macmillan, 1991)
Emsley, C., *The Longman Companion to Napoleonic Europe* (London: Longman, 1993)
Esdaile, C., *The Wars of Napoleon* (London: Longman, 1995)
Gates, D., *The Napoleonic Wars, 1803–1815* (London: Arnold, 1997)
Herold, J.C., *The Age of Napoleon* (Harmondsworth: Penguin, 1969)
Kemble, J., *Napoleon Immortal* (London: Murray, 1959)
Markham, F., *Napoleon* (London: Mentor, 1966)
Prinzig, F., *Epidemics Resulting from Wars* (Oxford: Clarendon Press, 1916)
Zinsser, H., *Rats, Lice, and History* (4th edn, London: Routledge, 1942)

CHOLERA AND SANITARY REFORM

Brockington, C.F., *A Short History of Public Health* (2nd edn, London: Churchill, 1966)
Durey, M., *The Return of the Plague: British Society and the Cholera, 1831–2* (Dublin: Gill & Macmillan, 1979)
Evans, R.J., *Death in Hamburg: Society and Politics in the Cholera Years, 1830–1910* (Oxford: Oxford University Press, 1987)
Finer, S.E., *The Life and Times of Sir Edwin Chadwick* (London: Methuen, 1952)
Halliday, S. *The Great Stink of London: Sir Joseph Bazalgette and the Cleansing of the Victorian Metropolis* (Stroud: Sutton, 1999)
Hamlin, C., *Public Health and Social Justice in the Age of Chadwick* (Cambridge: Cambridge University Press, 1997)
Lambert, R., *Sir John Simon 1816–1904 and English Social Administration* (London: MacGibbon & Kee, 1963)
Morris, R.J., *Cholera, 1832: The Social Response to an Epidemic* (London: Croom Helm, 1976)
Pelling, M., *Cholera, Fever and English Medicine, 1825–1865* (Oxford: Oxford University Press, 1978)

Porter, D. (ed.), *The History of Health and the Modern State* (Amsterdam: Rodopi, 1994)
Snow, J., *On Cholera* (reprint, New York: Hafner, 1965)

GIN, FLU AND TUBERCULOSIS

Bloch, M. *The Royal Touch: Sacred Monarchy and Scrofula in England and France* (London: Routledge, 1973)
Bryder, L., *Below the Magic Mountain: A Social History of Tuberculosis in Twentieth-Century Britain* (Oxford: Clarendon Press, 1988)
Crosby, A.W., *Epidemic and Peace 1918* (London: Greenwood, 1976)
Dormandy, T., *The White Death: A History of Tuberculosis* (London: Hambledon, 1999)
Dubos, R. & J., *The White Plague: Tuberculosis, Man, and Society* (Boston: Little Brown, 1952)
Fisher, R.B., *Edward Jenner, 1749–1823* (London: Deutsch, 1991)
Mann, T., *The Magic Mountain* (Penguin: Harmondsworth, 1960)
Rosenkrantz, B.G. (ed.), *From Consumption to Tuberculosis: A Documentary History* (New York: Garland, 1994)
Smith, F.B., *The Retreat of Tuberculosis, 1850–1950* (London: Croom Helm, 1988)
Sournia, J.-C., *A History of Alcoholism* (Oxford: Blackwell, 1990)

MOSQUITOES, FLIES, TRAVEL AND EXPLORATION

Brock, T.D., *Robert Koch: A Life in Medicine and Bacteriology* (Madison: Science Tech Publishers, 1988)
Crosby, A.W., *Ecological Imperialism: The Biological Expansion of Europe, 900–1900* (Cambridge: Cambridge University Press, 1986)
Curtin, P.D., *The Image of Africa: British Ideas and Action, 1780–1850* (Madison: University of Wisconsin Press, 1964)
——, *Death by Migration: Europe's Encounter with the Tropical World in the Nineteenth Century* (Cambridge: Cambridge University Press, 1989)
Foster, W.D., *A History of Parasitology* (Edinburgh: Livingstone, 1965)
Geison, G.J., *The Private Science of Louis Pasteur* (Princeton: Princeton University Press, 1995)
Gelfand, M., *Livingstone the Doctor* (Oxford: Blackwell, 1957)
Harrison, G.A., *Mosquitoes, Malaria, and Man* (New York: Dutton, 1978)
Jaramillo-Arango, J., *The Conquest of Malaria* (London: Heinemann, 1950)
McKelvey, J.M., *Man against Tsetse: Struggle for Africa* (Ithaca: Cornell University Press, 1973)
Vaughan, M., *Curing Their Ills: Colonial Power and African Illness* (Stanford: Stanford University Press, 1991)
Watts, S., *Epidemics and History: Disease, Power and Imperialism* (New Haven: Yale University Press, 1997)

QUEEN VICTORIA AND THE FALL OF THE RUSSIAN MONARCHY

Figes, O., *A People's Tragedy: The Russian Revolution, 1891–1924* (London: Cape, 1996)
Macalpine, I. & Hunter, R., *George III and the Mad Business* (London: Allen Lane, 1969)
——, *Porphyria, A Royal Malady* (London: BMA, 1968)
Massie, R.K., *Nicholas and Alexandra* (London: Gollancz, 1968)
Pares, Sir B., *The Fall of the Russian Monarchy* (London: Cape, 1939)
Pipes, R., *The Russian Revolution, 1899–1919* (London: Collins Harvill, 1990)

Potts, D.M. & W.T.W., *Queen Victoria's Gene: Haemophilia and the Royal Family* (Stroud: Sutton, 1995)
Seton Watson, H., *The Decline of Imperial Russia* (London: Methuen, 1952)
Taylor, E., *The Fossil Monarchies* (London: Weidenfeld & Nicolson, 1963)
Wilson, C., *Rasputin* (London: Barker, 1964)
Youssoupoff, Prince, *Rasputin* (London: Cape, 1927)

MOB HYSTERIA AND MASS SUGGESTION

Bracher, K., *The German Dictatorship* (London: Weidenfeld & Nicolson, 1971)
Bullock, A., *Hitler and Stalin: Parallel Lives* (London: HarperCollins, 1991)
Clark, S., *Thinking with Demons: The Idea of Witchcraft in Early Modern Europe* (Oxford: Clarendon Press, 1997)
Cohn, N., *Warrant for Genocide* (Harmondsworth: Penguin, 1970)
Kershaw, I., *Hitler* (vol. 1, London: Allen Lane, 1998)
L'Etang, H., *The Pathology of Leadership* (London: Heinemann, 1969)
Pernoud, R., *Joan of Arc by Herself and Her Witnesses* (Harmondsworth: Penguin, 1969)
Thomas, K., *Religion and the Decline of Magic* (London: Weidenfeld & Nicolson, 1971)
Trevor-Roper, H., *The European Witch-Craze of the 16th and 17th Centuries* (Harmondsworth: Penguin, 1969)

CURRENT PROBLEMS OF SURVIVAL

Bayer, R., *Private Acts, Social Consequences: AIDS and the Politics of Public Health* (New York: Free Press, 1989)
Fee, E. & Fox, D.M. (eds), *AIDS: The Burdens of History* (Berkeley: University of California Press, 1988)
Feldman, D.A. & Miller, J.W. (eds), *The AIDS Crisis: A Documentary History* (Westport: Greenwood, 1998)
Garrett, L., *The Coming Plague* (Harmondsworth: Penguin, 1994)
Gilman, S.L., *Disease and Representation: From Madness to AIDS* (Ithaca: Cornell University Press, 1988)
Grmek, M.D., *History of AIDS: Emergence and Origin of a Modern Pandemic* (Princeton: Princeton University Press, 1990)
Illich, I., *Limits to Medicine: The Expropriation of Health* (Harmondsworth: Penguin, 1977)
Kennedy, I., *The Unmasking of Medicine* (London: Allen & Unwin, 1981)
Kennedy, P., *Preparing for the Twenty-First Century* (London: HarperCollins, 1993)
Kissick, W.L., *Medicine's Dilemmas: Infinite Needs versus Finite Resources* (New Haven: Yale University Press, 1994)
Patterson, J.T., *The Dread Disease: Cancer and Modern American Culture* (Cambridge: Harvard University Press, 1987)
Proctor, R.N., *Cancer Wars: How Politics Shape What We Know & What We Don't Know about Cancer* (New York: Basic Books, 1995)
Rather, L.J., *The Genesis of Cancer: A Study in the History of Ideas* (Baltimore: Johns Hopkins University Press, 1978)
Wilkie, T., *The Human Genome Project and its Implications* (Berkeley: University of California Press, 1993)

Index